On the Plaza

The Politics of Public Space and Culture

by SETHA M. LOW

On the Plaza

 **University of Texas Press, Austin**

I am indebted to Marta Amighetti Lujan, who graciously gave permission to use La Fuente, *by Francisco Amighetti, San Jose, Costa Rica, © 1976, as the cover of this book.*

Publication of this book was made possible in part by support from the Pachita Tennant Pike Fund for Latin American Studies.

Copyright © 2000 by the University of Texas Press

All rights reserved

Printed in the United States of America

First edition, 2000

Library of Congress Cataloging-in-Publication Data

Low, Setha M.
  On the plaza : the politics of public space and culture / by Setha M. Low. — 1st ed.
    p. cm.
Includes bibliographical references and index.
  ISBN 0-292-74713-6 (cl. : alk. paper)
  ISBN 0-292-74714-4 (pbk. : alk. paper)
  1. Latin America—Civilization.   2. Latin America—Social life and customs.   3. San José (Costa Rica)—Civilization.
4. San José (Costa Rica)—Social life and customs.   5. Plazas—Latin America—History.   6. Plazas—Costa Rica—San José—History.   I. Title.
F1410.L69   2000
307.3´216´098—dc21   99-050899

To María Eugenia Bozzoli de Wille
Marlene Castro and Claudio Gutiérrez
Lucile Newman
Mentors and Friends

CONTENTS

Part III: Ethnographies

Part IV: Conversations

LIST OF ILLUSTRATIONS

■

Photographs

Credits: Photographs 7, 12, 20, 24, 25, 31, 42, 45, 47, 49, 50 by Joel Lefkowitz, copyright 1997; Photograph 21 by Bruce Newman; Photographs 23, 40 by Vicky J. Risner, copyright 1989; Photographs 34, 35, 36 courtesy of the John Carter Brown Library at Brown University; Photograph 37 by Marjory Dressler, copyright 1998; Photograph 51 courtesy of Oscar Arias; all other photographs are by the author.

The woodcuts on pages 1, 45, 125, and 205 are by Francisco Amighetti, San José, Costa Rica, courtesy of Marta Amighetti Lujan.

PREFACE

This book documents a personal journey to uncover the cultural and political significance of public space by focusing on the design and meaning of the plaza in a contemporary Latin American city. It encompasses a search for the architectural origins of the Spanish American plaza and the ethnohistorical meanings embedded in its urban location and spatial form. It includes an ethnographic analysis of the historical, political, and sociocultural context of the development of two plazas in San José, the capital of Costa Rica, and the meanings generated by their social production of space. First-person narratives and ethnographies present what people are thinking and doing in these public spaces, and what they say about the meaning of the plaza in their everyday lives. When confronted with losing their occupied places on the plaza, people talk about the meaning of such a loss and about their struggle to maintain their daily activities in other locations or at the edges of the redesigned form.

Another representation of meanings are poems and excerpts from novels and memoirs by Costa Rican authors who write about life in urban plazas. Some of the literary reflections portray San José in the early 1900s, capturing the ambience and meaning of the plaza in earlier historical periods. Other selections are contemporary, representing a diversity of perspectives on everyday plaza life and describing Costa Rican social dramas in the public spaces of the city center.

Based on data collected during twenty-five years of fieldwork in Costa

Rica that began in 1972 when I was an anthropology student there, this study traces changes in my perceptions and understandings of Costa Rican culture and the plazas of San José. During this quarter of a century, cultural anthropology and environmental psychology have been enriched by theorists who are concerned with the importance of space in social analysis, while, correspondingly, architects, landscape architects, and urban planners have turned their attention to social relations and cultural aspects of design.

I have written this book as part of this new synthesis, adding my own interpretations of what I observed, theories of the processes I document, and methods for the ethnographic study of the built environment. These theories of the social production and social construction of space; social and spatial boundaries of culture, class, and gender; and state responses to protest by closing, policing, and redesigning of public places further our understanding of the politics of public space. I conclude that these culturally and politically charged public spaces are essential to everyday civic life and the maintenance of a participatory democracy. The specific example of the Costa Rican plaza illustrates how urban public space embodies political ideals within a particular cultural milieu, and helps to explain why plazas arbitrarily located in North American cultural contexts are often not successful as socially or politically vibrant places.

There are a number of questions, however, that this analysis can not fully answer. For instance, is the availability of public space a precondition for any kind of democratic politics? What are the middle-range connections between the theories of the social production of space and the raw ethnographies? Is the threat to public space actually a threat to democracy? I address these issues in my current work on urban fear and the built environment, which focuses explicitly on the sociopolitical dimensions of public space and communities of exclusion (Low 1997a).

I begin this journey by taking the reader directly to Parque Central and Plaza de la Cultura in San José, Costa Rica, just as I arrived in February 1985 to begin the plaza study. Through a selection of field notes representing my experience during each subsequent field visit, I situate the reader in the ethnographic present of the field study. As a Costa Rican specialist who was initially unfamiliar with plaza life, my observations provide an interesting first-hand glimpse of these important public places. In my field notes I write as a "thirty-something," English-speaking woman from the United States, but also as an ethnographer with many years of anthropological training. I am confident that the reader can identify with my surprise of discovery, physical discomfort, social awkwardness, and pleasure in renewed acquaintances as I returned time and again over the next twelve years.

These notes also reflect how my experiences might be different from the readers' everyday experiences in that I am continuously comparing and theorizing what I observe. Thus, this account also communicates the phenomenological experience of being in the plaza from my privileged as well as professional point of view. In subsequent chapters, I retrace my steps by presenting a more formal historical and ethnographic analysis of the Latin American plaza in general, and of the development of the Costa Rican plaza in particular, punctuated with excerpts from Costa Rican memoirs, novels, and short stories that provide the data for my interpretations. I conclude with conversations from Costa Rican literature, with friends and colleagues, and finally with the readers about everyday life and meaning in this exemplar of urban public space.

Setha Low
East Hampton, New York
1999

ACKNOWLEDGMENTS

This book was written with the assistance of many friends, colleagues, students, and funding agencies. The research phase of the project began in 1985 when I visited Miles Richardson, who had studied the central plaza in Cartago, Costa Rica, and who encouraged my plan to study public spaces in San José. Upon my arrival in Costa Rica, María Eugenia Bozzoli de Wille welcomed me as a visiting scholar at the Universidad de Costa Rica, while Marlene Castro and Claudio Gutiérrez invited me to live with them during my numerous San José field visits. Lucile Newman, professor, colleague, and friend from my years at the University of California at Berkeley, also provided a home while I was tracking down maps and historical plans at the John Carter Brown Library in Providence, Rhode Island. I would like to thank them for their emotional and intellectual support and unrelenting enthusiasm.

Many Costa Ricans agreed to participate in this lengthy research project, and their insights contributed greatly to my understanding of the historical and contemporary processes at work in plaza design. I would therefore like to thank the architects and landscape architects Edgar Vargas, Jorge Borbón, Jorge Bertheau, Ibo Bonilla, María de los Angeles Barahona, Nora Flores, José Antonio Quesada, and Blanca Suñol; the heads of governmental offices Renato Cajas and Rudolfo Sancho; the government ministers Guido Sáenz, Carmen Naranjo, and Aída de Fishman; former president Oscar Arias; the writers and artists Gerardo César Hurtado, Alfonso Chase, Ricardo Ulloa, Alvaro Wille, Francisco

Amighetti, and Vilma Loría; the anthropologists Marta Pardo, Janilla Bonilla, María Eugenia Bozzoli, and Marlene Castro; the editorial directors Liliana Barrantes and Carlos De Vandas; the journalist Rubén Vega; and the directors of various public and private institutions Graciela Moreño, Eduardo Faith, Ana Cristina Castro, and Patrick McCoughlin. I would also like to thank the hundreds of Costa Ricans who were willing to talk to me—and in some cases befriended me—as I worked on the numerous plazas, especially Alfredo Rodríguez, "Jim," "the photographers," and the pensioners in Parque Central.

This project was supported financially by a series of grants, fellowships, and scholarly leaves. The 1985 field trip was funded by a sabbatical from the University of Pennsylvania. During 1986 I was a Fulbright Research Scholar in Costa Rica, and I returned again in 1987 with a grant from the Wenner-Gren Foundation for Anthropological Research. I completed plaza research in Spain, France, and Italy with funds from the Wenner-Gren grant-in-aid. From 1989 to 1990, with funding provided by a National Endowment for the Humanities Research Fellowship, I was a Senior Research Fellow at the John Carter Brown Library. I returned to Costa Rica in 1993 while on sabbatical leave from the Graduate School and University Center of the City University of New York, and again in 1997 while on academic leave funded by a John Simon Guggenheim Fellowship and a scholar incentive grant. I am very grateful to all these agencies for funding this project throughout its various stages.

I would also like to thank the colleagues who have worked and commented on this book. Dolores Hayden, Charles Rutheiser, and Neil Smith carefully read the entire manuscript and suggested changes that improved its focus and organization. George Foster read early drafts of my "origins of the plaza" argument and encouraged me to look more closely at the role of the *bastides* and at cross-cultural variation in plaza use and form. Robert Rotenberg, Gary McDonogh, Deborah Pellow, Denise Lawrence, Matthew Cooper, Margaret Rodman, Sharon Zukin, Anthony King, Sylvia Rodríguez, and Cindi Katz commented on or edited various papers as I worked out my theoretical ideas in articles and presentations. Audiences of students and faculty at the Graduate School and University Center of the City University of New York, New York University, Yale University, York University, Johns Hopkins University, and Brown University generously made suggestions, pointed out weaknesses, and added references to the ongoing work.

During the final year of this project, acquisitions editor and editor-in-chief Theresa May, assistant managing editor Leslie Tingle, and copyeditor Nancy Warrington played major roles in improving the manuscript and getting it to press. Nancy smoothed the rough spots and added her bilingual expertise to the correction and clarification of the Spanish. Leslie kept me on schedule, while Theresa encouraged me from the very start. Teresa Wingfield beautifully designed the book and cover. I greatly appreciate their dedication and support.

Costa Rican literature has generally not been translated into English. So, in order to include poems and excerpts that portray the plaza, it was necessary to create a translation project composed of bilingual colleagues, graduate students, and myself. Patricia Pérez and Marlene Castro translated the first draft of the stories by Fernando Durán Ayanegui, Manuel González Zeledón, and Ignacio Trullás y Aulet, while I translated the work of Vilma Loría and Gerardo César Hurtado. Vilma Loría and Gerardo César Hurtado reviewed my translations and made changes that have been incorporated. Michael Yomi translated the essay by Fernando Guillén Martínez. The poems by Alfonso Chase and Arturo Montero Vega were worked on by everyone on the team and reviewed by Mariana Díaz-Wionczek; because poetry is so difficult to translate, the Spanish versions have been included. Marlene and Ana Cristina Castro reviewed the translations of their interviews and the interviews with María Eugenia Bozzoli de Wille and Alvaro Wille. Suzanne Scheld transcribed all of the interviews in Spanish and translated the final interview with Alfredo Rodríguez. The translations of interviews and field notes are my own.

I am indebted to Stephane Tonnelat, a visiting doctoral student from France, who produced the CAD plans of Parque Central and Plaza de la Cultura, developed a system for clearly representing the movement maps, and created readable behavioral maps. Stephane also contributed to the theoretical discussion of the microgeographies of plaza life in Chapter 7.

While at the John Carter Brown Library at Brown University, Norman Fiering, librarian; Susan Danforth, curator of maps; and Dan Slive, reference librarian, were particularly helpful in locating and documenting plans and maps of early New World plazas. The photographs in Chapters 4 and 5 were taken by Richard Hurley and produced as a courtesy of the John Carter Brown Library. Resident fellows and faculty at that institution participated in a weekly seminar series that contributed to the ideas presented.

Selected photographs were taken by Vicky Risner, currently Head of Acquisitions and Processing of the Music Division at the Library of Con-

xx ■ on the plaza

gress and a specialist in dance ethnography. Vicky visited the field in 1986 in order to produce a series of movement maps presented in Chapter 7. She contributed greatly to my thinking about the role of movement in space on the plazas. Marjory Dressler took photographs of the plaza in Mérida that are included in Chapter 4. Oscar Arias contributed his photograph and granted me an important interview. Joel Lefkowitz visited the field in 1993 and 1997 in order to photograph the redesigned public spaces in San José. I appreciate their willingness to let me publish their photographs and to share their ideas about what they observed while in the field. I would also like to thank Arnie Kusnetz for editing the preface. Finally, I would like to thank Joel and Laurel Wilson for their intellectual insights and constant encouragement throughout the lengthy research and writing process, and for their tireless editing.

I would like to thank the editors of the following publications for permission to use excerpts that present earlier versions of the arguments found in Chapters 4, 5, 6, and 7:

"Spatializing culture: The social production and social construction of public space." *American Ethnologist* 23 (1996): 861–879.

"Indigenous architecture and the Spanish American Plaza in Mesoamerica and the Caribbean." *American Anthropologist* 97 (1995): 748–762.

"Constructing difference: Spatial boundaries and social change." In *Setting Boundaries,* ed. D. Pellow. Amherst: Bergin and Garvey, 1996.

"Cultural meaning of the plaza." In *The Cultural Meaning of Urban Space,* ed. R. Rotenberg and G. M. McDonogh. Amherst: Bergin and Garvey, 1993.

I would like to thank the Editorial Costa Rica for permission to translate and reprint excerpts from the following works:

Gerardo César Hurtado, *Los parques* (1975, pp. 111–115).

Alfonso Chase, "Casa del pueblo." In *Obra en marcha: Poesía, 1965–1980* (1982, p. 186).

Arturo Montero Vega, "Los parques." In *Poesía contemporánea de Costa Rica,* ed. Carlos Rafael Duverrán (1978, p. 197).

Manuel González Zeledón, "Un día de mercado en la plaza principal." In *Cuentos de Magón* (1994, pp. 23–31).

I would also like to thank Editorial Mujeres for permission to translate and reprint Vilma Loría's short story "San José de noche," published in *Relatos de mujeres,* ed. Linda Berrón (1993, pp. 67–69); and to thank Trejos Hermanos, S.A., for permission to translate and reprint an excerpt from Fernando Durán Ayanegui's novel *Mi pequeño bazar* (1989, 11–13).

The House of the People

Plazas are the palaces of the people.
On asphalt or stone
The passage way is a knife
and each lip a scream.
From street to street the world grows.
Animating the murmur of the crowd
Some gagged truth
discovered as soon as it hits the air.
I believe that in each plaza,
corner to corner and street to street,
people reveal themselves.
We look at one another face to face
we recognize each other
and make ourselves strong.
Take some forgotten word
and make it yours,
the same as when you are making love
or sensing the air.
The houses of the people are the plazas
and there we are, everyone and no one.

Casa del Pueblo

Los palacios del pueblo son las plazas.
Sobre el asfalto o la piedra
el paso es un cuchillo
y cada labio un grito.
De calle a calle el mundo crece.
Vivifica el murmullo del gentío
alguna verdad amordazada
y descubierta apenas en el aire.
Yo creo que en cada plaza,
esquina a esquina y calle a calle,
el pueblo se descubre.
Se mira rostro a rostro
y allí se reconoce
    y se hace fuerte.
Toma alguna palabra olvidada
y la hace suya,
igual que cuando hace el amor
    o siente al aire.
La casa del pueblo son las plazas
y somos allí todos y ninguno.

—ALFONSO CHASE

PART ONE   Introduction

1. Parque Central, 1986

The Parks

In the parks I added
the pines' height
and filled my senses with books.

Student of Josefino parks,
I promoted the trees
to keep them always with me.

In the parks I rhyme
the rose with the book,
human suffering
with children's smiles
while my friends
learned the legal code
and constructed syllogisms.

Los Parques

En los parques sumé
la altura de los pinos
y me llené de libros los sentidos.

Bachiller de los parques josefinos,
promoví a los árboles
para llevarlos siempre conmigo.

En los parques rimé
la rosa con el libro,
el dolor de los hombres
y la sonrisa del niño,
mientras mis amigos
se aprendían los Códigos
y construían los silogismos.

—ARTURO MONTERO VEGA

CHAPTER ONE

Notes from the Field
A Personal Account

■

Field Notes from Parque Central

Parque Central, weekday morning, February 20, 1985—
First impressions on field trip #1.
The bus stopped at Parque Central. I am struck immediately with how
ugly and strange the *kiosco* [bandstand] is; it is like a Precolumbian
Maya incense burner created in a giant form, or a Postclassic temple
with cut-out sides. The stairs are so steep and it is so tall that it re-
minds me of a temple at Tikal [a Maya site in Guatemala]. I start taking photographs as soon as I step out, shooting in a continuous circle
and also along the pathways and edges.

The park is full of people. Almost every bench is taken, mostly by
men, who stand or sit in groups around a bench or wall ledge; a few
are even stretched out full length on a bench. At each entry path there
are two to three shoeshine men, a few with customers (see Photograph
2). They look quite established and part of the scene. Most of the men
sitting are older, while the younger ones stand. One man is eating an
ice cream cone. I look for women and find only two on a bench, and
one *campesino* [country] couple sit silently with straight backs and severe faces. Two women have a flower stall, and one man is selling ice
cream. The men's behavior is a public display, full of symbolic postur-
ing, verbal play, and social exchange.

2. Shoeshine men and client in Parque Central

Parque Central, 8:00–10:00 A.M., weekday, May 19, 1986—
First day of section observations on field trip #2.

The day starts with waiting for the bus. The traffic is stop and go, and the wait seems forever. The bus creeps along letting everyone get on even if it means that people have to hang out of the doors. A man gets up to give me a seat, which is a stroke of luck, since I am having a hard time standing in the crowd. I arrive at Parque Central on the dot of 8:00 with the cathedral bells ringing. Mobs of people descend from the bus hurrying on their way as I try to find a place to start.

I circle the park once feeling uncomfortable in this male-dominated space. At this time in the morning there are hardly any women here, and those who are, walk through quickly. The park is littered with leaves and paper, ill-kempt and cluttered, looking rather worn and run-down. The benches are full even though there are eighty or more in the area of a square city block; and half of the area is taken up with the monumental kiosk. I circle the park again and notice that in the kiosk basement is a children's library.

I decide that it is impossible to describe the plaza all at once, so I start on the northeastern corner where there is the most action. The northeast corner is what I call the shoeshine men's corner. Each bench has one or two men who are either cleaning a customer's shoes or waiting, talking and joking nearby. The shoeshine men use the benches as props for all of their activities, work as well as recreation, and they circulate from one bench to another to exchange information, jokes, money, and stolen goods or drugs. If one bench becomes too full, they move again.

There is an "in-crowd" of five or six men with long hair, beards, and short-sleeved dirty tee shirts. They appear to be in their late thirties or early forties, and they move as a group. Other shoeshine men are more conservatively dressed and do not look very different from the people who are having their shoes cleaned. A couple of men carry plastic "suitcases" and unpack there in the park. The in-group men, however, carry their equipment in plastic coffee bags, which they hang on the backs of the benches. Some shoeshine men hang around a lot, talking and relaxing, while others aggressively try to get customers by inviting them to sit down so they can clean their dirty shoes. One common technique is for the shoeshine man to point to your shoes and tell you that he can make them look much better—even if you are wearing tennis shoes!

After about half an hour I move counterclockwise to the northwest corner, which is much sunnier and less crowded, with the majority of people walking through. The benches here are full of men reading newspapers or sitting and staring at the passersby (see Photograph 3). I see a street sweeper and his friends, who follow him as he works, talking and smoking cigarettes.

I move to the southwest corner, where everyone is meeting someone, with someone, or holding someone, and a lot of people are walking through on the diagonal. At this corner there are two couples and a woman—the largest number of women anywhere in the park except for the women who sell flowers. I notice the vendors, small boys walking through selling ice cream, candy, or bread. The pace of the walking is quickening as the day moves on.

The last half hour is spent at the southeast corner, back facing the cathedral. I am getting tired, but there is nowhere to sit because all the benches are taken. Everyone there seems to be waiting and looking at their watches before going back to reading their newspapers. The most frequent activity is reading the newspaper, staring into space, or talking to the person who is next to you. I see a family—father, mother, and four children—sit down on a bench, squeezing in next to a man they do not know. A young man comes over, offers me his seat, and then sits down next to me. He asks the time and then returns to reading his newspaper. He looks at me over his paper from time to time and notices if I glance back at him.

Parque Central, 10:30–11:30 A.M., Sunday, June 15, 1986—
Sunday in the park during field trip #2.

The band sets up slowly: first a truck pulls up and unloads the chairs, then the conductor's stand is arranged in the center, surrounded by a wider semicircle of the players' chairs. It looks like a full orchestra, and the sound is lovely. They play five different pieces of music on this sunny morning. Interestingly, most of the spectators stand on the platform of the kiosk in a circle surrounding the musicians (see Photograph 4).

I descended from the kiosk to take pictures of the people watching from the lower levels. The park is full of children running and playing, women talking, and older men looking on. There are many older

3. Man reading newspaper in Parque Central

4. Band playing on Sunday in Parque Central

Ticos [local slang for Costa Rican men] dressed up in their Sunday best, but I assume that this is because it is Father's Day!

I start to take a picture of three older men (over seventy years of age) who are talking (see Photograph 5); they smile and invite me to sit down. They also have come to hear the music, having gone to mass very early that morning. They ask me where I am from, if I am married, and whether I have children. I answer, "No, I do not have any children, but want to." They reply, "Then take your husband to Puntarenas. It is hotter there, and it will stick." They go on to talk about hot Ticas [Costa Rican women] and sex, chuckling that it is hard to get it up any more. They watch the girls walking by and add: "We watch more now than we did." I thank them for the seat and leave as another very old and quite feeble man with a cane comes up to join them.

As I walk around to the other side of the plaza an older woman, eighty-three years of age she says, hails me by waving her hand. She is

5. Costa Rican pensioners in Parque Central

putting everything that is in her purse on the bench beside her. She complains, "A woman robbed me of a 1,000 colón bill [Costa Rican money, about $7.38 if calculated at the exchange rate of 135.65 colones per U.S. dollar in January 1992] that was in my purse while she was helping to clean off. . . . A drunk had come up and thrown up on me, and the woman had been nice enough to help, but now you can not trust even someone who helps you." I tell her that it would be better to put the things back in her purse. She replies not to worry, that I was a big, strong girl who would protect her while she checked everything. I smile and wait for her to finish.

I go to see some children chasing pigeons and sit on the shoeshine corner with a tired-looking shoeshine man. The "gambler" comes over and says that he will show me the "cap game" [the "shell game" in the United States]. I had tried to watch the other day, but he had told me that I could not watch without playing. He spits on a tiny bit of paper, rolls it into a ball, and puts it under a Coca-Cola bottle cap. He then moves the bottle cap with the spit ball under it around, changing places with two other similar bottle caps. He moves the bottle caps slowly so that it is very clear where the spit ball is located. I choose the right one. Then he asks if I would bet 1,000 colones. I say that I do not have any cash on me. He tells me that I can bet my watch. Horrified, I react: "No, it was a gift from my boyfriend!" He smiles, says "OK," and walks off.

The tired-looking shoeshine man next to me asks me to bring him shoe wax from the United States when I return on my next trip. He has asked me out to dance or have a drink a couple of times, and wants to know if I do those kinds of things. I reply that I am "promised" [engaged to be married], and thank him for his invitation.

Parque Central, 6:00–9:00 P.M., Saturday, June 28, 1986—
Saturday night in the park during field trip #2.
It is very difficult to do fieldwork in Parque Central at night. It is cold and damp on the benches, and I feel quite uncomfortable as a woman alone. The same observations that I have made before seem confirmed: couples meet and fill the benches at 6:00 P.M. and slowly drift off between 7:00 P.M. and 7:30 P.M. Some go into the movie theaters that surround the park, and others finally catch a bus home. By 7:30 P.M. the park is occupied mainly by single adult men, some in pairs, but mostly alone.

The only new activity that I can now clearly pick out is a group of young women who are hanging around under the arbor, giggling and talking. They seem young, about fifteen to eighteen years of age, and most are wearing tight-fitting jeans. The older women who walk by wear even tighter, more provocative clothing; their style is tough and playful.

The young women get a man's attention by bumming a cigarette, teasing him, or planting a kiss on his cheek. The clearest pick-up is by a brunette woman in a floral dress and a sweatshirt. She goes over to a thin man, shakes his hand, and sits down. At first I wonder if he is her pimp. [I have since learned that in 1986 there were very few prostitutes with pimps, but that by 1997 prostitution had become more organized and dangerous, both to the sex worker and the client—see the short story in Chapter 3.] She bums a cigarette and smokes it dramatically, taking long, slow puffs. Two other men start to walk by, do a double-take, stop, and join them. She talks and flirts, commenting on the pleated pants of the well-dressed man of the pair, and the next time I look up they are walking off together. She swaggers and rotates her hips, and he smiles as they wave good-bye.

The most popular pick-up spot is the arbor. Everything is done pretty cautiously, as the Guardia Civil [local police] are everywhere, walking around and around the kiosk, so contacts are often in the form of shaking hands. Some women, however, are more direct: I see one jump on a man's lap and start kissing him before they walk off together.

Parque Central, 2:30 P.M., Tuesday, January 6, 1987—
First impressions on field trip #3.

The evangelical preachers who hold a prayer meeting every day under the arbor are just finishing as I arrive; I can hear their clapping all the way across the park (see Photograph 6). There is more business for the shoeshine men, and more women than during the last visit in the rainy season. One woman seems drugged, yet no one seems concerned. A policeman stops me and asks me if I am with the newspaper. I say no, and hurry on. All of the policemen are standing with girls; some were talking to prostitutes as they passed the time while on duty.

The same group of older pensioners are sitting on their bench. They salute me and invite me to sit down. I do not have time, so I smile and

6. Evangelist preacher clapping in Parque Central arbor

wave. Tourists wander by and sit on the steps of the kiosk. Policemen and groups of older men perch on the kiosk walls. The air is warm, not hot, and there is a breeze. It feels dry and very pleasant. Lots of children are playing on the kiosk, trying to slide down the curved, descending cement supports.

Parque Central, 1:30–4:30 P.M., Saturday, January 10, 1987—
Saturday afternoon during field trip #3.

Many more families, women, and couples are here; even the shoeshine men have their wives and children with them. Most people are sitting in the shade because the sunlight is so intense, except for one gringo [derogatory nickname for male North American] who is reading in the sun. The southwest-corner pensioners are still on their bench, but there are fewer on Saturday than during the week or on Sunday. And there are fewer shoeshine men. The one business that increases on Saturday is prostitution, and I notice one of my gringo friends wander off with a girl.

Young people lounge on the kiosk, girls and boys separately watching each other. Couples with children wrapped up as sleepy bundles walk by. The police also wander across the kiosk surveying the passersby.

The evangelists are preaching in the arbor, the sermon and the time of day are the same as during the week. Saturday just draws a larger crowd. I think the weather slows the movement and increases the sense of well-being for both me and other park users. More people are out enjoying the dry weather of January than during the rainy days of May, June, July, and August.

I sit with an eighty-eight-year-old man with whom I have become friendly. He comes every day and stays until late afternoon. I am greeted by another of my old friends, a pensioner, who is unshaven and dirty, wearing worn clothes, although he is smiling. I ask him what is wrong, as he is usually more well dressed; he points out that it is Saturday. During the week he comes every morning and afternoon before he goes to work at a hotel on 4th Avenue. He is proud that he still works, and he lives downtown so that he can go home for lunch, see his wife, and then return.

I map the slightly different sitting positions of groups on a Saturday. Families, couples, and singles all sit in different areas. People from out of town come here to rest before catching the bus home. The tempo of the traffic has increased on the edges of the park, but inside the pace has slowed to a standstill. The shoeshine men with their families are now having a picnic. One shoeshine man tells me that he is hopelessly in love with me. Another comes by to ask me how I am and where I have been for the past few months. They are funny and welcoming, and though I had felt some apprehension about talking with them last July, now they are part of my social world.

The strollers are languid in their movements, and girls smile on the arms of their boyfriends. People talk, look around, and then go back to reading. Children play everywhere, and only mothers and children walk through; everyone else is staying. There is a warm breeze that cools the hot sun. As the shadows deepen, the shoeshine men pack their bags and people stroll to the buses to go home. As it becomes too dark to photograph, couples begin to arrive, vendors set up for the evening crowd, and the tempo again picks up.

As I leave the park, I recognize two North American pensioners sitting on the inner circle of benches near the northwest corner. I walk over and say that I am surprised to see them here, as they usually go to the other plaza. Across the grass, in front of the Boruca Bar, are four more North Americans on their way to have a beer. I join them as they are getting ready to leave.

Both men are retired: the first, wearing a cap over his silver hair, worked for Standard Oil, and the second, for the Ford Motor Company. They love sport fishing and come here for four months each year to fish in Puntarenas [a city on the Pacific coast] or Río Colorado [an area on the Atlantic coast famous for game fishing]. They learned about Costa Rica from sport-fishing magazines and from friends. I walk on and then return to ask them a question: "Is it true that the gringos used to spend time over by the telephones in the park?" The man in the cap replied, "Yes, but then they moved to the Plaza de la Cultura." They get up to leave, saying that they want to go home for a nap before dinner.

Parque Central, 2:00 P.M., weekday, December 16, 1993—
Interview with Rudolfo Sancho, the engineer in charge of the
redesign of the park, during field trip #4.
[Parque Central was closed and under construction.]
I begin by explaining that I am interested in the remodeling and re-

construction of Parque Central. Rudolfo Sancho responds by saying that he got the original plans of the park from someone who came forth during the initial uproar about tearing down or preserving the kiosk:

> It was very interesting. It was quite a fight about the kiosk. If it were mine, I would get rid of it, but we should not throw it out, as it is part of our patrimony. And since they moved the fountain to the University [Universidad de Costa Rica, located in an eastern suburb of the city], and the University will not give it back, we will make a small copy of the original fountain to put in the park.

He continues:

> In 1889 we were the first city with lights in Central America. We were the first to have water. But by the 1940s the city decided that it was complete. There was no maintenance of the parks, and many beautiful details were lost.

I ask about the new design for the park, to which he replies:

> The idea is to raise the level of the plaza and just keep the lower part green where the pensioners and shoeshine men are located. Because of the monumentality of the kiosk, we are going to raise the entire level of the park, that way the kiosk will not look so out of scale. Since we see the park not as a place for sitting but [as] a ceremonial center, we made it "harder," covering more of the surface with cement to create a kind of *paseo* [walkway]. It should be a celebration of the city.

Parque Central, 11:30 A.M.–1:30 P.M., Wednesday, January 22, 1997—
A visit during field trip #5.
[The park has been redesigned since my last visit.]

I enter the park about 11:30 A.M. It is a bright, sunny day; the benches and ledges of the planters are full (see Photograph 7). The groups are more dispersed because of the new pattern of small benches. Benches now hold only two people, so there are often two seated with a third standing. The corners still provide a way to describe the park, even though the new design is more circular in orientation.

On the northeast corner there is only one shoeshine man left; he is

7. New sitting area in Parque Central

using a stand instead of a bench. Across the street there are four to five more on a sliver of sidewalk in front of the construction fence that is around the cathedral. The corner is only lightly populated, and it is quite warm there. I ask "What happened?" to the remaining shoeshine man, and he replies that they are no longer allowed in the park, that they have been banned by the municipality since the re-modeling. I ask, "Where is everyone, then?" and he responds, "In front of the Post Office and on the 'Boulevard.'"

Moving clockwise, there is a large group of older men along the planter wall and on the small benches. The men are deep in conversa-tion. I ask them about the changes in the park. One man comments that it is remodeled and prettier now. Overall, they have a mixed reac-tion to the design changes; they say that it is softer and more open, but less comfortable and green. The southern edge is also full of people waiting for buses. Even though buses no longer stop here, people still wait, and when they see buses arrive, then walk to nearby bus stops. There are more women now. The sense of "places" such as the arbor or the shoeshine corner has been lost and replaced with a se-ries of self-contained locations and isolated spaces. The southwest cor-ner, however, still has quite a few elderly men talking, and on the western edge there are forty people waiting to use the twenty-four newly installed telephone booths.

On the northwest corner, instead of praying and healing, there is a man called "Tango" doing acrobatic tricks with a soccer ball in front of a large crowd. I ask about the shoeshine men and vendors who used to be there, and everyone I ask confirms that they are now gone. A new security force is also very visible on the kiosk and on the park perimeter in their black uniforms. My photographer had counted four different uniforms yesterday when he was working, but I have seen only three: all black, all green, and the blue or khaki of the Guardia Civil. The men in the all-black uniforms must be the new municipal police placed throughout the center city to protect residents and tour-ists from the increased crime.

Parque Central, 10:00–11:00 A.M., Thursday, January 23, 1997—
The last visit on field trip #5.
I move clockwise around the kiosk to talk to some of the Costa Rican pensioners. I feel hesitant, but everyone is very friendly. I join a group of three men: the two older men are sitting and the younger one is

8. Photographer and the renovated kiosk in Parque Central

standing. One seated man has a camera and a briefcase, the second has some kind of photograph viewer or Polaroid camera (see Photograph 8). I ask the man with the camera if he is a photographer, and he answers, "Yes, I take pictures of people in the park—particularly the Nicaraguans." As he speaks, he takes out a set of his pictures to show me. I ask what he thinks of the changes in the park. He replies that it is fine, but that he likes it greener. The two other men agree that there is too much cement and not enough grass and flowers. They comment that there are no longer any vendors, but it keeps it cleaner, and without the shoeshine men, there are fewer illegal activities.

"Do you feel safer?" I ask.

"But you must be careful still because of the *chapulines* [members of young gangs]," he replies.

"Where are they?" I respond.

"Everywhere, there is one over there," he says, pointing to a young man in baggy pants sitting by himself, looking around. "They congregate here at 5:00 each evening."

I ask where the other pensioners are. The standing man replies that they are at the beach for the holiday. "Are they still there?" I ask, pointing to the southwest corner. "Yes," he replies, "they still come. One has died, but the rest come as before."

I move on and ask another older man why he comes here each day. He smiles and responds:

> Because it is agreeable, I can see and greet my friends every day. I see people I know to talk to. I used to come when there was a *ramada* [the arbor] and when there were dances in the kiosk on New Year's Eve, where those who could not afford to go somewhere expensive could go. The most important part, however, is to see your friends and family who you otherwise would not see. It is very agreeable.

Field Notes from the Plaza de la Cultura

Plaza de la Cultura, weekday, February 20, 1985—
First impressions on field trip #1.

At first I am shocked that the new plaza is so modern. It has a sunken fountain and is an expansive open space paved with cement tiles, lined with benches made of large metal pipes, and punctuated with small cement seats under a double row of fig trees. The space appears quite barren, denuded of greenery, and instead of plants, yellow and silver pipes stick up like periscopes from an underground submarine.

The plaza is multilayered, with offices below ground level where the Institute of Tourism's central office and a large marble exhibition space are located. The downstairs is closed, but the guard goes to get me a brochure that describes the plaza and its construction. The Gold Museum will eventually go into this subterranean space when there is adequate funding for guards. [In 1987 it was opened as Los Museos del Banco Central de Costa Rica (Museums of the Costa Rican Central Bank) and included the Precolumbian gold collection, stamp collection, and painting and sculpture collection.]

There are two distinct parts to the plaza: (1) the section between the National Theater (see Photograph 9; the edge of this turn-of-the-century building is visible on the right) and the Gran Hotel Costa

9. Plaza de la Cultura, 1986

Rica, which is for tourists and is full of vendors selling hammocks and other souvenirs (see Photograph 10), and (2) the plaza proper, which is a large, multilevel open space that extends along the side of the National Theater all the way to Avenida Central (see Photograph 9).

Plaza de la Cultura, weekday, May 26, 1986—
First impressions on field trip #2.

The first day at the Plaza de la Cultura is so slow that I decide to observe it by sections: the tourist plaza in front of the Gran Hotel Costa Rica, the shopping arcade and shaded tree-lined walkway of the upper plaza, the sunny open section of the upper plaza, the lower plaza areas, the section below the fountain, and the entrance to the tourist office.

The plaza is full of young people—even the shoeshine men are boys; it seems to be the domain of the adolescent and the tourist. There is an equal distribution of males and females here, lots of couples, and couples with children (see Photograph 11).

10. Vendors selling tourist crafts in Plaza de la Cultura

11. Couples and young people in Plaza de la Cultura

Children love this plaza, especially the fountain and the open areas where they can run and chase the pigeons (see Photograph 12). Furthermore, the low benches seem quite comfortable for them, and there is the attraction of the juggler/clown who entertains during midday. The children adore his jokes and tricks and clowning with his assistant/wife. Children of all social classes, from little boys who sell crafts or shine shoes to children in private school uniforms, come to see and listen to the juggler/clown. They all crowd forward to see while the adults line up behind them.

Another major activity is that of older gringos and other foreigners as well as some Ticos, who pick up young women, even girls, on Saturday and Sunday afternoon (see Photograph 13). A friend's brother-in-law said that Plaza de la Cultura is actually more dangerous than Parque Central because there are more drugs being sold and more male prostitution. So far I have only seen one clandestine activity on the plaza and at least three or four in Parque Central; however, it could be I have not been here at the right time.

12. Children and pigeons in Plaza de la Cultura

13. Gringos in Plaza de la Cultura

Plaza de la Cultura, 12:00 NOON–3:00 P.M., Thursday, June 12, 1986—
Sex in the afternoon during field trip #2.

I need to change a roll of film so I sit down on the shady pipe bench
next to three gringos who are looking at and talking about girls (see
Photograph 14). Finally I say something, and the smaller guy says, "I
wondered when you were going to admit that you speak English." I
then met "Jim," "the Canadian," and "the small man." Most of the
conversation focuses on their interest in the young Ticas.

> We like them younger—the older ones are not as nice. We come
> to the plaza because that is where the girls are—before we met
> them in the street. Now the plaza is the place—in the afternoon.
> . . . If you do not have one by evening, it is too late.

The men I interviewed think that there are about 1,000–2,000 older
North American men in Costa Rica looking for girls during the dry
season, and that most of them have been living here for years. They
get bored, leave, and then come back because of the beautiful young
women. They say [to me] that North American women are awful in
bed, and Ticas [Costa Rican females] know how to love. The conversation moves from sexual activity to "peckers," penis implants, and

14. Young women in Plaza de la Cultura

trouble with girlfriends. There is some joking and embarrassment that I would be shocked, but the conversation continues. It seems that young women and sex, or talking about it, are their main diversions.

Plaza de la Cultura, 5:00–7:30 P.M., Friday, June 13, 1986—
The great chain robbery during field trip #2.

Beautiful late afternoon, clear and cool. Tomás offers me a coffee, but by 5:00 P.M. I want to be back on my metal pipe bench. As I return, there is a lot of confusion and looking around. When I got off the bus I had seen three young men running down the street, and people shouting. I asked as many people as possible, "¿Qué pasó?" [What happened?]. The answers range from "a robbery" to a more precise description of "a girl's gold chain was torn off her neck." I have heard many stories about chain stealing, but this is the first case at which I am present. It happened under the trees of the shopping arcade. One man said that the robbers look for chains that they like, and then one stands in front and the other behind, working together to distract the unfortunate victim.

The plaza is filling up with high school students wearing uniforms and carrying musical instruments and banners. It seems that there is going to be a parade of high school marching bands along Avenida Central to celebrate the centennial of a private boys' school.

There are two groups of teenagers, both leaning along the fountain rail. Usually just one group is there and the other is on the planter seat with a portable radio. One group is predominantly male and Black— the leader wears a "do-rag" with tails. He speaks Spanish and English and something that I can not understand [probably a form of street slang]. The other group is mixed male and female with a rotating leader. The young male who looks like the rock star Prince, from Purple Rain [a rock music album by Prince], often takes the lead, but so does a kid in khaki pants or a small, dark-haired girl. It is hard to tell; they move around a lot, and the group composition constantly changes.

There are, by the way, a lot of police around everywhere, either because of the parade or because it is Friday night. The khaki-pants kid, with a bottle in a brown paper bag, signals the main group of six guys to "move over." They quickly go to the lower plaza in front of the entrance to the tourist office. It is darker and quieter there, and I follow. I am just wondering if they realize how many police are around when two Guardia Civil come up, take the bag, frisk two of the teenagers, take their identity cards, and line all six up along the National Theater wall. I go up to ask what was wrong, and the police curtly tell me to "move along." I move back and watch with a growing crowd.

Plaza de la Cultura, 8:00–9:00 A.M., Monday, June 16, 1986—
Morning during field trip #2.

Early morning seems to be a time when people sit on the benches to rest and then move on. They sit for two or three minutes, then stand, straighten their clothes, and move on. Some read or study, but most just sit and stare. I would call it waiting, but maybe this is what Tomás calls *meditar* [to meditate, reflect, think] (see Photograph 15). A couple of women begin to talk, but in general there is little interaction. Morning does not seem to be a social time, but rather a passage to work or an early break in the day. The most active group are the sweepers who are cleaning the plaza. They talk and call back and forth to one another. The food sellers and jewelry sellers are not out. The first gringo shows up, sitting alone on the benches under the trees.

One comes over and sits on the pipe bench. There is so little activity that it is hard to be a participant observer, and I am so sleepy that I treat myself to coffee at the hotel café.

Plaza de la Cultura, 9:00 A.M.–3:30 P.M., Tuesday, January 6, 1987—
First impressions on field trip #3.

The plaza is not filled up yet. There are very few people who talk or even walk by. The old woman who begs from tourists is sitting on the steps of the hotel café (see Photograph 16), and a few single men are reading the newspaper along the tree-lined edge. The hammock and whistle men begin to set up. Most of the tourists are still in the hotel restaurant (see Photograph 17), and the group of gringo men have not yet appeared. This morning is not very different from my previous early-morning observations.

By noon the plaza is packed with people. Early in the morning it was slow and sleepy, but now that I am back there is an apparently drunk man playing with a soccer ball and a long line of teenagers watching. There are a lot of young people, mostly males but some females, in groups and a few in pairs. This is a dramatic change because of the school vacation. When school is in session, teenagers usually do not come to the plaza until late afternoon or evening (see Photograph 18).

15. People reading newspapers in Plaza de la Cultura

16. Old woman in Plaza de la Cultura

17. Tourists having breakfast in the Gran Hotel café

18. Teenagers in Plaza de la Cultura

19. Peruvian singers in Plaza de la Cultura

By 1:45 P.M. the plaza is no longer loaded with people; there are fewer teenagers, but the gringos are now in full swing. Other things have changed but not the pick-ups. There is a group of Peruvian singers performing for tourists at the edge of the planter (see Photograph 19).

All of the gringos are sitting beside me on the center pipe bench trying to pick up three girls near us. One guy with a tattoo even speaks to the girls in Spanish. He seems to be doing pretty well; his conversation moves from Vesco [a well-known North American financier who fled to Costa Rica to escape prosecution in the United States] to chefs, restaurants, and then to girls.

I ask why they have come. A man in his fifties replies that they all have different reasons. He is a disabled veteran who had a "nervous breakdown." He has had the same girlfriend for over eight months. He says that most of the men are concerned about the Costa Rican women lying to them. Most have been divorced or widowed and are bitter and disillusioned about American women. He goes on: "They are looking for real love and trust, not just sex, even though they say that they are interested only in sex."

Just then two women and four small children who sell *chicles* [chewing gum] walk into the middle of the plaza. The youngest boy drops his tray of chewing gum, and one of the women beats him as he tries to pick it up. The gringos tell me that this mother sends her children out to beg every day and beats them if they do not sell enough. One man comments: "She is a hard woman." The men drift off to home and dinner. The plaza is quiet and dark.

Plaza de la Cultura, 3:30–9:30 P.M., Saturday, January 10, 1987—
Saturday afternoon and evening during field trip #3.
The tourist stalls are set up in front of the hotel for the Saturday handicraft market. Ceramics, leather, hammocks, blouses, and paintings predominate. The whistle boy begins to wrap up his merchandise.

There are only a few people here, especially compared to Parque Central. Lots of girls, groups of women, and a few gringos are sitting in the sun. Single men sit under the trees. The only excitement is the approach of two cute girls, who are greeted with howls and calls such as "Morena [brunette], come here" by a group of teenagers.

I greet the Gran Hotel bouncer, who is standing at the edge of the hotel café, as I go in for a soda. He says that he works every day from

20. Plaza de la Cultura with vendor stalls

3:00 P.M. until 10:00 P.M. I ask if there are people on the plaza at night. He answers: "Yes, after 7:00 P.M. people come out, particularly the teenagers."

I am making a sun-and-shade map and overhear a gringo talking about his most recent conquest. The air is clear, birds are singing as I sit in the afternoon shade. The mountains look as if you can touch them. A couple eating Pops ice cream [a popular Costa Rican brand of ice cream sold at the edge of the plaza] joins me. They murmur between bites. He keeps his hand on her shoulder. A mass of families walk through, everyone eating ice cream. I can hear children behind me screaming at the pigeons. Even *campesinos* [people from the countryside] come here to sit and stare at the sky.

"Vicky," a middle-aged performer I have seen before, is here playing his tiny guitar and telling lewd jokes to a large crowd. The rest of the area is quiet. I sit next to a gringo who visits Costa Rica with his wife. He tells me about his wife being mugged four years ago by a guy on a motorcycle who grabbed her purse and dragged her away. He was mugged on a bus during his first few days here.

I return later, about 9:30 P.M., to see if what the Gran Hotel bouncer had told me was right. As he had said, the plaza was full of people, too many to count, and many more than I expected. I could see and identify the teenagers, some single men, but no specific activities from that distance.

Plaza de la Cultura, December 13, 1993—
Interview with Renato Cajas, the head of tourism, during field trip #4.
I ask Mr. Cajas why the Plaza de la Cultura was originally designed and built. He responds:

> San José started without a plan, so it developed in response to commercial and industrial needs. More than half the population of Costa Rica lives here, over a million people. The transportation is terrible, you can not walk or breathe. This administration decided that it was necessary to reform the city government and to use 10 percent of the sales tax for the municipality. In 1990, Oscar Arias reformed the city governance so that we could create new policies for urban development. . . .
>
> We want to humanize the city. Something that we can do quickly and easily. The Plaza de la Cultura was the first project to attract tourism, and President Carazo got credit, even though President Oduber started it.

Plaza de la Cultura, December 16, 1993—
Interview with Rudolfo Sancho during field trip #4.
I ask Mr. Sancho what he thinks is going on with all the vendors totally covering the plaza (see Photograph 20). He answers:

> The 1974 design of the plaza was what was in style. The objective was to save the National Theater. Now what has happened is that the Guatemalan and Honduran vendors have a good lawyer to fight for them, arguing that foreigners have the same rights as Costa Ricans. We have had a year of this; there are at least four or five groups that are still fighting based on the "Bill of Rights." The result is that the Plaza de la Cultura is full of vendors and is no longer a plaza at all.

Plaza de la Cultura, January 22, 1997—
Interview with Ibo Bonilla during field trip #5.
[The Plaza de la Cultura was closed for renovation
during the last field trip.]

The plaza was entirely fenced off and full of rubble. The architect, Ibo Bonilla, greets me with a smile and offers to show me around. I am very disappointed that it is closed and concerned that it is being redesigned so soon after opening. He explains that he will not change the basic design, but wants to incorporate the observations that he has made concerning how people use the plaza. His objectives are to add color, redesign the pattern of groupings, that is, the way that people gather, and to correct some technical elements.

He feels that the first plaza was not a park but a "cultural space," and that the public was timid about entering at first. He felt that it looked like any internationally designed space and had little to do with Costa Rica. But now the public have claimed the space and are upset that it is closed. He has put windows in the construction fencing so that passersby can see the work going on and the changes he is making.

Later in the interview he comments that he is thinking about people coming from outside the city to meet and trying to give separate groups their own space:

> I want it to be a more closed space, but the openness of the plaza allows a sense of security because it provides many visual axes. When surrounded by high buildings, people feel less secure. The most dangerous place is the passageway by the National Theater.

I conclude the interview by asking why there are so many stories about the plaza being dangerous and unpleasant, to which he replies: "There are many myths about the plaza. The majority of people who talk about it do not use it, and negative information always travels fast."

CHAPTER TWO

Public Space and Culture

The Case of the Latin American Plaza

■

The plaza in itself, considered limited in space by its four sides, is the most exquisite expression of social life ever achieved by Man's [*sic*] city planning and architectural genius. The giant monuments of ancient cultures are grotesque and shapeless imperfections in comparison. The pyramids of Egypt, the palaces of Babylon, the temples of Greece, managed to convey a limited aspect of human life, but in so doing they sacrificed the wholeness of life. For that reason, they always bear within their beauty a mortal and definitive seal of sadness. They are closed circuits, frozen or gruesome perfections, because Man [*sic*] was never able to fully inhabit them, in spite of all their rich and complex existential temporality and eternity.

In contrast, the plaza affirms and resolves all things that are incompatible to pure reason; it preserves them, and gives them a voice and a future. The simplicity of its space is clearly an invitation to the social and moral freedom of the people. But its fortress-like lines are a definitive reminder that life and freedom can be lived only in a concrete and limited location, for a well-defined purpose. If those limits disappeared, there would be nothing left but the naked countryside, in which nature has absorbed and destroyed the essential freedom of human art and ingenuity.

—FERNANDO GUILLÉN MARTÍNEZ

The Latin American plaza has been an object of aesthetic inspiration and controversy since its inception. Its architectural beauty, political symbolism, and cultural importance have been discussed and debated by legions of scholars. As the above quotation illustrates, its architectural geometry has evoked philosophical treatises on the plaza as the ultimate architectural expression of social and moral freedom. It is seen as a testimony to human rationality, a defense against unbridled nature, and an example of enlightened urban design.

The plaza also provides a physical, social, and metaphorical space for public debate about governance, cultural identity, and citizenship. Journalistic reports of how politicians manipulate the political symbolism of these charged public spaces portray the plaza's power to elicit civic commentary and social action. For example:

> In all of Mexico, no place has been shaped by destiny or scarred by history more than the enormous concrete square in this city's heart that is known by some as the "gran tortilla" and most simply as the Zócalo.
>
> This is the very spot where Cortés sweet-talked the Aztec Emperor Montezuma into believing his intentions were noble; where General Winfield Scott declared the American victory over Mexico in 1847; where one Mexican President after another has come to receive the adulation—or scorn—of the masses.
>
> Because it is a potent symbol as much as a physical space, the Zócalo often succumbs to the ambitions of politicians who impose their own touches on the long stains of its history. Over the centuries, successive leaders have arrived and undone the work of their predecessors so their own efforts can be better seen. (DePalma 1998, A2)

This newspaper account goes on to report that an ostensibly benign proposal to plant trees in the Zócalo, the central plaza in Mexico City, engendered an intense reaction by those who viewed it as an attempt to reduce the plaza's effectiveness as a space for public protests and state ceremonies. Some people interviewed were concerned "that the only thing trees would clear the air of is civic expression" (DePalma 1998, A2) by restricting rallies and mass demonstrations that occur in front of the National Palace and Metropolitan Cathedral. There were, of course, others who agreed with the plan to transform it into a park to reduce pollution. The political symbolism of "greening" the open plaza could reflect the mayor's intention not to retain a monumental plaza traditionally associated with adulation and a cult of power, or his desire to make an environmental statement associated with left-leaning politics. In either case, the proposed new plaza design is politically significant, as evidenced by the amount of public debate and degree of national concern.

These purely aesthetic and macropolitical interpretations, however, are not sufficient for understanding the plaza because they leave out the people who use the plazas and its importance in their everyday lives. These perspectives exclude the indigenous archaeological and ethnohistorical past, as well as the memories, stories, and conversations that create the myths and meanings of plaza life. Instead, Eurocentric explanations of the origins of plaza architecture and formalistic readings of political symbolism determine what is known, while the local stories go untold.

Plazas are spatial representations of Latin American society and social hierarchy. Citizens battle over these representations because they are so critical to the definition and survival of civil society. Plazas are also centers of cultural expression and artistic display reflected in their changing designs and furnishings. And finally, plazas are settings for everyday urban life where daily interactions, economic exchanges, and informal conversations occur, creating a socially meaningful place in the center of the city.

[margin annotation: multiple def]

These aesthetic, political, and social aspects of the plaza are dynamic, changing continually in response to both personal action and broader sociopolitical forces. They are also contested through conflicts about the use, design, and meaning of the space. By tracing these changes and conflicts and their impact on plaza architecture, social activities, and political meanings, scholars can use the plaza to understand urban public space through the examination of this specific cultural form.

In order to address the importance of the plaza as a particular kind of public space and to provide a more complete narrative of plaza life, this book interweaves ethnography, history, literature, and personal narrative. These multiple genres are employed to create a more multivocal and multilocal representation of a place. Diverse scales, methodological strategies, types of narrative, and points of view purposely move the reader through the physical, social, and conceptual spaces of the analysis. The resulting dialogue includes the reader in an ongoing conversation about the importance of public space and culture in everyday life.

I explore three questions in this conversation: (1) Why is public space culturally and politically important—particularly urban civic spaces such as the plaza in Latin American cities? (2) What are the theoretical underpinnings of the relationship of space and culture, that is, of spatializing culture? (3) How are individual narratives, ethnographies, and histories interwoven into a loose fabric in which fragments of experience and memory are juxtaposed with theory and interpretation?

The conversation begins in Part I, Introduction, with an immersion in the setting of the plazas of San José, Costa Rica, through ethnographic field notes, followed by an overview of the book. Each question, then, is examined in the subsequent sections and chapters. Part II, Histories, uncovers the contradictory ethnohistories of the European and indigenous origins of the Spanish American plaza, and how the power of writing history, as well as of building the historical landscape, contributes to different interpretations of these ceremonial public spaces. Part III, Ethnographies, presents cultural descriptions of two plazas in San José, Costa Rica, that conceptualize the spatialization of culture, social and spatial boundaries, and commodification and artistic mystification of urban public space. Part IV, Conversations, explores various kinds of narratives—literary, conversational, and personal—in an effort to include Costa Rican voices and perspectives on the experience and memory of plaza life. The conclusion discusses what has been learned from this project about the importance of the politics of public space within a participatory democracy.

The Meaning of Public Space

There has been considerable concern about the demise of public space in the United States: civic spaces are no longer democratic places where all people are embraced and tolerated, but instead centers of commerce and consumption. The public's reaction to the loss of public space has been so dramatic that new communities such as Celebration, the Disney company's residential development in Florida, are being designed as ersatz versions of small-town America, including a town hall and a central square (Mark 1997). Even the Chicago suburb of Schaumburg, Illinois, a place synonymous with mall culture, is building a central square in a search for a sense of place, "a sort of civic soul" (Johnson 1996). But these suburban public spaces lack the diversity and complexity that residents seek, becoming theme-park versions of an idealized original.

Increasing privatization through collaborative public/private partnerships between municipalities and local businesses has transformed such places as Bryant Park and Union Square in the center of New York City into safe, middle-class environments maintained by strict surveillance and police control. The urban multi-use development of Battery Park

City in New York City has become yet another piece of the spatial board game in which the capitalist system is reproducing the central city as a homogeneous professional domain. The public space of Battery Park City is upper-middle-class space, not simply because only the wealthy can afford to live or rent offices there, but also because its design vocabulary and limited public access exclude other less affluent members of the city's population. Even city squares and village greens are no longer places for public discussion and casual loitering, but instead have become filled with regulated green markets, military reenactments, and seasonal county fairs.

There are observable differences between central urban plazas in Latin America or Europe that retain a vibrant public life and civic spaces of Los Angeles and New York. Unless North American urban spaces become commercially successful—the best examples being New York City's South Street Seaport, Boston's Faneuil Hall Marketplace, San Francisco's Ghirardelli Square and the Cannery, or Baltimore's Harborplace—or public/private models of center-city development such as Bryant Park or Battery Park City, their future remains in question. Commercialization and privatization, however, limit participation to those who can afford it and who conform to middle-class rules of conduct and appearance.

In contrast, the Latin American plaza has been identified as a preeminent public space, a source and symbol of civic power, with a long tradition as the cultural center of the city. The plaza represents the aesthetic of the city and is considered a metaphor of the urban cosmology (Da Matta 1984). In and around it are located the gardens and buildings most basic to the social life of the community: the church, representing religious power, and the government offices, representing political power. Traditionally, commerce was separated in another downtown area where impersonal transactions took place; however, over time, banks and businesses as well as theaters and restaurants have surrounded the plaza.

It is an arena where diverse social groups and social classes appear together in a highly structured way, segmented by space and time, yet intermingling and interacting on the same site. These rules of social encounter, of hierarchical complementarity and tolerance, however, are particular to the *cultura* (culture) of the plaza and are not necessarily obeyed in other parts of the city.

Moreover, this culturally distinct urban design tradition is also under attack from the pressures of global capital and generic architectural and planning vocabularies, but it has resisted commodification, or at least slowed its pace. In order to explain this seeming resistance to change, Part II unravels the confluences of history, power, and local politics that allow this form of public space to maintain its salience even in the large capital cities of Mexico and Central America. In these chapters, I trace the role of power and spatial symbolism in the evolution of the New World Spanish American plaza. Chapter 3 introduces the two plazas in San José, Costa Rica, and provides the specific ethnohistorical and sociopolitical context for this study. Chapter 4 presents evidence for European architectural models of plaza design, while Chapter 5 presents archaeological as well as ethnohistorical materials that argue for an indigenous origin of the plaza's spatial form. I conclude by highlighting the syncretic nature of Latin American plaza design and meaning.

Spatializing Culture

Theoretically, this work is about how culture can be understood spatially and what spatialization tells us about culture. Social and economic relations produce space. To think of the built environment as space rather than a collection of objects is useful because its parts become conjoined within a system, a kind of ecology. Through this ecology we begin to understand the causal relationships between economy, society, and culture on the one hand, and the urban environment on the other.

Theorists such as Pierre Bourdieu (1977), Manuel Castells (1983), Michel de Certeau (1984), David Harvey (1985), Anthony King (1980), Henri Lefebvre (1991), Neil Smith (1991, 1996), and Sharon Zukin (1991) have contributed to this discussion, linking political economic theory with the social production of the built environment at different urban scales. Anthropologists James Fernandez (1992), Keith Basso (1990), Fred Myers (1989), and Miles Richardson (1984) and the architectural historian Dolores Hayden (1995) have been more concerned with relating expressive culture to the experience of place. My objective is to bridge these understandings through spatializing culture, that is, integrating the social production of the built environment with the daily routines and ceremonial rituals of the cultural realm and the phenomenological experience of individuals.

Part III develops this theory and provides ethnographic examples of how spatialization works as an analytic framework as well as a method for uncovering spatially embedded aspects of culture. Chapter 6 sets out the larger theoretical agenda by proposing that social production of space and social construction of space must be understood as a dialogical process in which there is a high degree of conflict and contestation. Chapter 7 explores gender, class, and cultural differences that give shape and form to the world by permitting labeling and classification. Chapter 8 considers Costa Rican plazas both as artistic, architecturally designed expressions and as valuable commodities manipulated for political power and economic advantage, and it examines the contradictions that come to light when artistic style and political purpose are compared.

The Experience of Place

A final concern is how to link the history and ethnography of the plaza with the experience of being in the plaza. The sociopolitical and cultural forces that produce the plaza create an environment and an ecology in which the individual experiences the impact of these forces. Individual users and residents also generate their own memories, understandings, and feelings that color and shape the real and perceived environment. Further, other forms of expressive culture such as paintings, photographs, novels, short stories, autobiographies, and poetry represent plazas and urban public space in ways that transform an individual's perception and experience of a place. These memories, stories, and personal reflections create places within the constraints of local histories and social structure discussed in Parts II and III.

Throughout the book I include Costa Rican memoirs, short stories, poetry, and field notes that reflect alternative experiences and perceptions of being in the plaza. In Part IV, however, I focus on how Costa Rican conversations—both fictional ones found in novels and actual conversations I had with people who had lived near Parque Central—present still another dimension of the plaza experience. Talk is the centerpiece of the analysis, providing the reader with dialogue and personal accounts of plaza life. Chapter 9 presents excerpts from novels written by Costa Rican authors that portray conversations occurring in parks and plazas. Chapter 10 records conversations with five Costa Ricans about their experiences of growing up on or near the main plaza and the quality of the time they spent there. Chapter 11 concludes by weaving these various threads of conversation into the multistranded and textured fabric of plaza life.

Methodology

This project began with a methodological problem that was transformed into twelve years of ethnographic fieldwork and ethnohistorical research.

I was concerned with how public space was studied and represented in anthropology, environmental psychology, landscape architecture, and urban design and planning. Studies of public spaces were either behavioral, describing the numbers and kinds of people who used the space, or architectural, describing the physical characteristics and architectural history of the built environment. There were few ethnographic studies, and even fewer environment-behavior studies that emphasized sociocultural processes and social relations. Yet the theoretical questions I wanted to address required the integration of architectural, archaeological, historical, ethnographic, and phenomenological materials to construct a multilayered analysis and nuanced account.

RESEARCH METHODS

The ethnographic descriptions are based on long-term fieldwork in San José beginning in August 1972 through July 1974 (see Photograph 21), continuing during the summers of 1976 and 1979, and including five field visits that focused only on the urban plazas: the first, February through March 1985; the second, May through September 1986; the third, December 1986 through February 1987; the fourth, November through December 1993; and the fifth, during January 1997. By observing over a long period of time, I was able to record a variety of sociopolitical situations and changing social behaviors and designs—creating a series of natural experiments. By selecting different months, I was able to sample a variety of seasonal ecologies: summer months coincide with Costa Rica's rainy season, characterized by late afternoon showers or torrential downpours that interrupt plaza life. During these periods I would stand with other plaza occupants under the closest available shelter or visit one of the local cafés to wait for the rain to stop. The winter months are the dry season, with clear, sunny, and cooler weather. Especially around Christmas and New Year's Day, plaza use increases, and the plazas are filled with informal markets for seasonal gifts of nuts and fruits.

Two plazas were selected for study as particularly important public spaces and centers of civic life: Parque Central, located at the center of San José and bordered by the national cathedral, was the Plaza Principal (main plaza) during colonial times and is the preeminent symbolic space of San José. Plaza de la Cultura is a more recently designed and constructed modern plaza only two blocks northeast of Parque Central,

21. The author in the field in 1973

located next to the architecturally distinguished National Theater and the major tourist hotel, the Gran Hotel Costa Rica. These field sites and the surrounding city were the focus of data collection for the ethnographic and phenomenological portions of the research (see Photograph 22).

Observation

Because of my concern that participant observation in a public space might not capture all the ongoing activities, I utilized three different observational strategies:

1. Each plaza was observed by sector, and everything that occurred in that sector was recorded for a designated period of time. This time/place sampling provided a system for nonsequentially observing all the sites throughout the day on both weekends and weekdays. A series of behavioral maps locating activities and counts of people by location, sex, and age were also created.

2. After the first month of time/space sampling, a map of activity

[handwritten margin note: time-place sampling]

22. Aerial photograph of central San José, 1982

locations had emerged, so a second set of observations concentrated on documenting these activities and the people engaged in them.

3. During the third phase of participant observation, I carried a camera and map, spoke to people, and became more involved in everyday plaza life (see Photograph 23). By this time plaza users were quite used to seeing me with my clipboard and pen, and they were delighted that I was now taking photographs and involving them in my until then seemingly clandestine task. The camera gave many people an excuse to talk to me and to ask what I was doing. I began to make friends and hang out with some of the plaza occupants, even visiting them at home or joining them when they went for a drink or a meal.

Interviews and Historical Documentation

At the conclusion of these observations, I collected a series of interviews with plaza users, using questions that had emerged during the observational period (see Photograph 24). A systematic series of interviews with the managers, owners, and directors of local institutions located on or near the plazas were completed; and blueprints, design guidelines, and plans for the design of the plazas were collected and discussed. Interviews with local historians and archival work in the National Library and at the Universidad de Costa Rica provided documentation of the oral histories of Parque Central. Interviews with the current and previous Ministers of Culture, the previous Minister of Planning (President Oscar Arias), and the chief of Municipal Planning, as well as with the architects involved in the design of the Plaza de la Cultura, provided contextual data for the ethnographic descriptions and documentation of the design and construction process. Finally, Costa Rican literature and poetry, newspapers and magazines, television presentations, and conversations with friends and neighbors provided data on the broader context of public life. These phases of data collection were repeated during each of the five intensive field visits.

Ethnohistorical Archival Research

As a 1990 Research Fellow at the John Carter Brown Library, I uncovered the origins of the Spanish American plaza working with early North

23. The author interviewing in 1986

American and European contact documents, including original maps and plans. It was there that I was able to find evidence that the Spanish were influenced by indigenous architecture and urban planning in their New World urban designs. This separate project produced the ethnohistorical background for understanding the Spanish American plaza in indigenous as well as European terms.

Photographic Documentation

Throughout the field visits, photographs were taken to document the physical changes in the design and use of each plaza and the surrounding city. These photographs soon became an irreplaceable source of data as the plazas began to change. During each subsequent visit, I would

24. The author mapping in 1997

arrive in San José and unexpectedly find that the plaza I planned to photograph and field-check would be under construction or overrun with vendors and tourists. Thus, the original photographs and the data they contained became part of my personal archive of the plaza's history. It was fortuitous that the research project encompassed over a decade of observation, since it was the historical sequence that provided the most important clues to the meaning of users' resistance and response to plaza changes as well as the State's control of spatial design.

Analysis
These methodologies and procedures were effective in providing different kinds of data that could be compared and analyzed. The content

analysis of field notes, interviews, maps, photographs, and historical documents generated a series of themes and theoretical typologies that illuminate the cultural underpinnings of plaza design and use. The observations, interviews, archival documentation, and spatial and architectural maps and drawings provided distinct texts that could be read in relation to each other, uncovering areas of appropriation, conflict, and contestation over time. These analytic findings are the basis for the historical, ethnographic, and conversational chapters that follow.

High
written records
- descriptions (popular)
-        "   poetic/fictional
- description f construction, design
- architectural recs

visual images (plastic)
empirical records
interpretive

sonic

observations - in situ
in context (museum)

part - obs @ public meetings or org mtgs
concerned w/ space

part by being an personal role

phenomenological -
sensory experience + its repr/mediation

GIS - org tool for analyz org geog info
environ, economic

PART TWO   Histories

I began this project as a contemporary ethnography of two central plazas in San José, Costa Rica, and their meanings for the residents of that city. In order to understand contemporary meanings, extensive research on the history of Parque Central, the central plaza of the colonial city, was undertaken, which produced a series of contradictory and in some cases misleading explanations of the origin of this urban design form in the New World. The inconsistencies and discrepancies in the literature made it necessary to begin a second project on the ethnohistory of the origins, evolution, and, ultimately, the cultural meanings of the grid-plan town and central plaza complex in Spanish America.

Part II presents the findings from the ethnohistorical exploration organized into three chapters. In Chapter 3, I present the sociopolitical and economic history of San José, Costa Rica, in order to interpret the political symbolism of its public spaces and plazas. To contextualize the specific meanings of the Costa Rican plaza, I explore in Chapter 4 its European history and the power relations embedded in its spatial configuration as well as the scholarly writing about its design. Chapter 5 examines the Nahua and Maya derivations of plaza-centered designs and presents archaeological evidence that refutes the Eurocentric conclusions of the architectural history literature. I argue that cultural resistance to colonization can be found in the spatial appropriation and maintenance of indigenous spaces such as the plaza. These histories provide the broader Latin American cultural context for the ethnographies and conversations presented in Parts III and IV.

CHAPTER 3

The History of the Plaza in San José, Costa Rica

The Political Symbolism of Public Space

Introduction

Urban public places are expressions of human endeavors; artifacts of the social world are accommodated, communicated, and interpreted in the confines of this designed environment. Yet as an object of study they have been relatively neglected (Lennard and Lennard 1984; Whyte 1980), partially because their social messages are so complex, and partially because the theory and methodologies for making these messages explicit were not available. The past twenty years, however, have produced a number of new approaches to the interpretation of environment and landscape through the critique of social science practice and the application of contextual theories of space (Duncan 1990; Rapoport 1982; Ricoeur 1979). The conclusions of Miles Richardson (1978, 1980), Amos Rapoport (1980, 1982), and James Duncan (1985, 1990, 1993) suggest that interpretations of a place or landscape are constructed through the human ability to interplay (1) the past and present existence of a place, (2) the social behavior accommodated by the place, and (3) the symbolic and communicative aspects of the place.

The cultural landscape of the Costa Rican urban plaza offers an excellent opportunity to explore the relationship of cultural meaning to designed space. The public quality of the space provides a forum, or theater, for the performance of personal, social, and cultural dramas that can be observed, recorded, and analyzed. William Whyte's (1980) seminal work on the public plazas of New York City demonstrates that the vitality of small urban places is based on the presence of people sharing the space and using it in a wide variety of activities. Suzanne H. Crowhurst Lennard and Henry L. Lennard (1984) focus on how the uses of European urban plazas change throughout the day, week, or, in the case of festivals, the year. Both researchers suggest that these activities, plus their frequency and duration, tell the story of the city as a social place, and they utilize observational methods to describe and predict social behavior.

Anthropologists working in cross-cultural settings have focused more on the ritual and dramaturgical aspects of public behavior (Gonzalez 1970). The contexts of these studies are less formal, and space is defined in terms of its social action or symbolic meaning. Victor Turner (1967) uses spatial analysis as only one element of a symbolic ritual system, while Miles Richardson (1978) refers to space in terms of setting a stage for social interaction. Constance Perin (1977, 1988) employs a symbolic framework in her analysis of space as an indicator of social status. The processes of exchanging and allocating space become status rituals, as do the rules of property control.

James Duncan (1990) is even more explicit about the relationship of the control and design of space to the definition of social identity and the manipulation of social status. His work on the city of Kandy, Sri Lanka, illustrates how contemporary understandings of the urban structure and historical accounts of the creation and modification of public space can be developed into a theory of reading the landscape as a communication about social relations. Amos Rapoport also places increased emphasis on the designed environment as a communication system, thus, "the design of the environment can be seen partly as a process of encoding information so that users can easily decode it" (1980, 28). Miles Richardson (1980) explains how experience and image inform one another through the medium of the material culture.

Duncan, Rapoport, and Richardson agree that the urban environment is encoded with meaning, and each has presented a model or approach for its decoding. Richardson's phenomenological model of "being-in-the-plaza" suggests that the transformation of belief into image, which then reconstitutes itself as belief and appropriate behavior, can explain the meaning of the plaza as a place of culture (1980). Rapoport's contribution suggests that the meaning of the built environment can best be studied by models and methods with an emphasis on analogy or metaphor and nonverbal behavior (1982). Duncan, on the other hand, argues that the landscape is a form of text that becomes a "vast repository out of which symbols of order and social relationships, i.e., ideology, can be fashioned" (1985, 17). Duncan emphasizes the importance of history in the interpretation of the symbolic landscape, drawing upon literature, spatial design, and social commentary to decipher encoded meanings.

These theoretical models conceptualize how the built environment communicates meaning through experience and symbol, and offer methodological tools for its analysis. These tools—reading the landscape as a text, decoding the built environment through analogy and metaphor, and the phenomenological experience of place—enable the researcher to demonstrate that a built environment such as the plaza communicates specific meanings that can be understood.

A second theoretical issue concerns what can be communicated in the built environment and at what scale or level of analysis. At the scale of the individual, the social group, and local culture, the symbolic importance of the built environment is as an expression of culturally shared mental structures and embodied processes. A system of relationships among the spatial or physical attributes represents—by their configuration, content, and associations—aspects of social life. Symbolic theory approaches built forms as tangible evidence for describing and explaining often intangible features of expressive cultural processes (Turner 1967).

> As expressions of culture, built forms may be seen to play a communicative role embodying and conveying meaning between groups, or individuals within groups, at a variety of levels. The built environment may also act to reaffirm the system of meaning and the values a group finds embodied in the cosmos. (Lawrence and Low 1990, 466)

The examination of the built environment provides insight into meanings, values, and processes that might not be uncovered through other observations and offers a mechanism for exploring social and political forces of the past. Designed landscapes such as plazas are a living history of local cultural meanings and intentions retained through a mnemonic process of environmental memory encoded in space (Quantrill 1987).

At the scale of the city, state, and society, however, David Harvey (1985) argues that any spatial form, contemporary monument, or town plan is a product generated by conflicting sociopolitical and economic forces. There are political and economic implications at the root of all aesthetic sensibilities, and the design of a plaza is no exception in that it reflects the political agency of the state. Michel Foucault (1975), in his work on the prison, is able to examine how architecture contributes to the dominance of one group over others by encoding their unequal relationships in space in ways that allow for surveillance and control of the body.

Physical space at the urban level, then, is ordered by and reflects the power structures to which the community is subordinated, although the community may contest this subordination through local political action and use of the space. But, as Pierre Bourdieu (1977) points out, built forms structure the world and naturalize our experience of it in ways that are not always open to challenge, unconsciously reproducing the power relations of the past. Henri Lefebvre's (1991) distinction between the representation of space (the conceived) and spaces of representation (the lived) is an attempt to break down this illusion of realism and transparency of space. He argues that the assumed neutrality of space masks that it is produced and reproduced and is a site of social, political, and economic struggle (Keith and Pile 1993). Examining the origins and design of spatial forms, therefore, provides insights into the discourse of power relations and the ongoing, site-specific struggles.

It is these power relationships expressed in the built environment and their impact on the experience of everyday life that tie together the diverse geographical scales and levels of analysis to generate a more complete understanding of the political and cultural symbolism of public space. In the same way that Don Mitchell (1995) traces activists' struggles to maintain Peoples' Park in Berkeley, California, as a public place for the disenfranchised and homeless, the history of the creation and re-creation of the two San José plazas illuminates the political conflicts and disruptive social changes that have occurred over the past fifteen years.

Drawing upon these interdisciplinary perspectives, I propose that urban public space reflects the cultural order, not through a one-to-one correspondence between spatial arrangements and meaning, but through a complex culture-making process in which cultural representations are produced, manipulated, and understood by designers, politicians, users, and commentators within changing historical, economic, and sociopolitical contexts. These spatial/cultural representations express the power relations between different groups and reflect ongoing patterns of cultural change. This chapter presents a first step toward understanding how these representations come into being in the two plazas, Parque Central and Plaza de la Cultura, in San José, the capital city of Costa Rica.

The ethnohistory of the Costa Rican plaza locates this inquiry in a specific place and time, setting the stage for the ethnographic and historical analyses that follow. The historical context, however, is not just a backdrop for the ethnographies and interviews, but an integral part of the social production and social construction analysis presented in Chapter 6. Without the historical context, the embodied meanings and activities that I describe, and that Costa Ricans argue about, lose the nuanced meanings historically layered in the space itself and in related spatial practices.

The Spanish American Plaza

The Spanish American plaza usually was placed at the geometric center of the town or city, with the exception of coastal towns, where it was often located on the waterfront. In small towns there was one plaza, but as the town expanded, additional neighborhood or market plazas were added. Even though the historical plaza is no longer the physical center of many cities, it still remains the psychological focus of the community, while newer plazas for tourists and businesses are located in outlying shopping and entertainment districts (Gade 1974).

During the colonial period, the main town square was called the Plaza Mayor or the Plaza Real. In Mexico, the name Zócalo is used; in Northern Andean countries, Plaza Bolívar; in Peru and Chile, Plaza de Armas; and in Central America, Parque Central or Plaza Principal to designate the central public space (Gade 1974). Originally designed for religious processions, feats of horsemanship, or as a marketplace, a plaza often began as rudimentary open space, a square or rectangle cleared of trees and covered with grass. On the perimeter were the church and a few buildings. The grassy square was used to pasture and water animals, and transients could leave their animals there for the night. The local well was often located on the plaza, thus it also became a place for fetching water or doing laundry.

Over time the plaza took on special functions, becoming a market site where agricultural goods and laborers were exchanged or a ceremonial center of religious, governmental, or military significance. But regardless of its other functions, the central plaza remained the preeminent space for social interaction, and it is in this role as a social concourse that plazas were transformed into garden parks with grass, trees, flowers, and scenic walkways. Since the 1970s, some plazas have lost their ceremonial status and gardenlike qualities and have become traffic hubs to accommodate the proliferation of private automobiles and diesel-run buses in rapidly growing Latin American cities.

Historical accounts from the nineteenth century present contrasting depictions of the plaza as a setting for ritual promenading—the *corso* in Mexico and the *paseo* of Central America (Arreola 1982; Gade 1974; Jackson 1984)—or as centers of disorderly conduct by unemployed vagrants and idlers, police and military troops (Brading 1980). In these contrasting images, the urban contexts are also portrayed either as centers of an elite society living in a pastoral landscape (Arreola 1980) or as crowded agro-administrative centers where people shared housing and slept on the streets (Bronner 1986; Walton 1984).

Contemporary accounts based on ethnographic studies also provide conflicting descriptions ranging from the plaza as a place "where everyone in the province, from the wealthiest landowner to his hacienda serf or local water carrier, could be seen" (Oliver-Smith 1986, 49), to the plaza as a place abandoned by the upper and middle classes to create more social distance between themselves and the remaining lower-class users (Robertson 1981). European researchers suggest that these different social depictions are part of a historical progression: people shared public space "when the bourgeois and the noblemen lived side by side with common people without fear, precisely because social rules and hierarchies went unquestioned" (Korosec-Serfaty 1982, 15). But with the rise of the moralizing of the streets, associated with the Enlightenment, elite activities moved to more specialized and privatized spaces, such as the café or the theater, and families and children moved from the plaza to the playground and the neighborhood park.

The Costa Rican Plaza

In Costa Rica the development of the plaza has had its own trajectory, starting as a soccer field and slowly evolving into a ceremonial space and gardenlike cultural center. Costa Ricans themselves distinguish between *parques* and *plazas*: the *parque* is the Plaza Mayor of a town, a tree-shaded rectangle with walkways bordered by stone benches and with a bandstand (*kiosco*, or "kiosk") at its center (McLennan 1968). Most towns have only one Parque Central that serves as a focus of the community. The Costa Rican plaza, in contrast, includes a variety of public spaces that have a soccer field. In fact, in Costa Rica, the term *plaza* refers specifically to a soccer field, and almost all public spaces start with an open, undeveloped playing field.

Marshall McLennan (1968) groups Costa Rican plazas into six types: soccer field, residential plaza, *plazita,* neighborhood plaza, Plaza Central, and Parque Central. Each type evolves from the previous one— with the exception of the neighborhood plaza, which occurs only in cities—creating a hierarchy of public spaces that locate and represent social and economic status. Thus, a soccer field is a town's first plaza; when houses are added, it becomes a residential plaza. The addition of a church, school, and adjacent fields or pastures creates a *plazita,* a rudimentary plaza form. The Plaza Central is also quite modest and has a soccer field rather than a formal garden. The Plaza Central develops into a Parque Central through the landscaping of the open space into a formal garden. The Costa Rican plaza uniquely combines the soccer field and plaza, but lacks defining architectural features such as arcades and raised sidewalks often found in Mexican and other Central American cities (McLennan 1968).

The original colonial plaza in Costa Rican cities was the Plaza de Armas, a parade ground for soldiers that was converted into a park during the nineteenth century. Emperor Maximilian (1864–1867) of Mexico is credited with landscaping the Zócalo in Mexico City, and the idea spread southward throughout Central America (McLennan 1968). The military band retained its presence by playing music, *la retreta*—a concert of classical and popular music—in the kiosk for the citizens. The Parque Central was a place for public courting, which often took place after the military band had played. Its main function, however, regardless of the city, was that it served as a "means of expressing community identity" (McLennan 1968, 4).

The Parque Central has been remembered, imagined, and represented in Costa Rican literature. Memoirs written at the turn of the century provide a glimpse of what it was like to be there and of its social importance at the close of the nineteenth century. Ignacio Trullás y Aulet (1913) describes activities that no longer occur but are still remembered by older Josefinos (residents of San José). His reminiscences evoke the precise character, language, and habits of the *retreta* that was held in Parque Morazán, a neighborhood park a few blocks northeast of Parque Central.

The Retreta

Without a doubt, the most beautiful fiesta starts at 7:30 in the evening in Parque Morazán. All the military bands of the Republic participate; together they play pieces of light music.

All of San José, as well as people from the provinces and foreigners who arrived in the capital in order to participate in this public festival, comes together at this occasion, made even more distinguished by the number of people who attend and made sweeter by the atmosphere in which it is embedded; it is the most cultured of all events.

The older ladies and gentlemen are seated on benches constructed on either side along Avenue of the Ladies. The young ladies and other youths mill about going around the central walkways, conveniently laid down near the Central Avenue and covered with sand.

The splendid, extraordinary electric illumination and the luxury and elegance dispersed throughout the crowd give this part of the festivities a charming and lustrous quality.

All the latest fashions, all the imaginable whimsies of hats and coiffures, all the refinements of good taste parade in front of the amazed observer. The clothing ranges from a short simple dress to the most splendid fancy ones, and from ornate dresses made from the most humble fabrics to velvets and silks and brocades.

I saw passing in front of me, like a beautiful and undefinable vision, heads of angelic girls enveloped in admirable shawls; lovely young misses with blue eyes and blond hair, their sculptured heads covered with charming and elegant Cossack hats; proud, tropical beauties, half hidden underneath the big hats with flying brims; an astonishing variety of feminine ideals, dreamt in delicious rose-colored dreams; a legion of charming girls and gentle women, all smiling, disseminating looks and smiles that were a delicious delight; loud giggles, engaging their friends and acquaintances in confetti fights, the likes of which were always won by their incomparable beauty, their innocence, and their enviable youth.

The *retreta* lasts for two hours that pass like lightning and vanish as quickly as an enchanted dream, leaving in the spirit the feeling of the most pleasant memory and an irresistible desire to relive the enchanting vision the following night . . . and on the last night, weighs down the heart with the sweet longing of vanishing pleasure and the vehement desire to enjoy the coming Fiestas [the year-end parties]. (Trullás y Aulet 1913, 127–129)

The Costa Rican plaza, then, shares a common heritage with plaza complexes throughout Spanish America, yet it retains culturally unique features and meanings derived from its historical development and local social context. The remainder of this chapter presents the history and sociopolitical evolution of San José, Costa Rica, as well as the development of Parque Central and Plaza de la Cultura within this particular urban setting.

The Costa Rican Context

Costa Rica, with a 1996 population of 3,367,455, is the second smallest of the Central American republics, covering 50,900 square kilometers (Ministerio de Economía, Industria y Comercio 1996). Located between Nicaragua and Panama and bordered by the Caribbean and Pacific Oceans, the country comprises three distinct geographical regions: (1) the cool central highlands, (2) the warm Pacific lowlands and westward mountain slopes, and (3) the Caribbean lowlands and eastward-facing escarpments. The central highlands consist of a northern volcanic range and a southern mountain mass, between which lies the Meseta Central. Two small basins form the upland Meseta Central: the higher, eastern one of Cartago (at 5,000 feet) drains toward the Caribbean, and the western lower and larger basin of San José (at 3,000 to 4,000 feet) drains toward the Pacific. The Meseta Central, located in the *tierra templada* (temperate) altitudinal zone, benefits from the equable climate and the fertile volcanic soil that produces a wide range of crops and supports a dense population (West and Augelli 1966).

The population of Costa Rica is predominantly Hispanic, with a small English-speaking West Indian Black population on the Caribbean coast. Indigenous enclaves of Guatuso, Bribri, Boruca, Térraba, and Cabecar are found in the Talamanca region and other marginal areas. The majority of Costa Ricans live in urban areas; there has been a steady increase in urbanization since 1960, when only 37 percent of the population was urban, increasing to 40 percent urban in 1970, 46 percent urban in 1980, and 54 percent urban in 1990 (Rama 1996, 94–95).

In 1985, 97 percent of Costa Ricans identified themselves as Catholic, and only 3 percent as Protestant (Booth 1998, 213), although the number of Protestant converts has increased with the influx and success of evangelical Christian sects in the country and the region over the past fifteen years. This religious transformation, from a nation in which Catholicism was the state religion to one in which evangelical Christian preachers can be seen on most streets and in public spaces, has been attributed to the increasing penetration of North American capital and mores into the culture and even the religious life of the country.

During the colonial period, development of towns and cities in the highlands of the Meseta Central was slow, as it was dependent on a weak economy based on lowland cacao production and subsistence agriculture. In fact, ever since colonial times, Costa Rica has remained largely monocultural (Macleod 1973). The consecutive collapses of cacao, then tobacco, and then coffee, beef, and bananas are repetitions of a pattern of world-market dependence. However, Costa Rica's agrarian capitalist economy has changed dramatically since the 1960s, and a diminishing proportion of workers participate in the agricultural sector. From 1960 to 1989–1991, the percentage of agricultural workers had fallen from 51 percent to 24 percent, while during this same period the percentage of industrial workers increased from 19 percent to 30 percent, and the percentage of service workers increased from 30 percent to 46 percent (Rama 1996). By 1996, only 16 percent of the US $9,081,000,000 GNP was produced by agriculture, as compared to 34.4 percent produced by trade in goods and services, 24 percent by manufactured exports, and 23 percent by investment (World Bank 1998). The purchasing power of the comparatively high 1996 GNP per capita figure of US $2,640 is undermined, however, by an average annual rate of inflation of 18.4 percent (World Bank 1998).

The surge of world coffee prices during the early 1970s created an economic surplus that was reinvested in the expansion of social welfare and health care services. These services, along with the improvement of the population's nutritional status based on a government subsidy for basic foods and public health programs, produced one of the lowest infant mortality rates (13 per 1,000 live births in 1995) and highest life expectancies (77 years of age in 1995) in the hemisphere (World Bank 1998). Although the population growth rate of 2.5 percent per year in 1995 remains a source of concern for achieving sustainable development, it is well below its high of 3.9 percent per year in 1959 (Low 1985). Literacy and the completion of a primary school education, even in rural areas, is practically universal due to educational reforms institutionalized from 1885 to 1889; 93 percent of the population was enrolled in primary school in 1993 (Booth 1998).

This century-long tradition of social reform and welfare legislation has been sustained by the expansion of popular voting access, begun by political elites as early as 1913 and 1946. The establishment of universal suffrage, granted in the constitution of 1949, was reinforced by a mandatory voting law passed in 1971 (Booth 1998). Yet the argument that "Costa Rica es diferente" (Costa Rica is different), due to its social beginnings as an egalitarian and homogeneous society of small farmers, is not historically accurate, nor is Costa Rica entirely free from political conflict and instability. The country's national political mythology, however, does have some merit in that its early lack of resources and geographical isolation contributed to the development of civil self-government (Yashar 1997). Costa Rica did not have a large indigenous population available to create a militarily enforced, coerced labor system, and instead relied on family farms that had to pay high wages during periods of rural labor shortage throughout the nineteenth century. In addition, the elimination of a standing army, the establishment of an electoral tribunal, and the reestablishment in 1949 of no re-election of presidents further distinguished Costa Rica from other Central American countries with military dictatorships. "Ultimately, the stability of the new system rested upon a social democratic development model and widespread popular participation (but with a fragmented and subdued labor sector) to co-opt the mass public" (Booth 1998, 53).

During the 1980s, however, Costa Rica underwent a process of economic adjustment that transformed the nation's social policy agenda and shattered the country's urban system (Lungo 1997). An aggressive export-oriented development program based on tourism and industrial export processing zones accelerated the pace at which San José swallowed up adjoining municipalities, creating Central America's first megacity (Lungo 1997). The increasing population pressure and urban density, and the trend toward North American–style capitalism, has had social consequences such as further environmental degradation, class stratification, and increasing disparities between the wealthy and the poor. The recent emergence of greater socioeconomic differentiation is especially pronounced in Costa Rica, which has long considered itself a relatively egalitarian society, especially in relation to Nicaragua, whose more impoverished exiles appear so frequently in the Costa Rican plazas nowadays.

Sociohistorical Development of San José, Costa Rica

San José was first mentioned in the ecclesiastical record in 1708 as a nuclear population that did not fulfill its obligation to the Catholic Church. In 1711, Bishop Garlet y Arlovit asked the isolated families to group themselves together into a single settlement (Solís Zeledón 1969). This request was forgotten, but in 1736 a mandate by the church brought the dispersed population together and authorized a chapel to be built, forming the parish of Villa Nueva de la Boca del Monte consisting of 399 families, or 2,330 persons, not counting the indigenous population. The town's founding date is referred to as May 21, 1737, when a thatch hermitage was completed at the intersection of roads leading to different parts of the country. By 1751, Villa Nueva de la Boca del Monte was composed of the thatch hermitage and twenty-six dispersed houses, fifteen with thatched roofs and eleven with tiled roofs. An adobe church was built in 1776 in the same location as the present-day cathedral, and a parcel of land was located in front of the church (Fernández 1889).

The first colonists were descendants of the early Spanish settlers who migrated to the New World following the discovery of Costa Rica in 1508 by Columbus at Cariay (the present-day Puerto Limón on the Atlantic coast). Although the Spanish settlers were granted *encomienda* rights (rights to labor and land) by the Spanish Crown, the small indigenous population did not provide adequate labor to allow large landholdings, so most colonists were occupied with subsistence farming (Macleod 1973). Political posts, however, continued to be awarded to a small group of families, enabling this group to monopolize cacao and tobacco cultivation, and later coffee production (Stone 1974).

By the middle of the eighteenth century, San José was a center for the processing of tobacco (De Mora 1973). The town was expanded by a donation of land from Father Chapuí, and a tobacco factory was built there in 1784. The industry reached its zenith between 1787 and 1792 and then declined because of inadequate transportation, isolation, and labor shortages.

Nonetheless, San José continued to grow: in 1799 a new town hall was built, and the church was reconstructed in 1811. San José was elevated to the rank of "city" in 1813, and an expansion of the church was planned, but on April 10, 1821, an earthquake destroyed much of the original adobe structure, and its reconstruction was not completed until 1835. The importation and cultivation of three hundred coffee trees from Cuba in 1815 produced an excellent harvest, resulting in coffee's emergence as the country's principal export commodity by the 1840s (Hall 1985; Helms 1975). The coffee economy flourished with the building of the railroad and the growing European market, and the population of San José expanded from 13,867 in 1801 to 28,944 in 1844 (Fernández Guardia 1985).

Costa Rica's separation from Spain in 1821 precipitated a series of postindependence armed battles that resulted in San José's designation as the capital of the new republic in 1823. In contrast to Cartago, the colonial capital, San José was thought to be the center of republicanism and modernity, values identified as important to the growth of the new nation (De Mora 1973). Besides, the new elite of major coffee exporters and processors were already centered there, as their landholdings were located in the surrounding coffee-growing areas. During the 1840s their power was consolidated, and they began to influence the physical plan of the city.

In 1825, San José was made up of six blocks surrounding Parque Central in all four cardinal directions. By 1849, the lower classes who worked at odd jobs or as artisans were located on the outskirts of the city beyond Calle de la Ronda, while the upper-middle-class professionals, business people, and coffee farmers were located along the principal streets. The most important individuals were located to the north of Second Avenue and Parque Central and northeast of the city center (Vega Carballo 1981). John Lloyd Stephens, a traveler during that period, describes the city as

> the only city that has grown up or even improved since the independence of Central America. Under the Spanish dominion, Cartago was the royal capital; but, on the breaking out of the revolution, the fervor of patriotism was so hot that it resolved to abolish this memorial to colonial servitude and to establish the capital at San José. . . . The buildings in San José are all republican; not one is of any grandeur or architectural beauty, and the churches are inferior to many erected by the Spaniards in the smallest villages. Nevertheless, it exhibited a development of resources and an appearance of business unusual in this lethargic country. (1949, 289)

By 1862 there were 1,694 houses and 28 public buildings on sixty-nine *manzanas* (blocks) of land in the city center. In 1889, the engineer Salomón Escalante created a plan that extended San José to 23rd Street to the east, 14th Street to the west, 9th Avenue to the north, and 12th Avenue to the south. His plan included the addition of trolley car service, as well as the construction of the Atlantic railroad station, a customs office, and the Variety Theater (Sánchez and Umaña 1983). In 1890 the commercial and bureaucratic zones of the city were greatly expanded, and the coffee oligarchy had established itself on the best pieces of land around the Parque Central, forming a true urban elite (Vega Carballo 1981).

San José continued to grow at an accelerated rate: from 37,206 inhabitants in 1864 to 56,162 in 1883; 76,718 in 1892; 153,183 in 1927; and 281,822 by 1950 (Censo de Población de Costa Rica 1953). This urban growth was essentially fueled by the absorption of the surrounding ring of autonomous communities by the expanding city. The urban settlement pattern gradually merged into the countryside, creating a transitional sector inhabited by an agriculturally based subculture that acted as a buffer, delaying urban acculturation (Low 1985).

Opposition on the part of a growing middle sector to the monopolization of wealth and power by the traditional elite resulted in a brief civil war over a disputed election. The war ended in 1948 when José Figueres and his supporters took control of the government and created the National Liberation Party (Partido Liberación Nacional [PLN]). Under Figueres, elections were resumed, banks were nationalized, and the army was dissolved. A new constitution established a participatory democracy in 1949. Since the 1953 elections, the social democratic (PLN) and conservative, landowning parties have generally alternated their political control every four years with the presidential election. The National Liberation Party further consolidated its economic base by sponsoring legislation that provided interest-free loans from a nationalized banking system and encouraged foreign investment. The economy of San José began to change dramatically after the presidency of Figueres, when a sharp decline in coffee prices reduced the country's ability to import manufactured goods, and unemployment in the agricultural sectors began to drive rural peasants to the city. In response, a policy of *desarrollo hacia adentro* (internal development) was initiated to stimulate locally based, small-scale manufacturing companies and to establish better trade relations with other Central American countries. From 1950 on, the secondary sector of the economy gradually increased, and by 1973 it accounted for one quarter of the value of exports (Hall 1985, 79). The secondary sector, however, was mostly in the hands of foreign investors, thus a new class of industrialists, drawn from recent migrants to Costa Rica, emerged to compete with the landowning families of the coffee elite.

The post-1940 industrialization was capital intensive and could not absorb the overwhelming internal migration to the city (Morse 1980). Most of the job expansion occurred in the tertiary rather than in the secondary sector of the economy. The tertiary sector included a large number of service occupations, mostly governmental, petty trade, and personal services (Hall 1985). The growth in the tertiary sector and the explosion of informal-sector employment corresponded to the period of the most rapid population growth. The population of the province of San José grew from 706,419 in 1974 to 890,443 in 1983, and to 1,220,412 in 1996, while the metropolitan area of San José alone grew from 406,990 in 1970 to 471,736 in 1973, 579,136 in 1978, and 647,017 in 1982 (Ministerio de Economía, Industria y Comercio 1974, 1983, 1996). Estimates of the metropolitan population in 1997 range from 850,000 to over one million inhabitants. The figures used here allow for comparison to previous census numbers that were based solely on a count by province. After 1970 the term "metropolitan area" is used to refer to the urban areas of San José Province. These numbers are used whenever possible. If there is no designation of "metropolitan area," then the census figure refers to the number of people in the province, so these comparisons are only approximate but do give some idea of the magnitude of population growth.

The international economic crisis of spiraling inflation and debt default of the 1980s only worsened the economic situation in Costa Rica by forcing more people out of work and placing even the governmental price-controlled basic foods out of the reach of 70 percent of the population. The increase in petroleum prices in 1979 slowed Costa Rica's economic growth while accelerating inflation. A decrease in export trade, increases in interest rates, an unfavorable trade balance, and an economic recession impeded the payment of the foreign debt and resulted in President Rodrigo Carazo's refusal to negotiate with the International Monetary Fund (IMF) (Torres 1993).

By the time the Carazo administration (1978–1982) ended, "the economy was in a nosedive, and it hit rock bottom that same year" (Clark 1997, 78). Even though President Luis Alberto Monge (1982–1986) worked closely with the IMF and the U.S. Agency for International Development (USAID) on stabilization measures, his PLN administration disagreed over the need to pursue neoliberal economic reforms, particularly privatization of state enterprises and trade liberalization, given their historical success with public-sector employment and state intervention in the economy. Gradually, the economic leadership shifted from the Costa Rican government to a transnational alliance between the private Costa Rican bank BANEX and USAID. This alliance was further encouraged by the Reagan administration, which began to reorient United States economic policy toward improving the economic prospects of the region. The transnational alliance resulted in an increase of nontraditional exports such as textiles, fresh and frozen fish and shrimp, flowers, ornamental plants and foliage, and fresh pineapple (Clark 1997).

New challenges to democratic governance and economic stability have emerged in the 1990s: The PLN nearly lost two consecutive presidential elections, threatening the traditional pattern of presidential party alternation and personalist leadership. Increases in crime, violence, and corruption related to drug trafficking and anti-drug initiatives have resulted in a more active judiciary rather than effective legislative or executive responses. And, due to post-NAFTA trading-bloc conflicts, there are fears of a collapse of the economic growth stimulated by the neoliberal Caribbean Base Initiative (Gudmundson 1996). The *New York Times* reported that the European-style welfare state is "being dismantled by the son of the man who created it. Faced with huge deficits and a creaky government bureaucracy that . . . accounted for one of every six jobs, President José María Figueres is slashing away at the traditional cradle-to-grave protections and warning his people of continued austerity ahead" (Rohter 1996, A10).

These changes have had a tremendous impact on the lives of the working-class and poor residents, who have experienced a major decline in their standard of living and social safety net. Neighborhood life has also changed, with increasing illegal squatter settlements emerging under bridges and in vacant land along the railways and industrial areas. More important, the "relatively harmonious spatial blend of social classes in the city began to disintegrate" (Lungo 1997, 61), restructuring class relations and spatially segregating social groups.

> The spatial integration of social classes that traditionally characterized San José began to rupture during the 1980s. Until the late seventies, San José neighborhoods were characterized by a

high degree of spatial integration. Low- and middle-income families lived in close proximity and their daily rounds tended to overlap. (Lungo 1997, 69)

Lungo's survey of San José households found that while "bosses" perceived the quality of life as having improved over the past ten years (56 percent), the informal-sector workers and unemployed people perceived the quality of city life as having declined (55.3 percent and 67.4 percent respectively; 1997, 68).

Before the economic crisis, then, center-city neighborhoods had been relatively heterogeneous, but with the subsequent changes, wealthy residents moved farther from the central core, developing spatially restrictive means of protecting and closing their neighborhoods from the poor and working classes. This increase in the spatial segregation of class structure can be seen in the ethnographic and narrative descriptions of changes in the central plazas.

The impact of the economic crisis on the urban systems of San José has been catastrophic. Since there was no master plan, private commercial and industrial interests have increasingly driven urban development (see Photograph 25). Transportation systems remain rudimentary, and pollution from industry and individual automobiles and buses is reaching dangerous levels. The first planning document, completed by the Instituto Nacional de Vivienda y Urbanismo (INVU; National Institute of Housing and Urbanism) in 1983, called for the decentralization of city services, but without adequate funding, little could be accomplished.

Since 1948 Costa Rica's political system had been highly centralized, to the detriment of the municipal power structure. Much of the political apparatus of San José was dismantled in the 1950s, leaving the maintenance of urban infrastructure to the national ministries. Municipal authorities continue to be appointed by nationally elected representatives. This political division of labor set up a situation in which national authorities concerned with nationwide policy and planning decisions were also responsible for maintaining urban services (Lungo 1997). The results were that the needs of the city were overlooked and the infrastructure fell into disrepair. As one municipal official commented with regard to the redesign of the central plazas, the national leaders thought that the city's physical structure was complete and nothing else needed to be done.

25. Overview of San José, 1997

Since the municipality did not have the legal right to tax its citizens, all funds for urban development and planning came from the minimal 1 percent allocation from the federal budget for urban services. In 1990, President Oscar Arias reformed the city governance laws and instituted a 10 percent income tax on those living within the municipality. By 1991, a series of policies for sustainable urban development were legislated, and a land-use plan was put in place. The goals of this plan were to reconstruct the parks, rescue the rivers, provide clean air and water, and improve the overall quality of urban life. These governmental reforms and the 1991 plan created the basis for the renovation of many of the parks and plazas in San José.

This brief sociopolitical and economic history contextualizes the building and modification of the major central plazas in San José: Parque Central and Plaza de la Cultura. The unplanned development of urban infrastructure, alternating political agendas, changing social stratification, and waves of economic crisis produced a chaotic landscape of traditional and modern public spaces described in detail in the following plaza histories.

PARQUE CENTRAL:
A History of European Values and Economic Decline

Parque Central was first mentioned in a 1761 document in relation to the original town hall on the northeast corner of the plaza. In contrast to the Plaza de Armas, a plaza for military displays that was built a few blocks away, Parque Central was designated the ceremonial and civic center of the growing town. It began as a grassy, tree-covered rectangular public space used as a weekend market place, and it was oriented as a square city block, with north-south and east-west roads as its boundaries. Civic and religious institutions quickly surrounded it. The Iglesia Parroquial (the first church) was built on the eastern side of the plaza in 1776 (De Mora 1973) and became the National Cathedral in 1851 (see Photograph 26). The military barracks on the northern side were built next, and the new Casa del Cabildo (town hall) was completed on the northeast corner in 1799. At the same time, private buildings were being constructed; Captain Miguel Jiménez built a house on the plaza as early as 1761 (González Víquez 1973). By mid–nineteenth century, the remaining building sites were filled with private residences and small businesses, including the Botica Francesa and a small hotel on the southern edge of the plaza. Even as early as the beginnings of the nineteenth century San José was a relatively urban center, compared to other populated areas (Vega Carballo 1981; see Photograph 27).

Parque Central retained its colonial form and meaning until the emergence of the republican era in 1823. In 1861 Ramón Quirós, who was the governor, the chief of police, and the president of the municipality, created a public walkway shaded with trees in front of the cathedral (Delgado Rojas and Zúñiga Jara 1993). Workers planted forty-four large white fig trees, twenty-four fig saplings, and four mountain orange trees as a first step in the creation of Parque Central.

In the mid–nineteenth century, the plaza was redesigned and refurbished by President Castro Madriz with all the trappings of European bourgeois elegance: Francisco María Yglesias donated a fountain imported from England to supply water to the city in 1868–1869; an elaborate iron fence was added in 1870; and a wooden, Victorian Japanese-style

26. Historic photograph of cathedral

27. Historic photograph of Botica Francesa

28. Original Victorian kiosk

kiosk—in which the military band could play for the Sunday *retreta*—
was constructed in 1890 (see Photograph 28). An 1895 description of the
site says that it was 6,986 square meters encircled by a beautiful iron
fence, 334 meters long and 2 meters high (Marín 1991). Guards were added
and watchmen patrolled in the evenings calling out the hour and lighting
the gas lamps. The plaza was also famous for its large fig, palm, and mag-
nolia trees, so much so that when one was cut down in 1902, it incited a
public protest (La capital de antaño 1928). Electric lights were added in
1889, and by 1907 the dirt paths were paved into curvilinear walkways. In
1908 a complete renovation of the park was undertaken that replaced the
deteriorated kiosk with a copy in the same place, and installed mosaic
tiles along the walkways.

One way to capture the ambiance of Parque Central as an early marketplace is through the writings of Manuel González Zeledón, or "Magón,"
as he is known in Costa Rica, who depicts a late-nineteenth-century

vision of the main plaza. The idiosyncratic syntax and use of the local vernacular is characteristic of Costa Rican *costumbrismo,* a literary style of realism based on pastoral life at the end of the nineteenth century.

Market Day in the Main Plaza

The main plaza, with its iron railings, its lovely fig trees and fig saplings, and its monumental fountain—the only mute witnesses of the market scenes—was the place where buyers and sellers came, some hoping for a reasonable profit, others in search of their weekly bread.

The nearby streets were lined with booths made of wooden frames with cloth roofs, temporary stores, some of ready-made clothes, others of tin and metal artifacts, of knickknacks, and of course, of saints and religious posters. The big rectangle [of the plaza] was filled, in varied confusion, with huge mounds of potatoes, *ayotes,* pumpkins, and cabbages; dry pieces of leather were used as trays filled with corn and beans or splendid spreads of sweets smelling of raw sugar. Everywhere there were little stands of beans, *chayotes,* sweet corn, turnips, greens, radishes, representing all the delicious vegetables that used to fill our pots. The fruits were both abundant and incredibly inexpensive: mangos, limes, *pejibayes,* oranges, citrons, both ripe and unripened plantains, baby bananas, yellow and purple bananas, quince, peaches, green figs, *matasanos,* nuts, avocados, sapodillas, cashews, and *coyoles,* in short, a million wonderful gifts grown in this chosen corner of the world to sweeten generations of children.

In front of the main barracks, inside the Plaza, women vendors sat all lined up selling *melcochas* [local sweets], "*sobao,*" "*güesillas,*" *rosquetes* from Alajuela, cake, *empanadas de chiverre,* nougats, corn rings, cigars made of *iztepeque* and *bajeras,* their wares beautifully placed on huge baskets, covered with a cloth napkin decorated with doilies or three-stitch lace. Next were the poultry vendors selling eggs, chickens, turkeys, ducks, and other birds; next, the *molejoneros;* and finally the berry sellers, with their usual Prussian blue dresses with white dots and their jugs filled with tasty fruit.

On the east side, on large wooden boxes made into benches, with their rusted knives and little rulers or measuring slates, gathered the soap sellers, among whom figured young people from wealthy families. I remember that at twelve on the dot, they started drumming on the boxes with their knives, accompanying the barracks drummer, and not one bar of soap would be sold until they had finished their drumming task.

After these happy vendors were the rice growers and cocoa marketers, with their string packs hanging from their necks and closed at the chest, their hands dusty and blistered, always chewing the best coffee beans from Nicaragua or from the rosiest Matina [area on the Caribbean coast of Costa Rica]. Then the tin workers with their array of tin cans; pitchers and jars; plates with the alphabet around the rim and an elephant in the center; glass saints; and picture frames trimmed with soldering; mirrors studded with colorful stars and crescent moons, blue and green; a coil furnace together with its candles; and oil lamps, a vinegary old acid container, and a mixture for instant welding jobs.

"How much will it cost to frame the picture of our Lord of San José?"

"With or without glass?"

"With glass because it will fade without it."

"Six *reales*."

"Deal. I'll leave it now and pick it up on Saturday. Tell me, tomorrow could you fix a nasty water leak?"

"No ma'am. Only Maján or Mates [other tin workers] can do that."

Next came the blacksmiths, among whom were two figures that stood out: Mr. Berry and the master, Santiago Muñoz, with their racks filled with eyebolts, axes, hinges, tires, horns, cart rods—everything homemade and indigenous, with the color left by the forges and scratches of lime. Behind them were the child bird sellers, gathered near the steps of the fountain with all kinds of cages, some simple, some towerlike, in the shape of a fort, or of a cathedral with turrets, and of course a sardine can filled with rusty water and the bowl of birdseed.

"How much for the parrot?"

"Thirty."

"And how much for this other one?"

"It has to be forty-five; it's charming and sings beautifully."

"Is that *yigüirro* a male?"

"Of course, he's making his nest now, and he's molting."
And so every bird seller would bring out his sparrow, his *picudo* king, his tropical canary from the coast, or his orange chief.

And then, stumbling over old ladies, throwing big sacks of wares around amidst the cursing of the victims and the heckling of onlookers; his pine box hanging from his waist, held up by a wide leather belt full of unusual things such as buttons, needles, barrettes, faux pearl chokers, broaches, cigarette papers, Mason shoe polish, and a thousand other cheap knickknacks, and with a handful of dime handkerchiefs and glass rosaries; walking and jumping from place to place, selling his wares and making himself hoarse with shouting, the funny gadget man is everywhere, with his hat down to his ears, a lock of hair coming out through the holes in his hat, his shameless face in an arrogant and condescending grin.

"Large matches! Five for two boxes!"

"Come on, honey, buy this amber choker, real amber from Mompelas, and this pair of fine earrings that won't turn dark."

"This little guy is gonna buy Ms. Marie the rosary blessed by the Nuncio in Lima, they say it's made of wood from the Garden of Olives. For six *reales* I sold one to Bupedra, but for you, I'll sell it for four."

"Enough, give me a wick, one that gives a good light, glued, and don't bug me anymore."

And all these living paintings, filled with young blood and an athlete's energy, with the taste of virgin soil and perfumed by virtue and honor, passed by in the midst of a frightful clamor like the roar of the ocean, beneath the burning rays of a tropical sun, precursor of torrential rains, and having for ceiling the purest blue of a heaven that shelters us and is our pride, our welcome card, our noble banner.

Well, it was into that great turmoil that Charita and I ventured, she to buy groceries, and I to carry them home.

"How many eggs?"

"Two *reales*' worth; ten of yuccas, twenty of green beans, ten of *pacayas*."

"Go along and buy the beans: I'll wait for you here, and if you don't find me here, just put them in my bag and meet me at Mr. Bejarano's cocoa stall. Make sure they're not too sinewy or too stiff; and they should cost about four *reales.*"

My grandmother would give me the money, and I, relatively free, would quickly take care of the shopping and with a ten, sometimes from Mrs. Barbara Bonilla, at other times from Mr. Aquileo Echeverría or from my father, I would buy six handfuls of handpicked Nicaraguan cocoa, and with that old-fashioned coin, the kind that is not in use anymore, I would swap for *melcochas,* corn husks, mangoes, and limes. I would put away a nice flask of cheer from Mr. Matías Valverde and get two dozen little soaps that would end up next to the fruit in the bottomless bag of my childhood.

With the daily shopping finished—the big bag full, the basket packed with eggs, butter, and figs to make sweets; the couple of bitter palms and a short palm tree also in the sack and a bundle of onions from San Juan crowning the altar of nutrition—the difficult task of carrying everything home started.

"Mr. José, be kind and help me lift this bag over my shoulder."

"Which side do you carry it on?"

"The left."

The enormous bag weighed heavy on my fragile collarbone. Some damn pieces of raw sugar were digging into me, in spite of the beans that served as padding: I would grab the mouth of the sack with my left hand and put the basket in the crook of my right arm. My armpit already held down other supplies and the little palm tree, and I held on to the onions with my right hand. My straw hat shaded me, and I managed to see out of it through about four or five holes, enough to guide myself across the uneven brick sidewalk on my way home, two blocks away.

All of a sudden, a charitable passerby shouted to me:

"Little boy, the beans are falling out of your bag."

It took my whole body to be able to understand the warning; I put myself up against the wall to steady myself; the bitter palms and the little palm tree were falling from underneath my arm and, with a jerk, I tried to catch them. The sack fell over my back and was pressing horribly on the knots in my spine. My wrist was so cramped it gave way with a violent twist, and with a crash that in my imagination seemed like the final judgment, the enormous bag started falling to the ground, dispensing its contents in the middle of the street. The *ayote* finally stopped at the muddy sugarcane, and the jam jar broke into a million pieces, as did a number of eggs that were in the basket.

My face was like a chile, covered with sweat; my vision was blurred by huge tears, and my nose was dripping like a lit candle. I started to collect the runaway goods, putting them back in the damn bag, taking inventory of casualties and of those badly hurt. One pumpkin was unusable, and the onions were covered with mud. A round of raw sugar had made a fragile nest in a heap of cow dung, and the egg yokes and whites of a half dozen eggs were spattered all over the tile and part of the wall.

Finally, with the renewed help of Mr. José and some precautions, I was able to continue my calvary, but my happiness at seeing myself so close to the end of my journey—already at the corner of Mr. Juan de Jesús Jiménez, whose house faced mine—vanished, giving way to anguish. Cleto Herrera, Tatono Bolandi, Abraham Zúñiga, and others, so many that it seemed like a thousand outlaws, were ignoring my shouts and injuries, taking advantage of my state of complete vulnerability. Their tugs took my shirt from my pants, and my mangoes, *melcochas,* "*güesillas,*" limes, and dozen little soaps scattered at my feet and were stolen by the thieves. They had no regard for me as I watched them, laughing at my copious sweat and cries. And that wasn't even the worst part; with all the violence, they had taken off the button to my pants—the only thing holding up that precious article—and when I took the first step toward my house, my pants wriggled down until they bunched up at my calves, and in that embarrassing and sad state I approached the door of my paternal home.

"Grab the groceries!!! I can't go up the steps because my pants fell down! Gra . . ! Grab it!"

With my screams, my whole family came out and they took my sack, and with a couple of kicks for being so shameful, they pulled me inside by my ears.

"There is a jam missing and a pumpkin," said my grandmother.

"What happened was . . ."

"Be quiet! Telling lies again! Now, for your punishment, after you eat your lunch, bring in a cartload of firewood."

There was no hope for appeal, I was convicted, confessed, and sentenced. I thought for a while about the injustices of life. I ate lunch with a voracious appetite, and with the firewood inside, covered with scratches and scrapes on my ears and neck, I fell into the sleep of an angel on my mother's lap. (González Zeledón [1896] 1994, 23–31)

Another literary narrative that offers a glimpse of what it was like to be in Parque Central is Ignacio Trullás y Aulet's 1913 memoir of the drawing of the winning lottery numbers on Sunday. The depictions of shoeshine men cleaning shoes, the band playing on the central kiosk, and lottery ticket sellers filling the surrounding sidewalks are reminiscent of the Sunday scene in Parque Central in 1987 (see Photograph 29). So, although Parque Central has not retained a marketplace ambiance, this early-twentieth-century description suggests that there is a strong resemblance in both the actors and physical environment that was maintained until its remodeling in 1993.

The Lottery Drawing

On the first Sunday of every month something transcendental happens in this city that may completely change an individual's life or the life of a whole family. Something on which many people base their hopes and their dreams.

I am referring to the drawing of the lottery.

Since very early in the morning, vendors who sell the lottery tickets go into the streets literally attaching themselves to the pedestrians to reach every eye and ear to sell their tickets. The drawing today is the fat one, and they go around just short of deafening the space with their battle cries and high-pitched voices.

It is impossible to walk around the marketplace, it is so crowded. Pity whomever may be innocently strolling by. It would be impossible for him not to be attacked by the ticket sellers' mob. Right now, it's cool to buy; no, better, the selling is hot. One would have no other choice but to partake in some of the lottery fury; it would be hard to escape.

"Buy me a seven, sir," emphatically says a small urchin pushing up front, not letting anybody else get by.

29. Lottery ticket sellers in Parque Central

"Nine," screams another one, this one a little older, waving a fan of bills in front of his eyes.

"A six," breaks out another man, limping along.

"Don't miss your chance, gentleman," calls out a shoeshine man with his box of shoe polish and brushes in his shoulder belt. "It is going to be zero; Pedro Nolasco said it last night."

"Shut up, you fool," counters a teenager, smelling of *aguardiente* [cane alcohol], "Don't try to pull one over on us. What do you know? We know that it's going to be five. Buy me a five."

And so it goes. The impenetrable mass stifles every movement and does not let anyone pass. It rubs against you, shoves, steps on you until you give in, merely to get by. All this happens under the sly gaze of one lottery seller lazily propping himself up against the wall of one of the gates with a handful of numbers in his hand:

"You've just lost your money, sir, because the winning number will be four."

The scene goes on for hours and hours: No one who goes into

the market, not even a kid from Escazú who arrives to sell eggs, nor a girl from Desamparados who comes to bring poultry, nor the driver from Santa Ana who brought raw sugar—no one who enters innocently will come out without at least an eighth [a full ticket is made up of eight parts].

As the day goes by, the lottery atmosphere fires up in the *cantinas* [bars], in the barber shops all over town, at the gates of the church, and on every street corner, where shoeshine men have settled themselves this Sunday morning to do a general cleaning of the shoes of everyone wearing them. Throughout San José are heard the voices, young and old, of lottery vendors peddling their tickets.

"The fat one. Twenty thousand. Drawing tonight."

At a quarter to twelve people from all walks of life begin to flow into Parque Central. People of all kinds and colors, Josefinos and country folk, fill every seat available and all possible places. They sit anywhere in order to see what is going on.

The chalkboards for recording the winning numbers have been arranged in a semicircle since early morning. In the middle: two urns, the big one—"the fat one"—holds 25,000 numbers corresponding to the same number of tickets that make up the raffle; the small one holds the prizes, including the "big prize," the one that is the object of desire of almost everyone in the Republic.

With mathematical punctuality, the military band appears on one side, and on the other, the commission in charge of verifying and controlling the lottery drawing.

The rhythm of the *paso doble* [Spanish dance music similar to the quickstep or two-step] animates the faces of the audience, who welcome those in charge of the drawing and the music with a prolonged ah . . . . ! of satisfaction.

Everybody's eyes are anxiously fixed on the clock in the cathedral's watchtower. As the hands get closer to midday, they ready themselves for the drawing: both those who participate as well as spectators.

At the first chime of midday, at the same time that the usual bugle call of the Cuartel Principal [military barracks] begins, the band tears through the air thick with the masses, and the man in charge puts in revolution the 25,000 numbers by turning the crank of the big urn with a sound like crashing bones, almost like macabre applause.

The audience perks up their ears, taking out of their bags the tickets already purchased or slips of papers with their numbers written down on them.

The band quiets down and the urns keep spinning. First the big one stops for a moment to slingshot its first ball, which falls on a plate and then is picked up by the announcer, who calls out the number.

Then the smaller one is set in motion, and at the third or fourth spin, it stops to let go of its ball in the same manner, the ball that specifies the prize.

And the numbers keep rolling, and the prizes keep rolling, and they are written down on the blackboards.

And the audience watches the drawing of each number with great interest.

It is something to behold, the faces of those who win. During the few moments between the time when the ball comes out and the prize is given . . . everyone, everyone, everyone breathes in hope of winning 20,000 colones [Costa Rican currency]; and then when they hear the announcer say 60, in the look of disappointment on their faces, in their attitude, you can read that they feel they have been robbed of the big prize. The function keeps going for about an hour; nothing else goes on except the bellowing of the outcome by the announcer, followed by the *paso doble* of the band and an ah! from the crowd of spectators.

Many of the spectators who have not won get up to leave while making a mental promise not to buy another lottery ticket in their life; yet before they leave Parque Central, they hold another ticket for the next drawing in their bag.

I have noticed two things: at the end of the event, you do not notice the difference in the noise at the turning of the large urn; that is to say, so few balls have come out that you don't notice the difference in prizes. At the beginning of the drawing, there are many happy faces . . . but at the end, they turn sad.

These observations show that there are few prizes, but unmet expectations are in abundance; and from this I deduce that in lotteries, as in life, luck never reaches the one who looks for it, only the one that stumbles upon it, and that the number of the unlucky is much greater than the number of the lucky.

At the end of the raffle, the people go up to the kiosk to compare their tickets with the written numbers, and it is worth mentioning that the grandstand is totally covered with bits of paper that the wind drags through the Parque Central; and since in the final hour it usually rains, those little pieces of paper, on which moments before rested hopes of a lifetime of comfort, are suddenly converted into wet paper.

The lottery in Costa Rica is not to blame, because it has a charitable end; but what does deserve criticism, and severe criticism, is that a large part of Costa Rican people place their hopes of prosperity on the lottery without observing that the number of winners does not reach even 11 percent [of ticket holders] and that the number of losers is 89 percent [of ticket holders]. They don't think about the best lotteries, the ones that never disappoint us and that truly deliver riches and comfort, the ones that are called the trilogy of fortune: Work, Constancy, and Savings. (Trullás y Aulet 1913, 30–36)

This turn-of-the-century version of Parque Central was not changed until the late 1930s, when the verandah was removed during the paving of the city streets. Increased automobile traffic and, more recently, diesel bus transport have added to the noise and congestion of the surrounding area. In 1944 the fountain and the Victorian kiosk were removed to make room for a modern cement kiosk donated by Anastasio Somoza, the Nicaraguan dictator (although there is some dispute about whether it was Somoza or a Nicaraguan industrialist named Masagoza). It was constructed by Alfonso Peralta Esquivel and Ernesto Arroyo Cascante, and elaborated by Carlos Savater during the administration of Teodoro Picado Michalski (1944–1948). Below the kiosk was a nightclub that scandalized many Josefinos; it was eventually replaced by the Carmen Lyra Children's Library.

Throughout this period and into the 1950s the edges of the Parque Central retained a number of the original private residences of elite families, the Botica Francesa, and the military barracks, now in the guise of a school. Cafés lined the northwest corner, and people still went to the Parque Central on Sunday for the evening *retreta* of the military band.

But the shift in the major symbols marks the change in cultural focus of the society. New industrialists' interests and alliances with other Central and North American countries were beginning to be reflected in the urban landscape.

The dramatic economic changes of the 1950s included an increase in urban density, crowding, and pollution. Upper-middle-class families sold their homes and moved to the suburbs. Residences were torn down and replaced with banks, symbols of a new kind of economy, one based on debt and banking controls and dependent on North American capital and culture. The growth of the tertiary sector of the economy and an increase in unemployment because of the decline in agricultural exports were reflected in the proliferation of informal occupations in Parque Central. Shoeshine men who controlled the northeast corner, ambulatory vendors along the sidewalks and pathways, small-time salesmen who used the benches as an office because rents were so high, and construction workers who waited behind the arbor in hopes that some employer would drive by to hire them are all examples of how the Parque Central was used as a place of employment. Their stories and spatial identities reflect the increasing unemployment and decreasing opportunities of capital-intensive industrialization and the expansion of the service sector discussed in the previous section on the history of San José.

By the mid-1990s, Parque Central was located in the most densely populated district of San José, with 10,669 inhabitants per square kilometer in 1992 (Departamento de Planificación 1992). The park now encompassed 7,569 square meters (based on my pacing of the plaza in 1993, 6,400 square meters, or 80 meters by 80 meters, was used by the city for the redesign in 1994) surrounded by a Burger King as well as the traditional Soda Palace and Soda La Perla. The overcrowding, the high levels of pollution from diesel buses, and the increase of petty crime contributed to the perception that Parque Central reflected the deteriorating center city of San José that resulted in its 1993–1994 redesign and the renovations discussed in Chapter 8.

PLAZA DE LA CULTURA:
The New Culture of Liberation

The Plaza de la Cultura has a much shorter history: it was begun in 1976 during the administration of President Daniel Oduber, and was completed in 1982. The history of the Plaza de la Cultura, however, is one of conflicting interpretations that have not had an opportunity to

30. National Theater and plaza

fade, and there remain many different points of view about why it was constructed. The idea of having a plaza in front of the architecturally prominent 1897 National Theater had always been a concern of the theater's board of directors (see Photograph 30). Oscar Arias, who was then the Minister of Planning, was concerned that the development of San José was disorderly and unplanned; he was interested in revitalizing the downtown area. Carmen Naranjo, a well-known writer and head of the newly created Ministry of Culture, Sports, and Recreation (Ministry of Culture), wanted to change the upper-class image of San José and make downtown a place for all Costa Ricans. The future director of Plaza de la Cultura, Eduardo Faith, saw the new plaza as an open space to breathe, a place where the middle and lower classes could enjoy the city. And Bernal Jiménez, the head of the Central Bank, wanted a new home for the Costa Rican Precolumbian gold collection.

These individuals who were involved with the creation of the Plaza de la Cultura were members of a new kind of elite politically tied to the

National Liberation Party and with a mission to reconstitute Costa Rican culture based on local customs and arts. These same individuals, however, were also connected to North American values and symbols, as much of their financial backing came from foreign commercial and industrial interests described in the San José history.

The process that led to the construction of the plaza started when the Central Bank acquired the land next to the National Theater to build a museum for the Precolumbian gold collection. A design competition was held, and three architects, Edgar Vargas Vargas, Jorge Borbón, and Jorge Bertheau, were given the commission. Vargas had been on the National Theater board of directors, and he said that they had had an inside line on the competition. A building for the museum was designed and under construction when Guido Sáenz, the new Minister of Culture, saw the cleared site; he was so taken with the open view of the National Theater that he insisted that the gold museum be placed underground. He said that he rushed to see President Oduber and the head of the Central Bank to show them what he had seen: a plaza that would have the "jewel" of the National Theater as its crown.

The Plaza de la Cultura took six years to construct because of a series of delays and setbacks. All the plans had to be redrawn and redesigned after the decision was made to put the museum underground. A retaining wall had to be built so that the construction would not disturb the foundations of the National Theater. The engineering required to build an underground building in an earthquake zone was technically complicated and had to be reworked many times. And then the conservative party came into power in 1978, blocking money for what was seen to be a Liberationist project.

One incident illustrates the ambivalence with which the media and interviewed citizens viewed the lengthy project. During the construction, a large hole was dug to put in the retaining wall. The hole then filled with water during the heavy winter rains, and all construction was stopped. The media portrayed this delay as the "*hueco de la cultura*," the cultural gap, and satirized the venture as a public swimming pool that at least the public could use.

The final design included an open space of approximately 9,785 square meters (based on my pacing in 1993) for public events on the side of the National Theater, and left a smaller space in front of the theater as an entrance plaza and café area for the major tourist hotel. The design included a large, flat fountain that functions as a skylight for the underground museum, decorative pipes for the exhaust system, an underground office for the Tourist Bureau, uncomfortable pipe benches along the periphery of the fountain and the planters, and molded cement benches under a row of trees running along the arcaded hotel shops.

As I discuss in Chapters 6 and 7, the reaction to the opening of the Plaza de la Cultura was mixed. The new space became the province of teenagers and tourists, as well as the arena for sexual cruising and solicitation. One depiction of this new public space is found in a contemporary short story by Vilma Loría. I was struck immediately by the similarity of her story to what older North American men told me about their experiences in the Plaza de la Cultura.

San José at Night

To return to your native country as a tourist. It happened to me.

After thirty years of living in New York City, I had to return to Costa Rica on a business trip. It was my first time back after so many years. I had gone to the United States in search of better horizons. When I left, I had a dead-end government job. I worked Monday to Friday. On Saturdays, I went to Puntarenas Beach by train with the neighborhood gang to dance, drink, and other such pleasures. If I had no money, which was often, I stayed in San José: Mass at twelve to see the young fillies, four o'clock movie at the Palace or the Raventós, and a little dancing at the Sesteo with one who would stand up to me. One day I got tired of it all, even the Trianón, which was like a second home to me. I was very lucky in the United States. I married an incredible woman who worked so that I could study, I found a good job, and we had children. My life changed radically. From a sad employee, I went on to become an executive who wore $200 dollar suits and had a promising career.

The airplane landed at the Juan Santamaría Airport. I was surprised by the large buildings and the modern highway we took to reach San José. I thought the cab driver had gone crazy when, after passing San Juan de Dios Hospital, he drove onto Central Avenue going the wrong way. "In this government, everything is done backwards," he said, as an explanation. I smiled, remembering that one of the local pleasures in Costa Rica is to badmouth the government and insult referees at soccer games.

On our way down Central Avenue I felt as if I was reading a book backwards. Looking from east to west I could not recognize a single building. When we passed the Hotel Costa Rica I finally knew where I was. I tried to find the Bazar La Casa and the Mariano Jiménez Drugstore, and I got to see the formerly hidden facade of the National Theater made much more visible thanks to the great view provided by the spacious Plaza de la Cultura that now frames the architecturally majestic construction. I checked into a hotel in the center of town.

At eight that night, after a rest and a shower, I went out to conquer San José at night, the same San José where I had been without a nickel in my pocket. About a block from the hotel two little creatures of the night approached me; I'm not a saint, but they looked as young as my twelve-year-old daughter. It hurt to see them with so much makeup on and dressed to show off their bodies and talking dirty. This was not for me. I walked over to the Plaza de la Cultura and got more of the same, only this time it was young boys who propositioned me.

I walked the town, hoping by chance to see one of my old friends. No such luck. Finally, I walked into a bar; it was packed with gringos drinking piña coladas, which probably makes them feel very tropical. One of the women smiled at me. "Do you speak English?" We started a silly conversation; the gringa was pretty and very forward. We ended up making love in some room. She was satisfied thinking that she had found a native, and I felt like an idiot for coming all the way from New York to whore around in English.

The following night I found an attractive companion—with American dollars it's very easy—and we went around the Amón neighborhood, where my great aunts still live, and where a lot of nightclubs now are. My "girlfriend" introduced me to some of her friends, who called me *mae* [a Costa Rican term that indicates someone of your group or gang] all night. I understood less than half of what they were saying. We drank like crazy, danced, and smoked weed. When things were getting good . . .

I came to on a lonely road, totally naked, barefoot and freezing to death. I tried to stop a car for help. "Bum! Pig! Filth!" They screamed everything at me.

I had to stay a couple of days longer in San José to replace my documents. I spent the nights in my room at the hotel watching cable television from New York. (Loría 1995, 67–69)

The Plaza de la Cultura continues to be a space of ambivalence and perceived danger. It has become overrun with vendors selling foreign goods and local handicrafts, and a hangout for teenagers and foreign pensioners and visitors. As of January 1997, it was closed for renovations. The complete story of the plaza's design and closing is presented in Part III.

Conclusion

In this first history chapter, I have presented the two plazas in their local sociopolitical and ethnohistorical context. But in order to understand the meaning of the plaza—both as an urban design form and as a cultural artifact—a much broader history must be invoked. The origins of the grid-plan plaza design span both European and indigenous histories, each contributing to our understanding of the cultural and political derivation of the built form.

Plazas have been important spatial representations in many societies, not just Costa Rica, and they have been centers of conflict and contestation during critical moments of many peoples' struggles for freedom and sovereignty. Thus, the question of influence in the design of the built environment is part of the larger question of what a place means, and how a place represents a people, and re-presents a people to themselves. This historically created symbolism of public space is central to our understanding of the ethnographies and personal narratives that follow. In order to accomplish this task, though, the histories of the European and indigenous development of the plaza must first be introduced.

CHAPTER 4

The European History of the Plaza

Power Relations and Architectural Interpretation

■

Introduction

The grid-plan town with a central plaza built under the direction of the Spanish throughout their colonial domain has been interpreted to be an architectural representation of colonial control and oppression. This urban form is thought to be based on Renaissance rules of rationality and order and is not a traditional cultural expression in the colonizing country (Foster 1960). Valerie Fraser even suggests that

> it is as if the Spanish colonists were drawing on some sort of cultural memory, an inherited, almost instinctive knowledge. Under the special circumstances of America the sense of what was right and proper in architecture and town planning comes to the surface to be transformed into physical reality. (1990, 7)

According to Dora Crouch, Daniel Garr, and Axel Mundigo, the central square of space ringed by the cathedral, administration buildings, arsenal, and customs house, and later the residences of the social elite, represented the double hierarchy of church and state "conceived and executed as propaganda vehicles, symbolizing and incarnating civilization" (1982, xx). The plaza "was[,] and in many places still is, a manifestation of the local social order, [of] the relationship between citizens and citizens and the authority of the state" (Jackson 1984, 18). In the colonial city, this relationship was one of social and racial domination reflected in the structure of the built environment (Gutiérrez 1983; King 1976).

These interpretations are based on a tacit assumption that the plaza-centered urban design was of solely European derivation. Researchers identify the 1573 Laws of the Indies or the writings of the Italian Renaissance as the main sources of New World plaza design, even though they were published many years after the establishment of the first Spanish American towns. In fact, the redesign of Spanish cities under Philip II was partly stimulated by the urban-design experiments of the New World. Jesús Escobar argues that when Madrid was chosen to serve as the political center of Spain in 1561, it became an architectural laboratory in which ideas received from Spanish-controlled cities were tried and developed and then sent out again into the Spanish realm (1995, 63). The implication is that European and North American architectural historians have overlooked the Precolumbian architectural and archaeological legacy, and by doing so have constructed a Eurocentric narrative of the evolution of this urban form (Benevolo 1969; Borah 1972; Borah, Hardoy, and Stelter, 1980; Couch, Garr, and Mundigo 1982; Foster 1960; Hardoy 1973; Hardoy and Hardoy 1978; Kubler 1976; Morse 1987; Palm 1955, 1968; Ricard 1947; Schaedel, Hardoy, and Kinzer 1978; Stanislawski 1947; Zawiska 1972).

Even Fraser in *The Architecture of Conquest* is unclear about the role of the indigenous planning influences, though at the same time she provides archaeological and ethnohistorical evidence that many, if not most, Spanish American towns utilized the existing indigenous settlement pattern and buildings. Yet she agrees that indigenous towns and architecture were greeted with admiration and appreciation for the skill and knowledge it took to design and build such magnificent urban centers.

> Many early travellers in South America were impressed by indigenous towns and indigenous architecture, but this seems not to have weakened their confidence in the superiority of their own culture. . . . As the Spanish colonies are consolidated, so this cultural confidence is in fact strengthened rather than weakened. Once the Indian towns have been appropriated and recognizably Europeanized, then there is less evidence of a non-European urban society to upset this confidence. The unsettling possibility that a completely different, non-European people might also have developed a form of town based on straight streets, square blocks and a central plaza surrounded by important political and religious buildings could be set aside, to be dealt with by later historians. (Fraser 1990, 80)

But later historians have not dealt with this problem. Even though Fraser provides a plausible psychological interpretation of why the Spanish did not acknowledge the contribution of indigenous planning, she still argues that the new town forms were basically European, coming from an almost subconscious impulse to create order.

This chapter addresses the history of the Spanish American grid-plan and plaza-centered design through a reexamination of the European historical, architectural, and ethnographic evidence. In the same sense that Susan Gillespie (1989) suggests that she is searching for historical "truth" so that she can present a more accurate picture of both the events and their cultural interpretation, I attempt to present a more inclusive view of the evidence in order to argue that the Spanish American grid-plan-plaza urban design had its roots in a multiplicity of architectural and cultural traditions.

The reanalysis suggests that the grid-plan-plaza town is not a unique and therefore difficult-to-explain occurrence: there has been a continuity of grid-plan-plaza forms across time and cultures. Most ancient towns in China, Japan, Korea, peninsular India as well as in Precolumbian America were planned according to a gridiron pattern (Braudel 1981, Stanislawski 1946). Only two civilizations produced large, irregular towns—Islam and medieval Europe—and even in Europe grid plans were being produced in new towns (such as *bastides*) throughout the Middle Ages. From this perspective, the question of the style's uniqueness recedes, and the question of its ubiquitousness from many cultural sources emerges.

Even within the European ethnohistorical and architectural research there is considerable disagreement as to the derivation of the grid-plan, plaza-centered urban design form. The most plausible argument was made almost forty years ago by the anthropologist George Foster (1960), who, as part of his concern with selective cultural transmission during the Spanish Conquest, identified a series of Roman and garrison towns in Spain as the urban-planning models for the development of towns in the New World.

The grid-plan-plaza urban plan is found throughout Europe in fortress and frontier towns that were built to consolidate borders as well as to protect religious settlements. As such, their designs reflect the power relationships that are seen in the later Spanish American plaza form. The power relations of plaza design form are not just about its spatial and architectural production, however, but include the hegemony of

Eurocentric scholarship and writing found in architectural history. The published word has had more influence than the commonsense examination of the landscape. Thus, power relations are embodied in language as well as in physical design, and written "history"—rather than the examination of multicultural histories—has the greatest power of all.

Finally, the evidence suggests that there were multiple forces affecting the planning and building of each city and town because of differences in available information, individuals involved, chronology, local materials, geographical site and history, and environmental context. By examining the case example of Santo Domingo, the first city in the New World, the interplay of these forces becomes clearer. Santo Domingo was probably designed based upon Spanish models, making it one of the foundational architectural examples drawn upon by architects throughout the colonial period.

This chapter is divided into three sections: an overview of the existing European architectural, historical, and cultural evidence pertaining to the origin of the grid-plan-plaza urban design form; a section focused on the case study of Santo Domingo, including a discussion of the indigenous Taino traditions that Columbus encountered; and a brief discussion of the implications of these findings for an understanding of the role of power relations in the attribution of landscape design forms.

European Ethnohistorical Evidence

The European evidence revolves around weighing the importance of the contributions of the Italian piazza, the writings of the Italian Renaissance, and the role of the *bastides* in France or exploring whether the plaza could be explained based solely on Spanish sources. Unfortunately, there are almost no references to what the early designers might have seen or read or to what was known about architectural sources outside of Spain. The New World explorers, though, provide some clues of the cities with which they were familiar in their allusions to Salamanca, Rome, and Seville.

Italian

Italian planning traditions influenced the design of Spanish American grid-plan towns indirectly through Etruscan Greek and Roman architectural planning and directly in the post-1550 period of town development based on Renaissance planning ideals. The Etruscans followed cosmological principles in orienting their temples, and they were concerned about town planning, passing on ideas about both surveying and cartographic practice to the Romans (Aveni and Romano 1994). The Greek architect-philosopher Hippodamus is credited by Aristotle with designing the first regularized agora—a rectangular space 400 ft. by 540 ft., surrounded by porticoed civic buildings, with a single street entry—in his native city of Miletus between 475 and 470 B.C. (Webb 1990; Zucker 1959). Allegedly, he also laid out the plans for Piraeus, the harbor of Athens, introducing this regularity and grid plan to mainland Greece as early as 446 B.C. (Webb 1990, 29). "The Hippodamean plan consisted of a street grid split into wide parallel strips by a few major north-south running streets" (Aveni and Romano 1994, 546). Paul Zucker comments that Hippodamus merely introduced into Greece "a concept developed from earlier Oriental [*sic*] examples in Ionic settlements of Asia Minor. There the *economic advantages of a regular distribution* of lots may have contributed to a preference for organized planning in the process of orderly colonization" (1959, 33; emphasis in original). He adds that it was Pausanias, the Greek traveler and geographer of the second century A.D., who emphasized repeatedly the difference between the older agoras and the post-Hippodamic ones, which were reported to have been regular and surrounded by colonnades (34).

Although there is considerable disagreement among scholars, the Roman version of this scheme is thought to have featured a central intersection of a pair of major axes as used by Greek traders (Stanislawski 1946). The Romans developed a standard plan called the *castrum,* made up of a grid-plan military camp with a small central square for the mustering of troops, for their settlements across Europe, North Africa, and the Middle East (Stanislawski 1946; Ward-Perkins 1974; Webb 1990). Vitruvius, in his *De Architectura* (1931 translation), offers specific rules on how to build these new cities and Roman colonies. The Romans thus created a planning model through their building foundations as well as their writings that by the twelfth century was influencing the layout of new towns throughout Europe.

From 1299 to 1350 a series of new towns were founded by the city of Florence for defense, protection of roads, development of new markets, and increased communication with outlying territories. The records show that some architects designed these new towns with an orthogonal street system, a transverse piazza, and a back-to-back block system (Friedman 1988).

By 1346 there was a shift in the architectural importance of the plaza with the building of the famous Siena piazza, which was designed as a public open space for purely aesthetic and prestige-related motives (Cosgrove 1982). Between 1459 and 1462 Bernardo Rossellino built the piazza of Pienza based on Renaissance scenographic principles described as "an early Renaissance painting of an ideal city come to life" (Webb 1990, 68). The Pienza piazza, which is only 100 feet wide and 75 feet deep, brings the linear perspective of the composition together (Webb 1990). In 1492, the same year that Columbus departed for the New World, the piazza of Vigevano was redesigned based on Renaissance principles of urban planning. The facades were made uniform and the space regularized to conform to new ideas of proportion and perspective (Lotz 1981).

Leon Battista Alberti's interpretation of Vitruvius's writings ([1485] 1986) in the context of emergent Renaissance advances in mathematics, engineering, and aesthetic theory, combined with practical notions of auspicious astrology and weather, was published in 1485 (1452, according to Webb 1990), further expanding the influence of Renaissance urban design ideals. Quoting Vitruvius, Alberti argued that a square should be twice as long as it is broad, surrounded by buildings between a third and a sixth as high as the square's width, with porticoes where old men could relax in the heat of the day. In fact, a copy of Vitruvius was found in a library of Mexico City as early as 1550 (De la Torre 1978; Kubler 1948). Yet Renaissance planning ideals and utopian writings did not have a direct impact on the design of Spanish American towns until the second half of the sixteenth century with the writing of the 1573 Laws of the Indies.

French

The French contribution to New World planning derives mainly from the building of the *bastides* and the influence of the design of Valbonne on Mendicant towns in Mexico. The European population increase of 1220–1250, the reorganization of governmental and agricultural institutions, and the responsibility of supplying the crusades necessitated the building of *bastides,* population centers established for trade, defense, and administration, particularly in southwestern France but also in Spain and England (Calmettes, Cornu, and Calmettes 1986). *Bastide* actually means "rural landholding" (Kubler 1978), and *bastides* were agricultural communities based on land grants and built by "royal authority, either to impose itself over dissident parts of its territory, or to extend its domain" (Morris 1974, 82–83). The *bastide* form was a transitional stage between the feudal castle and the massive formal styles of the seventeenth century; it was characteristically an open town with narrow streets, a fortified church or walled perimeter (Kubler 1948), a gridiron plan of rectangular shape depending on the terrain, and limited size (Marshall 1973).

The most commonly cited *bastide* with the characteristic grid-plan and plaza-centered design is Monpazier in the Dordogne. Built in 1285, Monpazier has lost its walls but retains its twenty rectangular blocks, including an arcaded square about 210 ft. by 190 ft., with the church and a smaller square off the northeast corner (Webb 1990; see Photograph 31). The plan illustrates the centrality of the arcaded square to the grid plan and the separation of the church, which has its own side yard, from the central square. Monpazier continues to use the arcaded square as a central marketplace and meeting place, although the demands of automobiles continue to erode the integrity of this prototypical public space (Aubarbier, Binet, and Bouchard 1989).

The plans of these *bastides,* similar to the new towns of Italy, Germany, and Holland, are evidence of a continuous history of European town planning from the Roman colonies through the medieval period to the Spanish garrison town of Santa Fe, Granada, described below. The importance of this European medieval planning tradition as a model for new town planning in the New World has been generally overlooked (exceptions include Kubler 1978 and Foster 1960). Researchers have been too concerned about establishing a direct link to Spain, which has actually always been there in the *bastides* of Navarre and in the sequence of Spanish town planning identified by George Foster (1960).

A later French influence discussed by Kubler (1978) was the model of new, unwalled gridiron towns, which included Valbonne (1519), Mouans-Sartoux (1504), and Vallauris (1501), built on the initiative of the Benedictine abbey of St. Honorat of Lérins. These high Renaissance towns resemble the *bastide* but are argued to have influenced the development of the Mendicant towns of sixteenth-century Mexico through links to the Spanish Court. The physical resemblances of this open-city plan to the colonial Spanish town are close enough in time and in political connection through the Grimaldi family to provide an alternative design influence (Kubler 1978).

31. Central marketplace of Monpazier, a bastide *in France*

Other European Influences

Other European influences include those from the Germanic region. The Dutch market town of Haarlem was expanded in 1426 in an ordered and planned manner with a rectangular market center and straight streets alternating with canals (Hardoy 1978, 329). The Dutch, as well as the Germans, built an extensive network of new towns along their expanding frontiers.

Other theoretical sources said to have inspired Renaissance town planning include the writings of the utopian philosopher Thomas More, whose *Utopia,* published in 1516, describes cities of uniform row houses. Eximenic, the Catalan Franciscan who published in 1381–1386, describes the ideal city as a square fortified city with a large central open space and four smaller plazas in the four quarters of the town (Foster 1960, 44; Reps 1965, 6). The direct effect of these writings is unclear, although Morse (1987) argues that it is considerable. Germán Arciniegas (1975), a Latin American historian, presents an interesting argument that information and travel accounts from Vespucci were what stimulated Thomas More to write his account of an ideal country as a protest against what existed in Europe. Often colonial planning is more of a protest against what exists in the imperial country than a reflection of the needs of the colonial situation (Rabinow 1989). The colonial situation allows for the expression of both social and architectural utopian ideas that are generated by dissent about the traditional European order but are not acted upon in the home country because of the existence of well-accepted norms of building and behavior.

Spanish

The primary Spanish influence on New World town planning is usually considered to be the codification of Spanish American planning practice in the directives from Philip II and the 1573 Laws of the Indies, but other influences include the design of Islamic palace gardens and the garrison town of Santa Fe, Granada.

Spain, like most of Europe, retained vestiges of early Roman settlements. The grid-like plans of early Roman towns were subsequently built over in the course of the series of invasions that culminated with the Moorish conquest and nearly seven hundred years of Islamic settlement. However, the Spanish knew of the Roman foundations from a number of ancient cities, including Barcelona, where the urban core is designed as a grid such as is found in the Plaça Real.

Most of the cities of medieval Spain are characterized by their irregular plan and lack of open spaces (see Photograph 32). The cities of Al-Andalus, Muslim Spain, were built resembling Islamic cities, with winding streets ending in cul-de-sacs, blocks of houses irregular in shape and length, and an absence of defined squares—all features of the walled-in central nucleus, or *medina,* of any Islamic city. According to John Brookes, "The traditional Islamic concern is primarily for the feel of space within, defined by its building materials. Volume is more important than mass. . . . The result is an internal architecture, inseparable from the fabric of the city, less concerned with buildings in space, more with space itself" (1987, 21).

The influence of the Islamic garden is often overlooked by architectural historians searching for the origins of the gridiron plan, undoubtedly because the Islamic city is known for its lack of planning and maze of streets. Nonetheless, paradise gardens have had a strong influence on the decoration and form of plazas, especially from the point of view of landscape architecture (Brookes 1987). The private gardens of large houses and palaces such as the Alhambra in Granada were organized in gridlike

32. Winding streets of Seville, Spain

patterns with designs that were drawn upon by the Spanish for their gardenlike plazas (*parques*) of the New World.

The internal courtyard garden was the form commonly used in Al-Andalus urban dwellings. This enclosed garden became the prototype for the home as well as the mosque and *madrasa,* or "college" (Brookes 1987, 23). A specific example of a courtyard garden that might have influenced the design of New World plazas is the Patio de los Naranjos in Córdoba, Spain. The courtyard is claimed by C. M. Villiers-Stuart (1936) to be the oldest existing garden in Europe (A.D. 976), and it represented an early urbanization of the standard Middle Eastern concept with its rows of orange trees planted in a grid plan (Brookes 1987, 39). The side yard of the Patio de los Naranjos, an original feature of the Mezquita Great Mosque/Cathedral, retains the internal courtyard design features of its Islamic design (see Photograph 33). Interestingly, the spatial relationship between the Mezquita Great Mosque/Cathedral and its side yard in Córdoba is the same as the designed relationship of the central cathedral and side-yard plaza found in Santo Domingo, Dominican Republic, the first city built by the Spanish in the New World.

The medieval cities of Spain, therefore, were not the models for the plaza-centered grid-plan town. The plaza is a normal form in very old Spanish cities, but even in the sixteenth century it remains small and irregular (Kubler 1948, 99). In fact, the plazas of Andalusian cities were added as part of the redesign of urban centers in response to the New World planning, rather than the reverse. And even today, the streets of Spain, such as Sierpes in Seville, are the centers of social life rather than the plazas.

Ramón Gutiérrez (1983) argues that the design of the Plaza Mayor in Madrid, completed in 1619, was a response to the beauty of the designed plazas of the Spanish American New World. More recently, Jesús Escobar, an architectural historian, describes Madrid as an architectural laboratory of ideas received from Spanish-controlled cities and adapted to the needs of the new capital (1995). In his discussion of the Plaza Mayor as an important site of architectural experimentation, Escobar suggests that New World ideas were imported to Spain and incorpo-

33. Patio de los Naranjos, Córdoba, Spain

rated into a Plaza Mayor that had social as well as symbolic political significance:

> The planned city square came to symbolize the urban order sought by the Spanish government in the capital and beyond. In the illustrations of Andean towns by the colonial author Felipe Guamán Poma de Ayala for his *Nueva Corónica,* a manuscript completed in 1605, the geometrically regular plaza mayor signified the achievement of "buen govierno [good government]."
> (1995, 63)

The strongest argument in favor of a Spanish origin for the grid-plan town with a central plaza has been proposed by George Foster (1960). He traces the *bastides* of southwestern France and Navarre, Spain, to the design of the garrison town of Santa Fe, Granada, built by the Catholic Kings during the final phase of the reconquest of Andalusia in 1491 (Foster 1960; Reps 1965; Zucker 1959). Christopher Columbus signed the *capitulaciones* (articles of agreement) for his first voyage in Santa Fe in April 1492, and the physical design form of this city is generally agreed to be the basis for the urban design of Santo Domingo, built in 1502 (Bronner 1986; Crouch, Garr, and Mundigo 1982, 43; Elliot 1987; Palm 1955). Thus, even though Spain was basically a country of unplanned Islamic and medieval cities, there is some evidence of Spanish influence in the design of New World grid-plan towns from thirteenth- and early-fourteenth-century *bastides,* Islamic gardens, and the garrison town of Santa Fe, Granada.

The most commonly cited evidence of Spanish derivation of the grid-plan plaza has been the Laws of the Indies, a set of planning decrees published in 1573 that collected previously executed directives from 1509 and 1523 into a codified form. These so-called laws or directives were written by Philip II of Spain, who was heavily influenced by the writings of Vitruvius, as translated by the practicing architect Leon Battista Alberti. But, as has been pointed out by many scholars, by 1573 the majority of the major cities in the New World had been built, and the Laws of the Indies only reflected what was already established practice. Further, they state that the cathedral was not to be placed on the plaza, while common practice was to have the cathedral facing the plaza as a central symbol of the city or town (Crouch, Garr, and Mundigo 1982, xx).

To further explore the influence of these various European design forms, the circumstances of the building of the first New World city, Santo Domingo, and the design of its plaza must be examined.

The Case Study of Santo Domingo (on the island of Hispaniola)

In December of 1492, Christopher Columbus built a crude fortress known as La Navidad from the timbers of the wrecked *Santa María* on the northern coast of the island of Hispaniola (Columbus 1493). This first primitive military outpost of Europeans in the New World did not survive long, and it was not until 1496 that Columbus's brother Bartolomé Colón founded Santo Domingo on the southern side of the island (Reps 1969).

Columbus and his crew found a number of indigenous Taino towns on the island. The towns had attained a size that could only be explained by the enormous wealth of good land suitable for cultivation. The streets were generally straight, and plazas were built for ceremonial use (Las Casas 1951). Fray Bartolomé de Las Casas identifies a definite Taino building design in which, after felling the trees to clear a place for the plaza, four "streets" were hewn out in the form of a cross. However, not all of the towns were large enough to have real plazas, and many houses, except those of the *cacique* (chief), were built in an irregular pattern and without streets (Loven 1935). Many early chroniclers, including Las Casas, Columbus, Fernández de Oviedo y Valdés, and Martyr, recorded seeing these plazas and house sites (Fernández de Oviedo y Valdés 1959; Parry and Keith 1984; Wagner 1942; Wilson 1990).

From the writings of Las Casas (1951) and Fernández de Oviedo y Valdés (1959), and from archaeological evidence of the West Indies, it can be concluded that there were plazas situated in front of *cacique* huts where ball playing, and in some cases ancestor worship, took place. The majority of these excavated plazas are described as quadrilateral or rectangular and are enclosed by flat stones standing on end (Loven 1935). Some of these plazas were very large, about 258 yards long by 96 yards wide; however, their relationship to the overall settlement pattern is not always clear (Wilson 1990).

In his description of the villages of the Tainan islands, Las Casas (1951) states that the house of the king or gentleman of the town was in the best location, and in front of this royal house was a large plaza, very level and well swept for ball playing. There were also houses near this plaza, and if it was a very large town, there would be other plazas for smaller ball games (Loven 1935, 94). Las Casas's writings have been critiqued as revisionist history written to empower the native populations, thus presenting a counterdiscourse to the early conquerors' self-serving depictions of the native peoples (Arias 1993; Merrim 1993). Even so, it appears from these accounts that we can establish that there were plazas in the Taino villages, although their relevance to the planning of Santo Domingo is unclear.

Bungled administration and the failure to establish a permanent settlement on the island prompted the Spanish Crown to send Fray Nicolás de Ovando as governor. In these early settlements, the Crown gave little direction, and Ferdinand's instructions to Ovando in 1501 state only:

> As it is necessary in the island of Española to make settlements and from here it is not possible to give precise instructions, investigate the possible sites and, in conformity with the quality of the land and sites as well as with the present population outside present settlements, establish settlements in the numbers and in the places that seem proper to you. (Stanislawski 1947, 95)

Ovando arrived in 1502 with 2,500 settlers. When after two months a hurricane destroyed his capital, he re-sited it on the right bank of the Ozama River. Ovando developed a geometric layout that he used as the model for a network of towns on Hispaniola for which he "coordinated selected urban sites, controlled municipal appointments and determined the disposition of lots around the plazas" (Morse 1987, 171). Ovando's experiences with the laying out and administration of towns informed the Crown's 1513 instructions to Pedrarias Dávila, which directed him to choose healthy places with good water and air, divide plots for houses according to the status of the person, and arrange the houses in relation to the plaza, church, and pattern of streets. These instructions have been interpreted to imply a grid plan (Stanislawski 1947).

Gonzalo Fernández de Oviedo y Valdés describes Santo Domingo as superior even to Barcelona and all the other Old World cities that he had seen. Kathleen Myers (1993) has recently noted that Oviedo uses the first person so that the reader is allowed to see through his eyes, creating a visual epistemology that justifies his representation of New World phenomena. This literary technique is particularly convincing in his descriptions of cities and towns; nonetheless, these passages should be read as descriptions written for the king, and therefore also represent a political as well as social reading of the scene:

Since the city was founded in our own time, there was opportunity to plan the whole thing from the beginning. It was laid out with ruler and compass, with all the streets being carefully measured. Because of this, Santo Domingo is better planned than any town I have seen. (Fernández Oviedo y Valdés 1959, 11)

The earliest plan of the first permanent city in the New World reveals that the rather impressive settlement described by Oviedo was centered around its plaza and cathedral (see Photograph 34). Straight, wide streets divide the town into rectangular blocks containing the homes of the settlers, warehouses, barracks, and buildings for religious orders. In the engraving, the plaza's relationship to the cathedral is as a church side yard. This cathedral/plaza relationship resembles the Patio de los Naranjos side yard of the Mezquita in Córdoba, Spain, and the church/plaza relationship of the *bastides* and Santa Fe, Granada, more than the front-facing cathedral and plaza design of later Spanish American cities (Low 1993). Even though the accuracy of the Bigges (1588) depiction of the early plan can be questioned based on the differences of plan representation, even in 1989 Santo Domingo's plaza retained this side yard/plaza design (Williams and Lewis 1993).

The colonists' relationship to the native population must also be considered in an interpretation of the origins of the plaza in the Santo Domingo design. Irving Rouse's (1992) overview of ethnohistorical and archaeological research on the Taino documents the abuse, violent subjugation, and mass killings by Ovando and other colonists in their attempts to use the native peoples as laborers. In this first encounter, the indigenous population and their cultural traditions did not survive. The enduring influence of Taino architecture and planning was limited by the devastating impact of Spanish domination and control.

Thus, Santo Domingo's plaza appears mostly derived from Spanish/Islamic models, primarily the design of a mosque/cathedral side yard, with some possible reference to the indigenous Taino cultural pattern of placing a plaza in front of the *cacique*'s house. Santo Domingo was a frequent way station for travelers to the New World, so there were opportunities for voyagers to compare the open plazas of Precolumbian cities with the marketplaces and parvis (an irregular open space in front of a cathedral) of medieval European cities. It is particularly frustrating that there is no direct evidence for the derivation of the Santo Domingo

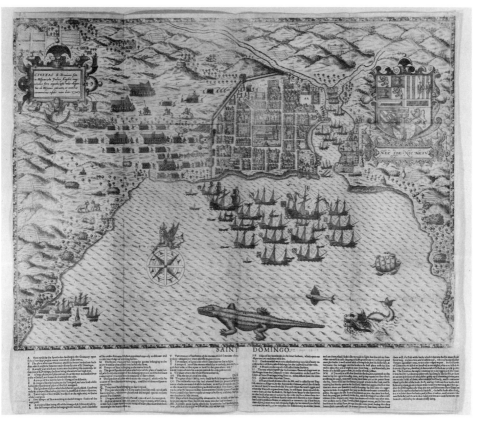

34. Santo Domingo by Walter Bigges, 1589

plaza because, as the earliest European New World urban design, it provides one of the models for later Spanish American cities.

Conclusion

Ovando's plan of Santo Domingo most closely resembles the Spanish
bastide-like garrison town of Santa Fe, Granada, although the plaza itself is reminiscent of the side yard of the mosque/cathedral in Córdoba,
Spain. There is indirect evidence of indigenous influence on its design
in that Taino towns had ball-playing plazas that are described in voyagers' accounts, but there is no direct evidence that they were architectural
models for the Spanish.

Santo Domingo is one of the few examples of predominantly European influence on an early grid-plan, plaza-centered urban design in the New World. In the next chapter, however, I trace the wealth of evidence indicating that other New World cities and towns, such as Mexico City and Mérida, were based on indigenous architectural plans. Revisionist historians have even asserted that the design of Spanish plazas was based primarily on New World models throughout the late sixteenth and seventeenth centuries (Escobar 1995; Gutiérrez 1983; Low 1993, 1996). In other words, the ethnohistorical analysis of European documentary materials tells us more about the power relations of the writing of architectural history than about the history of the plaza itself. The Europeans produced the architects, built the plazas, and wrote about their designs, so that even though the plans were derived from a variety of sources, including existing New World designs, the architectural history records only the European story.

Thus, the control of spatial meaning can be maintained through the design of the public space, as well as through the writing of its history. The European plaza provides the first step in understanding the culture and politics of public space by illustrating the dual avenues of control—materially through plaza design, and metaphorically through writing (Smith and Katz 1993). But in the New World, the instances of the former, contrary to popular opinion, have been much less prevalent than the latter, while both contribute to a hegemonic architectural design tradition.

CHAPTER 5

The Indigenous History of the Plaza

The Contested Terrain of Architectural Representations

Introduction

Within anthropology, the assumption that the Nahua and Maya of Mexico and Central America were passive recipients of colonial Hispanic culture has been thoroughly refuted (Jones 1989; Weeks 1988). "It is now widely understood that the recognition of colonial exploitation does not preclude a recognition of the colonized as being capable of acting to influence their own destiny" (Weeks 1988, 73). This insight has particular significance in the domains of architecture and urban design, where the ascendancy and control of the Spanish colonizers remains unquestioned.

Nahua and Maya peoples' resistance to colonial domination took spatial and architectural forms that can be traced in the archaeological and historical record. Cultural conflict and contestation is semiotically encoded in the built environment and provides material evidence that the plaza and its spatial relations are a cultural production of these struggles. The importance of the struggle for the control of public space and its attributed meanings is highlighted by the contemporary debate concerning the allocation of space and rights of excavation in the Zócalo, the historic Plaza Mayor of Mexico City.

The tension between Spanish colonial and indigenous, particularly Nahua, cultural hegemony and their spatial and architectural representations can be seen in the struggle for the restoration and preservation of the remaining architecture and archaeological materials. The archaeological excavation of the Templo Mayor of Tenochtitlan Stages 1 through 6 (the seventh stage was destroyed by Cortés to build the current colonial plaza and buildings) and the building of the new Museo del Templo Mayor have caused considerable concern among architectural historians and other scholars interested in the history and architecture of the colonial period. A number of important colonial buildings were torn down in order to excavate the Mexica site and to make room for the new museum that interprets the archaeological remains. Further, the archaeological excavations are said to have disturbed the foundations of a number of the remaining colonial buildings on the Zócalo, including the cathedral and the National Palace, causing serious damage to the facades of some colonial buildings. The archaeological site itself is rising, apparently due to the removal of the weight of the colonial buildings and the expansion of the spongy soil of the original lake bed. Colonial historians and architects are worried that with the continued excavation there will be even more damage from the emerging ruins. Some of the architects would like to stop or at least slow down the plans for additional archaeological projects in the area.

Although this preservation dilemma provides insight into the sociopolitical struggle for representational control of space in the symbolic center of Mexico City, the most interesting part of this story is that the contemporary conflict recapitulates the colonial struggles of almost five hundred years ago. The emergence of the Templo Mayor has created considerable cultural capital for the indigenous Indian representation of Mexican identity (Lomnitz Adler 1992). In response, the historians and architects who are involved in the cultural conservation of the Spanish colonial past and the preservation of the colonial symbols of Mexican identity are attempting to reappropriate the Zócalo, the most sacred, and political, of Mexican spaces. The irony, of course, is that Cortés attempted to erase the indigenous past when he tore down the seventh stage of the Templo Mayor, only to have the temple's re-emergence become a vindication of the indigenous culture that was submerged. The plaza remains a contested terrain where the ongoing dialectic between the indigenous presence and Spanish appropriation continues to be played out. Other dissenting groups, not tied to an indigenous ideology, also appropriate this space to oppose the state. These struggles illustrate how important these symbolic spaces are for the formation and maintenance of cultural identity, and how meanings from the past are encoded in the built environment and manipulated through spatial representations and architecture to create the sociopolitical present.

This chapter identifies, albeit indirectly, the Mesoamerican architectural and urban design precedents of the plaza. It contributes to the dialogue about the meaning and interpretation of the built environment as a visual representation of colonial dominance, cultural resistance, and spatial control in the New World. Drawing upon architectural and archaeological data, I argue against the dominant view that the plaza was of European derivation, and present a syncretic view of the plaza urban design form.

The Paradox of the Plaza in the New World

Large cities such as Tenochtitlan (Clendinnen 1991) and Cuzco (Hyslop 1990) were centered on ceremonial plazas surrounded by major temples and residences of the ruling elite. The Spaniards, upon their arrival, admired these exceptional models of urban design and wrote about the grandeur, order, and urbanity of these newly discovered cities. Even though there were major differences between the Valley of Mexico and the tropical lowlands in that straight streets did not characterize the lowland urban form, a hierarchy of central plazas and temples was found in most Mesoamerican cities. The ceremonial and commercial use of these plazas, as well as their sacred and civil meanings and regular form, contrasted with the irregular and functionally dispersed spaces of the medieval European city, and yet were similar to the subsequent colonial plazas built after the Spanish Conquest.

The question of the origin of the plaza urban design has implications for the cultural interpretation of the meaning of the plaza complex. The case of Tenochtitlan provides a revealing example. David Carrasco (1990b) states that for the Mexica, the ideal city type was a sacred space oriented around a quintessentially sacred center and that the design of the city is a replica of cosmological space. Eduardo Matos Moctezuma reiterates the cultural significance of the sacred center:

> The Mexica's first act upon settling in this place was to build a small shrine to Huitzilopochtli. They thus established their "center," the navel of the world, the sacred space from which would emerge the four fundamental divisions of the city. Within this supremely sacred space they attempted to reproduce architecturally the entire cosmic order. (1990, 56)

Further, there was a symbolic relationship between nature and architecture such that the main pyramid was considered a sacred mountain (Matos Moctezuma 1992; Townsend 1992, 182). This correspondence of natural and supernatural places with architectural sites also is evident at Quiriguá, Guatemala, where a stela erected in the main ceremonial plaza specifies the place where it was set, that is, "Black Water Sky Place" (Grube, Schele, and Fahsen 1991). This stela reference suggests that place-names refer to supernatural and natural locations, and that Maya—as well as Mexica—believe that their cities replicate features of the supernatural world.

If the central plaza and Great Temple of Tenochtitlan was the sacred space of the Mexica world, then what happened to the sacredness of the space when Cortés decided to rebuild the city on the ruins of this space, thus, re-presenting (re-creating) the Mexica ceremonial plaza and Great Temple in a new Spanish American plaza and cathedral form? Can it be argued that each time an indigenous plaza is reconstituted or rebuilt maintaining some aspects of its original spatial form and integrity, the new form retains and conserves some of the original cultural meanings of the space? Are the uses of the plazas so different from how native residents used the plaza before? Why isn't the plaza treated as a representation in which the forms and cultural meanings merge the two traditions?

To answer these questions it is important to consider the temporal scale of what is being studied. Michael Smith (1992) points out that there is often a confusion between ethnographic and archaeological time. Similarly, there is often confusion when architectural historians lump two hundred years of colonial life into one period. The study of the built environment and its cultural meanings is best achieved by breaking down the temporal scale, as in the (1991b) work of Inga Clendinnen, which chronicles the year-by-year decisions and movements of Cortés and his soldiers in order to interpret his actions and their consequences. In the case of the origins of the Spanish American plaza, this is often difficult to do because the data are incomplete and rudimentary. One place to start, however, is to examine, city by city and site by site, the data that *are* available. There are multiple cultural sources and architectural models for plaza design. Ethnohistorical research has reinforced the perspective that the origins of any cultural artifact are based on a complex set of influences (Gillespie 1989; Todorov 1984; Williams and Lewis 1993). Further, studies in the social production of built form suggest that many of these forces are latent rather than manifest and must be teased out of the data, or may be found in other, tangential data sources (King 1980). Issues such as what the role was of indigenous laborers who were building these new towns, what models the Spanish had in their new environment, and what influence these models had on form and style have not been adequately researched, but they must be to illuminate other dimensions of the research question (Matos Moctezuma 1990). By examining a number of specific sites, the interplay of forces becomes clearer, and questions can be answered based on the history of a particular place.

In this chapter, I focus on the development of the Spanish American plaza in three case studies: two cities, Mexico City and Mérida, and one archaeological site, Negroman-Tipu in Belize (hereafter referred to by its colonial period name, Tipu). I begin with a brief overview of the nature of Mesoamerican traditions of building and architecture and then turn to the individual cases. I conclude by returning to a discussion of the larger project, that is, of the politics of public space and the symbolic meanings of spatial representations as a way of explaining why origins and influence have such cultural and political importance.

Architectural and Urban Design Traditions

Many researchers have argued that "the design of colonial capital cities has nothing to do with local traditions, or with persistence of pre-Columbian town planning concepts" (Gasparini 1978, 274). Yet Angel Gracia Zambrano (1992) argues that hidden in the space and concepts of urban design are physical and ideological elements of Precolumbian cultural practices. Many of the indigenous cultures were already employing domestic or ceremonial urban designs that the Spanish would have seen either in Postclassic/Conquest period towns and cities or in the ruins of previous civilizations uncovered in their explorations. So, to balance the Eurocentric view of plaza design and to set the stage for a discussion of the Spanish American plaza as a new syncretic form, the evidence from Mesoamerica needs to be incorporated.

Much of the ethnohistorical evidence presented is based on firsthand Spanish accounts that have been criticized for their representations of the native peoples encountered based on models and myths from Spain and Europe (León-Portilla 1992; Williams and Lewis 1993). These critiques have been helpful in clarifying and deconstructing the European image of the New World. Nonetheless, a recent review by Angel Delgado-

Gómez (1993) found that most of these Spanish accounts try to be clear and to show interest in and respect for the natives. The accuracy of the physical descriptions of cities, towns, and ruins encountered has not been directly challenged, although Clendinnen (1991) comments that Cortés was very strategic in how he presented his descriptions of the wealth and grandeur of Tenochtitlan in his letters. Yet these descriptions are a major part of the fragmentary body of evidence that we have about the perceptions and reactions of the early Spanish soldiers and colonists, and this brief exploration does not allow for a full discussion of the interpretative limitations of these materials. Therefore, I have used the descriptions as published, with few commentaries, and treat these chronicles as one kind of evidence about what these Spaniards thought they saw or cared to write about during their early New World conquests.

The same but even more complex problem confronts us when working with maps, plans, and visual representations produced by Europeans about the New World (Williams and Lewis 1993). These representations are best understood in the context that they were made and should not be used uncritically. However, their interpretation is not the object of this discussion, so no detailed exegesis of the maps and plans is presented.

Mexica Building Traditions

Tenochtitlan, established in 1325, is probably the clearest source of evidence for Mexica influence on architecture and urban design. Tenochtitlan was a monumental urban center of 200,000 inhabitants in an area of 13.5 square kilometers, with straight causeways that ran directly into the main ceremonial plaza (Smith 1994). Firsthand accounts suggest that the Spanish colonists were impressed by the regular plan and urban design of the city, with its centrally located ceremonial temple-plaza complex (see, for example, Díaz del Castillo 1963).

Other Indian towns were also planned with a central grid-plan-plaza system and had at their center a fortified temple enclosure with a plaza that stood upon the intersection of a social thoroughfare. Based on archaeological evidence, Michael Smith (1996, 1997) has found that towns outside of Tenochtitlan conform to a general Mesoamerican urban pattern in which there is a formally planned ceremonial center surrounded by a more informal residential area, a temple-pyramid facing west onto a public plaza, and often a palace or ball court constructed around the plaza. Spanish observers also commented on the formally planned plazas of local Indian towns. Toribio Motolinía comments that

> in the whole land we find that the Indians had a large square court in the best part of the town; about a crossbowshot from corner to corner, in the large cities and provincial capitals; and in the smaller towns, about a bowshot. (Motolinía 1951, 174)

One of the explanations for the central design of Mexica ceremonial sites is the use of the four cardinal points in much of Mexica cosmology (Toussaint, Gómez de Orozco, and Fernández 1938). The cosmos was re-created in the architectural structure of the Great Temple; it "was the place, real and symbolic, where Mexica power was centered" (Matos Moctezuma 1987, 25). The twin shrines that faced the plaza were dedicated to the two great deities—Tlaloc, god of rain, water, and agricultural production, and Huitzilopochtli, god of war, conquest, and tribute—who represented the economic structure of the Mexica state. These gods symbolized the two sources of Mexica income: agricultural production and tribute paid by subject communities (Matos Moctezuma 1987).

The Mexica were developing principles of general city planning in order to achieve an efficient urban organization (Hardoy 1973, 178). The plan of Nahua towns was roughly rectangular and evolved from the division of land among the clans. The central plaza was destined for communal gatherings and as a marketplace, and it simultaneously represented the courtyard of the central temple. This pattern is found from the Maya lowlands to the Zapotec highlands (M. Smith 1996) and is not unlike the representational and functional use of the Spanish American plaza that replaced it.

Both Paul Zucker (1959) and Edward Calnek (1978) suggest that social status among the Mexica was reflected in the architectural markers and the distance of houses from the plaza, with the highest status locations being those on the perimeter and surrounding blocks of the central plaza. A similar organization of social status was later employed by Cortés in his plan for Mexico City. William Schell (1986) argues that, with the exception of the Yucatán Maya, Mesoamerican culture and economic structure resembled that of Iberia in a number of ways, including landholding systems, governance by city-states, and market laws, which explains some of the ease with which Cortés was able to conquer and govern and some of the spatial congruency that arose.

Maya Building Traditions

Preclassic and Classic Maya sites were less rectangular in their plan and in the placement of their ceremonial plazas than Mexica plans. However, even though the ceremonial sites were not in a grid, lowland Maya house sites were organized around plazas (Ashmore 1981). The social status of house sites was also determined by their proximity to the plaza in Maya designs (Becker 1982; Tozzer 1907). Plazas were the focus of community life and were pivotal gathering places, whether adjoined by temples or houses.

Excavations at a number of sites reveal that the earliest form of the ceremonial center consisted of a small plaza and associated structures. The Maya plaza was an open space, cleared of trees and artificially leveled; this leveling and paving of the open space of the plaza was an important architectural statement and became an essential aspect of Maya cities (Andrews 1975).

In the Yucatán, late Classic and Postclassic Maya sites show a cosmopolitan mix of influences evident in the material culture, which may account for the design of the main plazas such as is seen at the site of Chichén Itzá. The Yucatán Maya town of Izamal illustrates how in the Maya region the Spaniards—in this case Diego de Landa—built the Spanish church and monastery next to the massive Maya ceremonial platform topped with a pyramid. The case study of the Maya site of Tipu also illustrates the phenomenon of the building of the colonial church and plaza near Postclassic temples. At the Belize site of Lamanai, the first church was superposed directly over a Postclassic temple platform (Graham, Pendergast, and Jones 1989; Pendergast 1986).

Descriptions from firsthand accounts throughout the Maya region suggest that the Spaniards were aware of the design and grandeur of the abandoned indigenous sites. In a quote from a geographical description of Guatemala by Diego García de Palacio on March 8, 1576, he described the plaza in the ruins of Copán:

> Near here, on the road to the city of San Pedro, in the first town
> within the province of Honduras called Copán, are certain ruins
> and vestiges of a great population and of superb edifices, of such
> skill, that it appears they could never have been built by a
> people as rude as the natives of that province. . . . Near this, is
> a well-built plaza or square, with steps or grades, which, from
> the description, resemble those of the Coliseum at Romes [*sic*].

In some places it has eighty steps, paved, and made in part at least of fine stones, well-worked. In this square are six great statues. (Parry and Keith 1984, 3: 546)

Wendy Ashmore (1987a, 1987b, 1989) presents a partial rationale for the site planning and plaza organization of Copán and other Precolumbian Maya centers. She argues that Copán was designed based on principles of architectural arrangement and their directional associations deriving from Maya cosmology, and suggests a site-planning template for testing this idea (Ashmore 1991b). Maya cities were laid out as microcosms, with buildings arranged so as to symbolically equate the architectural center of civic power with the center of the universe (Ashmore 1991b). Architectural meaning was determined by the spatial relationship of the supernatural with the hierarchy of the state (Coggins 1980). This "sacred geography" encoded in the urban architecture may account for the striking regularities found in these sites. Further, sites such as Quiriguá copied the Copán civic layout with its monument plaza and Acropolis, maintaining these architectural arrangements but in some cases making them even larger than their original model (Ashmore 1991a). The centralization and hierarchical arrangement of plazas at Tenam Rosario, Chiapas, also show evidence of master planning in the repetition of architectural elements found at other Maya sites (Agrinier 1983; De Montmollin 1989).

Although the Maya evidence is not as clear as that of the Mexica tradition, the research suggests that there was a Maya site-planning tradition replicated throughout the region. Architecture was used by Maya elites to symbolically encode their affiliation to more powerful neighbors (Ashmore 1987b). Although the impact of the Maya architectural and site-planning traditions is not clearly documented in the ethnohistorical and archaeological record, Spanish references to existing sites and indigenous architecture in letters and travel accounts suggest that the Spanish were aware of these design traditions.

Archaeological and Ethnohistorical Case Studies

Two cities and one archaeological site have been selected as examples of how different combinations of cultural models and influences were important at different sites. Tipu, Belize, is one of the few excavated examples of places exhibiting continuous Postclassic to Historic period occupation. Lamanai in Belize was also continuously occupied, but it differs from Tipu in the degree and form of colonial impact and is discussed only to provide a context for the Tipu material (Pendergast 1991). Tenochtitlan/Mexico City is the earliest well-documented city in the Mesoamerican region, and the last case, Mérida, although it is poorly documented, is reported to have been built on the indigenous ruins of Tihoo in the Maya Yucatán. These cases illustrate how each plaza evolved in its own historical moment and within distinct sociopolitical and cultural contexts.

Tipu, Belize

The site of colonial Tipu, known in Belize today as Negroman (Graham 1991; Graham, Jones, and Kautz 1985; Graham, Pendergast, and Jones 1989), provides an opportunity to combine ethnohistorical and archaeological evidence to study Maya and Spanish influences on a colonial frontier town: "The identifications of the Late Postclassic-Spanish Colonial period component at Negroman as Tipu itself is based on the conjunction of ethnohistorical and archaeological data" (Graham, Jones, and Kautz 1985, 206). Spanish documents used to locate small *visita* churches built in the region under Spanish direction led investigators to Tipu's general locus, and anomalous mound configurations, very different from nearby Classic and Postclassic features, helped investigators to pinpoint the site (Graham, Pendergast, and Jones 1989).

Tipu is one of the few Maya sites—Lamanai is another (Pendergast 1986, 1991; Pendergast and Graham 1993)—that documents continuous occupation from the Pre-Conquest to the Colonial period. The area was occupied during Preclassic and Classic times, but the Late Postclassic/Colonial period occupation was the focus of investigation and is best understood (Graham, Jones, and Kautz 1985). The Historic period structures themselves are arranged around a plaza bordered at one end by the church (Graham, Pendergast, and Jones 1989).

The reconstruction of the colonial encounter at Tipu depicts a long period of resistance by the native population to Spanish control, marked by violent and bloody rebellions (Jones 1989). The documentary, architectural, and ceramic evidence together suggest that the Spaniards established nominal colonial rule in 1544 and modified existing structures for their use (Graham, Pendergast, and Jones 1989; Jones 1989). Spanish pottery was recovered from the core of church walls, and the church itself was erected over the corner of a Precolumbian building, the remaining portion of which was modified and used in Historic times (Graham, personal communication; Graham, Pendergast, and Jones 1989). It was not until the pacification of the rebellions of 1567–1568 that a major reorganization of the community took place, "represented by the laying out of a European-style, ground-level plaza around which the church and other buildings, entirely colonial in style, were arranged" (Graham, Pendergast, and Jones 1989, 1256).

By 1638, Tipu was joined in a widespread rebellion that expelled the Spaniards from most of Belize until 1695 (Jones 1989). During this period of rebellion, a Precolumbian-style platform was built in the nave of the church, apparently for the purpose of carrying out rituals of some kind (Graham, Pendergast, and Jones 1989, 1257). After the violent conquest of the Maya at Dzuluinicob, Spanish interest in Tipu waned, and after 1707 Tipu was no longer an occupied town. However, Precolumbian-style vessel fragments found in the collapsed debris of abandoned buildings indicate that Pre-Conquest habits persisted (Graham, Pendergast, and Jones 1989, 1257).

Spanish power was reflected mostly in community planning and construction techniques (Graham, Pendergast, and Jones 1989). Traditional groups of inward-facing structures were replaced in part by a single central plaza surrounded by the most important buildings, and the style of masonry was changed during the Colonial period. However, based on observations of other aspects of material culture such as pottery, stone, and shell, Spanish material culture formed a relatively small part of the artifact inventory, and, instead, indigenous preferences, materials, and styles predominated (Graham, Pendergast, and Jones 1989, 1258; Pendergast 1993).

Evidence from excavations at both Tipu and Lamanai shows that the local Maya continued to be concerned about Precolumbian rituals and, by extension, Precolumbian beliefs. At Lamanai, an animal effigy (bat or jaguar) was placed into the platform that was about to be incorporated within the first Christian church, and a Late Postclassic–style effigy pendant and marine shell were placed together as a cache in the foundation of a building constructed during the Historic period at Tipu (Graham, Pendergast, and Jones 1989, 1259; Pendergast 1993, 121, fig. 5). Similar evidence has been cited from archaeological excavations at the Great Temple in Mexico City, where the guidebooks identify Mexica deities carved in the stones that made up the foundation of the Colonial church and plaza. The guidebook text suggests that the Mexica were concerned that their old gods be appeased even in the colonial context (Matos Moctezuma 1990).

Thus, Tipu provides a documented example of a continuously active Colonial population living in the shadow of Postclassic temples standing "only a stone's throw away from the Historic central plaza" (Jones, Kautz, and Graham 1986, 43). During the Colonial period, one of these temples, by then partly in ruins, seems to have been the site of some Precolumbian-style ritual activity, because Spanish olive-jar sherds were found in platform debris along with Late Postclassic–style censer ware fragments (Jones, Kautz, and Graham 1986, 47). Elizabeth Graham (1991) comments that, from an architectural perspective, what we may be witnessing at Tipu is an amalgam of Maya and Spanish traditions rather than any dominance of one tradition over the other. The portable material culture recovered from excavations is more equivocal, and the documentary evidence sheds little light here because the Spaniards "were least interested in recording those things that loom largest in the archaeological record: the components of Maya material culture" (Graham 1991, 332). Thus it is difficult to resolve not only the archaeological and ethnohistorical data but the architectural and artifact data as well.

Lamanai in Belize, another site of continuous occupation from the Middle Preclassic until 1675 or later, also provides archaeological and ethnohistorical evidence that outside influences were blended into preexisting native practices (Pendergast 1993). In the Lamanai case, however, the first church was superposed on a native ceremonial platform after destroying the original Maya temple (Pendergast and Graham 1993). "Superposition had the eminently practical aim of perpetuating precontact patterns of activity while supplanting one form of religious practice with another" (Pendergast 1991, 343). The frontier situation of both Lamanai and Tipu resulted in European buildings interpreted within a Maya architectonic tradition, built by Maya masons with little guidance or oversight by infrequently visiting priests (Pendergast 1993, 122–123).

The combined ethnohistorical and archaeological study of these sites does present some interesting insights into Maya and Spanish interaction. It certainly suggests that the Spaniards utilized Maya buildings until they could construct their own, and that even when some architectural changes were made by the Spanish, the Maya workers incorporated these buildings into their own religious system. Further, it seems that the building of the church and plaza on the edges and foundation of the Precolumbian Maya settlement at Tipu, or superposed on the ceremonial platform at Lamanai, served only to add another cultural dimension rather than to eradicate existing Maya ritual and belief—particularly in this rebellious Maya region.

Tenochtitlan/Mexico City

Tenochtitlan, the capital city of the Mexica, was first encountered by Cortés and his men in 1519 when they entered the city and were given temporary quarters by Moctezuma II. At that time, Tenochtitlan was probably the largest city in the world. Interestingly, the rulers of Tenochtitlan did not follow the normal Aztec civic-center pattern; instead, they walled off the temples and shrines in an inner sacred city, and built palaces for each ruler adjacent to the inner city (Smith 1995). According to Michael Smith (1996), the limiting of public access to the sacred precinct was part of the Mexica plan to elevate their religion to the level of a state cult. Yet, unlike the layout of most towns and cities, the urban area of Tenochtitlan was planned according to political, religious, and pragmatics principles (M. Smith 1996). The grid pattern used demonstrated the power of Mexica rulers to impress their will on the city; the cardinal directions (the orientation of streets was 6.5 degrees east of true north) and their symbolic significance were extended to the entire city; and the rectilinear grid provided a practical layout for a rapidly growing city (M. Smith 1996).

Chroniclers' descriptions emphasize the size and grandeur of the original Mexica city as well as the design and importance of the main plazas. Bernal Díaz del Castillo marvels at the scale and order of the plaza in his memoirs written many years after he returned to Spain:

> Some of our soldiers who have been in many parts of the world, in Constantinople, in Rome, and all over Italy, said that they have never seen a market (plaza) so well laid out, so large, so orderly, and so filled with people. (1963, 235)

The Anonymous Conqueror writes:

> There are in the city Temistitan (Tenochtitlan), Mexico, very large and beautiful plazas where they sell all of the things which the natives use. There was especially the great plaza which they call the Tutelula (Tlatelolco) which may be three times the size

of the square of Salamanca. All around it are porticos where every day from twenty to twenty-five thousand people come to buy and sell. (Saville 1917, 65)

Cortés also is impressed by the city and conveys this to the king in his second letter:

The city itself is as big as Seville or Cordoba. The main streets are very wide and very straight; some of these are on the land, but the rest and all the smaller ones are half on land, half canals where they paddle their canoes. . . . This city has many squares where trading is done and markets are held continuously. There is also one square twice as big as that of Salamanca, with arcades all around. (Cortés 1986, 102–103)

Inga Clendinnen (1991b) notes that the reader must interpret the glowing commentaries of the Spanish colonizers about the "planned" nature of Tenochtitlan in the context of the Spaniards' experience of cities as places filled with organic clutter and filth. The Mexica city grandeur was planned in scale and orientation in a way that was unknown among Spanish and most European cities of that time.

The conquest of Tenochtitlan and the seventy-five-day siege left the city destroyed. According to George Kubler, Cortés originally had wanted to rebuild the city on a better site:

In 1521 he said the city must be depopulated and transferred, and that any Indians seeking to resettle there were to be hanged. Cortés persisted in this intention until November of 1521, so that between November, 1521, and January, 1522, he changed his mind and gave orders for the rebuilding of Tenochtitlan. In Cortés's words, "as the city was so renowned and was so important it seemed well to us to rebuild it."
(1948, 70)

Kubler goes on to explain that there were three interlocking considerations: economic, strategic, and historic prestige. Even though the economic capacities of the site were disadvantageous, separating the city from its subsistence activities, it had positive strategic values—the Aztec were able to resist the European and Indian allies' siege of four months—reinforced by an appeal to tradition and prestige. "The triumph of Christians over Saracens in Spain had long been manifested in the European occupancy of Moorish towns" (Kubler 1948, 70), and in Tenochtitlan, the motives for reoccupation were perhaps similar to those of the Reconquest in Spain.

Clendinnen (1991a), on the other hand, argues that Cortés did not want to destroy the city but wanted to present it to the king. Regardless of which interpretation of his intent is more accurate, by occupying Tenochtitlan, the Spaniards not only changed its appearance but also identified themselves with the space of the political and governmental center (Kubler 1948, 71). In this rebuilding, the religious, administrative, and civic importance of Tenochtitlan's center buildings was maintained: the colonial plazas replaced the markets, the cathedral was built next to the Templo Mayor, and the National Palace covered the destroyed houses of Moctezuma II (see Photograph 35; Matos Moctezuma 1987). This kind of successive dominion over core space became a crucial part of the Spanish strategy of conquest and is repeated throughout the Mesoamerican region.

There is also some dispute about the master plan (*traza*) of Mexico City. Manuel Toussaint (1938) states that Alonso García Bravo authored the plan following his expedition with Pedrarias Dávila in 1513. He is said to have modified the Mexica plan by opening up new streets, widening some streets, and bringing in new streets at right angles (Boyer 1980; Toussaint, Gómez de Orozco, and Fernández 1938). Kubler (1948), however, argues that the surveyor, García Bravo, was not called in until 1524, when land titles were discussed in connection with the assignment of municipal lands, and that, at the very least, the master plan had not been established in 1523. So by the time the master plan was drawn (1523–1524), the cardinal thoroughfares had already been laid out and a year of building had taken place. Thus, the original Mexica plan rather than the Spanish master plan must have guided the earliest phase of urban development.

During the next one hundred years Mexico City grew in importance and size to become a city visited by travelers whose accounts give a detailed description of its physical and social character (see Photograph 36). Thomas Gage's account of Mexico City describes the plaza during this period:

> The chief place in the City is the Market place, which though it be not as spacious as in Montezuma's time, yet is at this day very fair and wide, built all with Arches on the one side where people

> may walke dry in time of rain, and there are shops of Merchants
> furnished with all sorts of stuffes and silks, and before them sit
> women selling all manner of fruits and herbes. (1655, 59)

This account describes the physical evolution of Mexico City, which to
this day maintains the central plaza with the cathedral in its sacred ceremonial center.

Mérida, Yucatán

Mérida was built on the ruins of the Maya town of Tihoo, near the
Mayan sites of Uxmal, Chichén Itzá, and Tulum. It was and still remains the principal city of Spanish Yucatán. According to the Relaciones
Geográficas (1890–1900), this land was first encountered in 1517 by Francisco Hernández de Córdoba, who reported fine cities of masonry houses,
abundant populations, plantations, and gold (Wagner 1942). Governor
Diego Velázquez then sent Captain Juan de Grijalva in 1518 to explore
what was to be called New Spain. Hernán Cortés passed through in 1519
on his way to Tenochtitlan, and, finally, Fernando de Montejo was sent
in 1527 to settle the region.

35. Tenochtitlan by Hernán Cortés, 1524

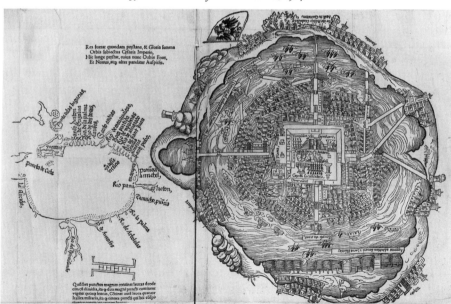

In Peter Martyr's account of the discovery of the Yucatán, he writes:

> The Spaniards discovered a fortified town on the shore of such importance that they named it Cairo after the capital of Egypt. It possesses houses with towers, magnificent temples, regular streets, squares and marketplaces. (Wagner 1942, 33)

This description has been attributed to the site of Tulum. Other nearby sites also had a rectangular ceremonial plaza center and straight causeways leading to the plaza center. Chichén Itzá, a Postclassic site, is even more regular in plan, but while Tulum still functioned as a trading center, both Uxmal and Chichén Itzá were abandoned and only appeared as ruins.

Although there are few early plans of Mérida, there is rich textual material concerning its founding and development. The Maya resisted Spanish invasion and resettlement throughout the Yucatán region (Jones 1989), and the city of Mérida was not founded until January 6, 1541. Diego López de Cogolludo, in his *Historia de Yucathan Compuesta* published in Madrid in 1688, describes the founding of Mérida following a great battle at Tihoo during which 60,000 Maya warriors were finally

36. Nova Mexico by John Ogilby, 1671

subdued (1688, 137). The Spaniards replaced the chief of these people and built the Spanish city on the same site so that people would know that the Spaniards' success would be permanent (López de Cogolludo 1688, 137–138). This superposition appears to have been undertaken with the same strategic intent described above for Mexico City, rather than for the practicality of using the same site, as referred to in the frontier area of Lamanai (Pendergast 1991).

In 1548, Fray Lorenzo de Bienvenida describes Mérida in these terms:

> After the beautiful buildings [Tihoo] contains: in all the discoveries in the Indies none so fine has been found. Buildings of big and well-carved stones—there is no record of who built them. It seems to us they were built before Christ, because the trees on top of the buildings were as high as the ones around them. Amongst these buildings, we, monks of the Order of St. Francis, settled. (Bienvenida, quoted in Hammond 1982, 33–34)

In 1605, with the birth of King Philip IV, Mérida was given the title of Noble and Loyal City of Mérida. According to Clendinnen (1987), the center of life and the city was the plaza, which was the main stage for social display and verbal exchanges. The center of the city was organized around the plaza, with the cathedral on the eastern flank of the plaza, the government buildings—royal and municipal—constructed on the northern edge, and the grandiose mansion and houses built for Francisco de Montejo, Captain-General of the royal government, along the southern part. To the west was a large hill of rocks where many years ago Indians offered sacrifices.

Today residents still pass the day exchanging news and commentary on the plaza benches (see Photograph 37). It is possible that the plaza of Mérida/Tihoo, much like those of Tipu and Lamanai, reflects a confluence of Maya ceremonial center and Spanish colonial design in which Maya cultural practices were maintained even as the new plaza was constructed from the stones of the Maya Precolumbian ruins.

Patterns of Urban Plaza Development

The above three cases—Tipu, Mexico City, and Mérida—illustrate the complexity of determining the architectural and cultural influences on the development of the Spanish American plaza. The first example, Tipu, was a continuously occupied town that flourished in the period prior to the conquest, although it did not have the number of masonry buildings or architectural density of the other two cases. It documents in greater detail the way in which Maya and Spanish architecture was interrelated. Further, Tipu reaffirms my earlier contention that even though Spaniards built a new plaza near the original Postclassic temple—or superposed a church on a ceremonial platform in Lamanai—this did not necessarily represent a break with earlier traditions, and the Maya continued to practice their own religion and follow their earlier cultural beliefs, even while building for the Spanish priests. Contemporary ethnographic evidence from Chiapas further confirms that Maya belief and practice only went underground. Today's Zapatista rebels are building Maya sacred ceremonial centers called Aguascalientes (discussed in Chapter 8) to proclaim their political and ethnic identity (Gossen 1996).

Mexico City's plan, designed by Cortés and executed by Alonso García Bravo, is derived from the structures and foundations of the Mexica city of Tenochtitlan. The Zócalo of Mexico City and its surrounding buildings retain a close relationship to the original order of Mexica governmental and religious architecture.

37. Central plaza in Mérida, Mexico

Mérida is another city that was built on top or close to an indigenous town, in this case Tihoo, but there is no evidence about the details of the indigenous town plan nor are there archaeological excavations of the original site. Maya models existed in the form of nearby ceremonial sites with large ceremonial plazas, but by 1541 there were also many examples of Spanish American town plans and skilled surveyors were available. The design of the plaza at Mérida, like that at Tipu, most likely reflects elements from both indigenous and Spanish architectural and planning traditions.

It seems apparent, then, that the central-plaza design of Spanish America must be interpreted in terms of both indigenous and Spanish architectural and urban design traditions. Unfortunately, we have only limited evidence about the process by which this syncretism took place, and few texts discuss the process of spatial appropriation other than the naming and establishment of towns (Seed 1993). It could be argued that, especially for Mexico City and archaeological sites like Tipu and Lamanai, the spatial relationships that are maintained by building on the ruins using the same stones and foundations allowed for elements of the Mexica politico-religious cultural system to remain. These latent meanings were not necessarily acted upon publicly, but they may have been useful in reinforcing aspects of indigenous identity, self-esteem, and spiritual power that helped to preserve indigenous folkways, beliefs, and practices. But even in areas where there were no indigenous architectural forms, the new syncretic urban design was used as a model for planning and building Latin American cities.

Thomas Patterson (1996) offers another interpretation, citing the literary critic Terry Eagleton, who notes that "the object of historical knowledge is some complex conjunction of past and present, rather than some autonomous region of antiquity quite unmodified by the contemporary" (1986, 271). Patterson goes on to reflect that archaeologists in both Mexico and Peru place their "object of inquiry—ancient societies—in the period preceding the arrival of the Spaniards. This effectively disconnected the pre-Columbian past from the present and denied that pre-Columbian history had any direct effect on or immediate relevance for the present" (1996, 502). He suggests that the ideas and categories used by archaeologists are shaped by the ruling hegemony of the state—in this case, the United States—and that each nation-state has its own political hegemony and intellectual discourse that must be examined as part of the analysis. These considerations echo my assertion of the importance of the political hegemony of the writing of history, which in this situation distorts the observable continuities of Precolumbian and Spanish ethnohistories found in the built environment.

Wendy Ashmore (1987a) has suggested that there are three patterns of archaeological site growth in which social evolution may be detected. Her goal is to systematize observations of site growth regularities in order to compare Precolumbian architecture in southeastern Mesoamerica. Since architecture reflects changes in power and social relations, and is a representation of cultural beliefs and power relations, Ashmore's patterns also seem appropriate for the examination of the architectural evolution of contemporary plazas and city centers as well as the evolution of archaeological sites.

These patterns of site growth are:

> (1) Simple expansion—the evolution of a civic center in which the original plan is essentially preserved or modified gradually through time. This usually occurs when there is linear growth and continuous occupation of a center by the same society.

> (2) Engulfment—the development of a center in which an early structure or structure group is preserved unmodified while the surrounding structures and groups develop through simple expansion. Her example is taken from Quiriguá, in Guatemala, where "Group 1B-1 includes engulfment of a single structure within growth of a single group" (Ashmore 1987a, 4).

> (3) Lateral displacement—the establishment of new focal civic groups adjacent to, but without direct spatial association with, antecedent construction. The older center seems to be recognized and may allude to even more ancient power, but is not included in the newer development (Ashmore, pers. comm. 1994; Helms 1988). The cases of Izamal or Tipu could be considered examples of lateral displacement. Certainly, Santo Domingo on a larger scale creates a new town and plaza center displacing any former Taino organization or settlement hierarchy.

A fourth logical category, the "establishment of a new center after destruction of the old," is added but not dealt with in Ashmore's text (1987a, 3). It seems that the two remaining examples, Mexico City and Mérida, fall into this fourth category. And recent archaeological excavations reveal that in some ways Mexico City/Tenochtitlan may also be considered a particular kind of lateral displacement. Even though the Mexica site of the Great Temple and ceremonial plaza was destroyed, there are extensive archaeological remains under the colonial overlay. The lateral displacement and establishment of a new center architecturally represent examples of colonization or the incorporation of outside influences in order to maintain local control (Ashmore 1989). This cursory analysis suggests that it is possible to develop theoretical and methodological analyses of the built environment that encompass archaeological, ethnohistorical, and contemporary architectural materials.

Conclusion

Returning to the larger topic of the politics of public space, I would like to conclude by pointing out how limited our knowledge about the meaning of these plazas will be until we uncover how each was designed and built, by whom, and for what purposes. The politics of the indigenous as well as the colonial plazas must be grounded in the study of their use. Many of these plazas became sites of executions, while others became markets or places designated solely for mestizo and Spanish elites. For example, in Costa Rica the plazas began as marketplaces or soccer fields and later became the civic and ceremonial centers we ordinarily perceive them to be. The ethnographies that follow complete our understanding of the cultural and political importance of these public spaces.

Even so, numerous questions about the significance of "sacred" space built upon by colonizers can not be completely answered. Does the re-emergence of the Great Temple in Mexico City mean that the Nahua meanings and cultural significance were always there just waiting to be uncovered? Does architecture frequently obscure as well as highlight what happened in the past, such as in Tipu, where the architecture changes but indigenous beliefs and everyday religious practices remain just as before? What relationship does the sacredness of the built environment of the past have to the experience of everyday life then or now?

These questions have been partially answered in this historical exploration of Mesoamerican influences on the design of the plaza. The ethnohistorical and archaeological evidence suggests that the colonial plaza evolved from both indigenous and Spanish influences and models that created a new urban design form. This new form, the Latin American plaza, is syncretic in the sense that it is no longer Spanish or indigenous but, through a series of historical and sociopolitical processes, has become emblematic of Latin American culture.

The historical analysis of the plaza's built form demonstrates that the plaza retains architectural, spatial, and physical elements from both traditions such that the tensions of conquest and resistance are symbolically encoded in its architecture. Thus, the plaza is a contested terrain of architectural representation and provides an excellent example of how cultural and political meanings of the past are represented in the built environment.

The history of the plaza, however, also illustrates that spatial representations of the dominant, in this case colonial, culture may in fact obscure representations of the less powerful culture. But this obfuscation can be remedied by the investigation of specific places utilizing historical, ethnological, and archaeological research. The exploration of the indigenous history can illuminate indigenous peoples' political and cultural resistance in the face of Spanish hegemonic practices.

The ethnographies that follow illustrate how plazas, as significant public spaces, are continuously reconceived, redefined, and reworked by citizens and the state. Within the confines of the plaza, class-, age-, and gender-based social differences are spatially contested and renegotiated. Microgeographies of everyday plaza life etch meaning and memory, literally and figuratively, onto the social and physical structure of this sacred public space. These contemporary ethnographies suggest, even more forcefully than the historical data, that plazas, like other significant public spaces, are centers of urban civility that provide a forum for the social and political exchange necessary to democratic life.

PART THREE   Ethnographies

Part II presents three histories that provide the background for understanding the historical contingencies, spatial configurations, and political symbolism of the Costa Rican plaza. Part III, Ethnographies, analyzes the specific findings gleaned from twelve years of participant observation and interviewing in Parque Central and Plaza de la Cultura and develops a series of theoretical frameworks. The concepts of spatializing culture, social and spatial boundaries, and commodification and demystification of public space organize the data and explain the sociocultural patterns found in these significant urban public spaces.

In Chapter 6, I attempt to "spatialize" culture, that is, to physically and conceptually locate social relations and social practice in space. By employing the perspectives of the social production of space and the social construction of space, I demonstrate how public space becomes meaningful reality to users and urban residents. In Chapter 7, I turn to the idea of spatial boundaries and examine how differences in the use of space define social groups and separate ideological differences through the physical realm of spatial relations. These plazas are inhabited by distinct groups of people who change places and uses throughout the day. The distinctions made between and among groups take on spatial form and ultimately have social consequences.

In Chapter 8, I explore how designed spaces are manipulated for political and economic ends under the guise of their artistic contribution to urban improvement. Plazas are a social good that enhances the life and well-being of urban users and residents, but the improvement of the urban fabric is not the only objective of these highly politicized places. I demystify the objectives of landscape design by analyzing the decision-making processes involved in building the Plaza de la Cultura and in redesigning Parque Central.

CHAPTER 6

Spatializing Culture

*The Social Production and Social Construction
of Public Space*

Introduction

Contemporary debates concerning ethnographic methodologies and writing strategies emphasize the importance of characterizing social actors in terms of their experience of the theorized phenomena. The coproducers of the ethnography must be given a voice and a place in the written document, and ethnographic research is increasingly judged by its ability to portray the impact of macro- and microprocesses through the "lived experience" of individuals (Appadurai 1992; Rodman 1992). Thus, an effective anthropological theory of the spatialization of culture and human experience must integrate the perspectives of social production and social construction of space, contextualizing the forces that produce it and showing people as social agents constructing their own realities and symbolic meanings. But it must also reflect both of these perspectives in the experience and daily life of individuals.

By "spatialize" I mean: to locate—physically, historically, and conceptually—social relations and social practice in space. In this chapter, I am using the specific analysis of Parque Central and Plaza de la Cultura to explore the use of the two complementary perspectives of social production of space and social construction of space as tools for understanding how public space in urban society becomes meaningful reality.

To clarify this discussion, it is important to distinguish between these two terms that are often used interchangeably. The *social production of space* includes all those factors—social, economic, ideological, and technological—that result, or seek to result, in the physical creation of the material setting. The materialist emphasis of the term *social production* is useful in defining the historical emergence and political/economic formation of urban space. The term *social construction* may then be conveniently reserved for the phenomenological and symbolic experience of space as mediated by social processes such as exchange, conflict, and control. Thus, the *social construction of space* is the actual transformation of space—through peoples' social exchanges, memories, images, and daily use of the material setting—into scenes and actions that convey meaning. Both processes are social in that both the production and the construction of space are contested and fought over for economic and ideological reasons, and understanding them can help us see how local conflicts over space can be used to uncover and illuminate larger cultural issues.

The contestation over the meaning of the plazas is the focus of this ethnographic inquiry. The plaza as a site of civic expression becomes a space of opposition and resistance in response to state and local efforts at social control. Steve Pile suggests that when we think of "resistance" we think of "unemployed people marching to demonstrate their plight . . . or a lone man standing in front of a tank as it rolls onwards to Tiananmen Square" (1997, 1); these events "take place," creating "geographies of resistance." I agree that it is critical to understand the material setting of resistance and to document the events that occur on the plaza. But I am arguing that the contest over public space is also about plaza meaning, which reflects differences in a war of cultural values and visions of appropriate behavior and societal order. Discussions of architectural style, plaza design, and nostalgia are equally important indicators of local struggles for political and social control (and resistance to control) of public space. Thus, this ethnography traces historical and contemporary conflicts in the design, use, image, experience, and meaning of the Costa Rican plazas.

There have been many macrolevel approaches to spatialization. David Harvey (1985, 1990) and Manuel Castells (1983, 1989) examine the spatialization of social conflicts, focusing on class-based struggle with state-imposed spatial regimes. They provide historical and contemporary examples of grassroots and labor organizations fighting to maintain control of housing (Castells 1983), urban sacred space (Harvey 1985), and neighborhood real estate (Castells 1983; see also Smith 1991 and Peattie 1969, 1987). In their analyses, the local population is portrayed as having a role through social movements that resist the control of the dominant classes and planning elite. The concern is with the way in which capital reformulates social relations and space. Within this system, space is constitutive of power, and resistance takes the form of social movements and local activism.

Michel Foucault, in his work on the prison (1975) and in a series of interviews and lectures on space (1984; Rabinow 1984), takes a historical approach to the spatialization of social control through analysis of the human body, spatial arrangements, and architecture. He examines the relationship of power and space by positing architecture as a political "technology" for working out the concerns of government—that is, control and power over individuals—through the spatial "canalization" of everyday life. The aim of such a technology is to create a "docile body" (Foucault 1975, 198) through enclosure and the organization of individuals in space.

Continuing this approach, Paul Rabinow (1989) links the growth of modern forms of political power with the evolution of aesthetic theories and shows how French colonists sought to use architecture and city planning to demonstrate their cultural superiority. He focuses on the ordering of space as a way to understand "the historically variable links between spatial relations, aesthetics, social science, economics, and politics" (Rabinow 1982, 267). James Holston (1989) develops this argument further by examining the state-sponsored architecture and master planning of Brasília as new forms of political domination through which the domains of daily life become the targets for state intervention. These writers successfully illustrate how architecture contributes to the maintenance of power of one group over another at a level that includes both the control of daily movement and the surveillance of the body in space.

Michel de Certeau takes resistance as his starting point, setting out to show how people's "ways of operating" constitute the means by which users reappropriate space organized by techniques of sociocultural production (1984, xiv). These practices are articulated in the details of everyday life and bring to light the clandestine "tactics" used by groups or individuals "already caught in the nets of 'discipline'" (De Certeau 1984, xiv–xv). By tracing out the operations of walking, naming, narrating, and remembering the city, he develops a theory of lived space in which spatial practices elude the discipline and constraints of urban planning. The pedestrian's walking is the spatial acting-out of place, creating and representing public space rather than being subject to it.

In a more ethnographic effort to link human agents and resistance to domination, Pierre Bourdieu (1977) looks at the spatialization of everyday behavior and how the sociospatial order is translated into bodily experience and practice. He proposes the key concept of *habitus,* a generative and structuring principle of collective strategies and social practices, which is used to reproduce existing structures. In his examples, the Kabyle house becomes the setting in which body space and cosmic space are integrated through metaphor and symbolic homologous structures. Through the experience of living in the spatial symbolism of the home, social structure becomes embodied and naturalized in everyday practice. Since the concept of habitus, like Foucault's *dispositif* and De Certeau's walking, spatially links social structure to the human body and bodily practices, the possibility of individual resistance to these practices becomes more apparent.

These theories of spatialization provide a basis for working out how spatial analysis would satisfy the anthropologist's need to link experience, practice, and structure. Nonetheless, it is difficult to derive ethnographic research strategies solely from these conceptual approaches. One intermediate step is to identify domains of action and endeavor that allow for empirical analysis. I have chosen to concentrate on the historical emergence of the space, the sociopolitical ideologies and economic forces involved in its production, including the role played by planning and architecture professionals in its design, the social use of the space, and its associated affective and symbolic meanings. To categorize these domains in terms of their generative processes, historical, sociopolitical, economic, and professional understandings refer to social production of space; social use and affective meanings refer to social construction of space (Richardson 1982). I must point out, however, that it is always necessary to keep in mind that this sorting is somewhat illusory. I agree with Henri Lefebvre (1991) that social space is a whole and that any one event or illustration has within it aspects of that whole. The complex and contradictory nature of space is that "space is permeated with social relations; it is not only supported by social relations but it is also producing and produced by social relations" (Lefebvre 1991, 286, cited in Hayden 1995, 31).

In this chapter, then, I examine the theorizing power of these perspectives by focusing on the ethnography of the two Costa Rican plazas. Applying these analytic tools to the ethnographic material, I demonstrate that there is a relationship between the circumstances of the production of public spaces such as plazas and people's experience of them; that this relationship is dialogic rather than dialectic, in spite of the high degree of conflict and contestation often found in the Costa Rican plazas; and that the plazas act as containers, thus permitting resistance, counterresistance, and change to occur publicly and with relative safety. In addition, the negotiation of the form and meaning of spatial representations is illuminating as a public forum for the working out of larger conflicts stemming from the growing impact of globalization, increased tourism, and the struggle by both individuals and the state to maintain a distinct cultural identity.

The Ethnography of the Spanish American Plaza

Parque Central represents Costa Rica's Spanish colonial history in its spatial form and context. Its relatively long history spans the colonial, republican, and modern periods, and a number of historical photographs and portrayals of earlier periods of plaza design and social life were available in local archives. During the research period of 1985 through 1987, Parque Central was a vibrant center of traditional Costa Rican culture, inhabited by a variety of largely male workers, pensioners, preachers and healers, tourists, shoppers, female sex workers, and people who just wanted to sit and watch the action. This chapter focuses on this fieldwork period. When I returned in 1993 and 1994, the plaza was under construction: the cement kiosk was being renovated and the surrounding benches, pathways, and gathering spaces were in the process of being redesigned. By 1997 it had reopened, and its design and use had changed, as discussed in Chapter 8.

The Plaza de la Cultura, a contemporary plaza only one block east and one block north of Parque Central, is a recently designed urban space heralded by Josefino boosters as an emblem of the "new Costa Rican culture." Because it was opened in 1982, I was still able to interview individuals involved in its design and planning, while at the same time it could be studied as a well-established place. The Plaza de la Cultura proved to be an excellent comparison to Parque Central, providing contrasts in style of design, spatial configuration, surrounding buildings and institutions, activities, and the kinds of inhabitants and visitors. It is a site of modern consumption, a so-called landscape of power (Zukin 1991). North American culture is consumed by Costa Rican teenagers carrying radios blaring rap music, and North American tourists "consume" Costa Rican culture by buying souvenirs, snacks, theater tickets, and artworks as well as the sexual favors and companionship of young Costa Ricans.

These two urban spaces were socially produced—planned, built, designed, and maintained—in different historical and sociopolitical contexts, and both were constrained by limits imposed by the available resources as well as by the central government's political objectives. The environments thus produced are observably different: Parque Central is a furnished and enclosed space of trees, paths, and benches, while the Plaza de la Cultura is an open expanse with few places to sit, providing a magnificent open vista leading to a view of the National Theater.

These plazas were also socially constructed through contested patterns of use and attributed symbolic meanings. The social uses of the plazas, which at first glance appear similar, are fundamentally different in the age, sex, ethnicity and interests of the users. The degree and form of social contestation and conflict between the regular users and the agents of the municipal government—the police, the planning agency, and the directors of surrounding institutions—also vary, most visibly in terms of the kind of spatial control that is maintained. Even the experience of "being-in-the-plaza" (Richardson 1982) is distinct and voiced in different ways in the two spaces.

The differences in the plazas' material production and experiential construction have created very different urban spaces that are distinct in physical design as well as use, and that are controlled, experienced, and thought about differently by both users and nonusers. These distinctions provide a vehicle to contrast the ways in which urban space is socially produced, both materially and metaphorically, and socially constructed, through experience and social interaction.

Parque Central

The plan and urban design of Parque Central was part of the establishment of the Spanish American colonial empire, which repeatedly created a type of urban space that has continued to be "produced despite the vicissitudes of imperialism, independence and industrialization" (Lefebvre 1991, 151). Its history is a perfect illustration of the production of space in Spanish American towns based on the 1573 *Orders for Discovery and Settlement,* as characterized by Lefebvre:

> The very building of towns thus embodied a plan which would determine the mode of occupation of the territory and define

how it was to be reorganized under the administrative and political authority of urban power. . . . The result is a strictly hierarchical organization of space, a gradual progression outward
from the town's centre . . . from the inevitable Plaza Mayor a
grid extends indefinitely in every direction. Each square or rectangular lot has its function assigned to it, while inversely each
function is assigned its own place at a greater or lesser distance
from the central square: church, administrative buildings, town
gates, squares, streets . . . and so on. (1991, 151)

Lefebvre characterizes the building of Spanish American towns such as
San José as the "production of a social space by political power—that is,
by violence in the service of economic goals" (1991, 151–152). While I
agree with his theoretical analysis, the details of the origins of the plaza-
centered grid-plan town deserve further examination.

I argue in Chapter 5 that the Spanish American plaza and grid-plan
town are syncretic spatial forms derived from European architectural
traditions of medieval *bastides,* and the Mesoamerican plaza-temple complexes and urban plans of the cities encountered during the conquest of
the New World. Many of the earliest Spanish American plazas were in
fact superposed on the ruins of their Aztec or Maya antecedents. The
European and Mesoamerican plaza designs had similar aims: both were
produced to display military conquest and market domination by the
conquering rulers, whether those rulers were Aztec, Maya, or Spanish.
Therefore, although the Spanish American plaza is a product of colonial control that was consciously produced as a means of spatial domination, its form also derived from indigenous forms of political and
economic control expressed in the Mesoamerican plaza-temple complex. Since the spatial relations of plaza to buildings, hierarchy of spaces,
and functions of the plaza remained the same from the Mesoamerican
to the Spanish American plaza, the symbolic meanings of the spatialized
material culture reflect aspects of both cultural histories.

Parque Central retained its colonial form and meaning until the mid–
nineteenth century, when it was redesigned to become the civic center
of San José. By the late nineteenth century it became the social center
for elite families who met after attending mass at the Catholic cathedral
on Sunday mornings and Friday afternoons. It is from this late-nineteenth-century period that there is textual and photographic evidence
of class-based social constructions of the appropriate use (and appropri-

ated use) of public space. The accumulated wealth of coffee growers and a republican government made up of landed elite began to impose a class-based conception of public space and spatial representation.

Historical texts, retrospective interviews, and diaries from this period describe Parque Central as a place where the elite would gather and stroll in the evening; at night it was locked and patrolled (Fernández Guardia 1985). However, this elite image is contested in other sources. For instance, photographs from 1870 show workers in open shirts and barefoot boys resting in the plaza (see Photograph 38), and a well-known 1915 portrait of middle-class men with their children sitting on the ledge of the fountain captures a barefoot boy standing on the side of the scene (Banco Nacional de Costa Rica 1972). Photographs from 1917 of street scenes along the fenced edge of the plaza include barefoot campesinos as well as well-dressed urban businessmen (Banco Nacional de Costa Rica 1972); and novels of the period describe street children and poor people living in or along the edges of plaza (Trullás y Aulet 1913).

This conflict between the images of Parque Central as an elite strolling park or a socially heterogeneous public gathering place has contin-

38. Historic photograph of workers in Parque Central, 1870

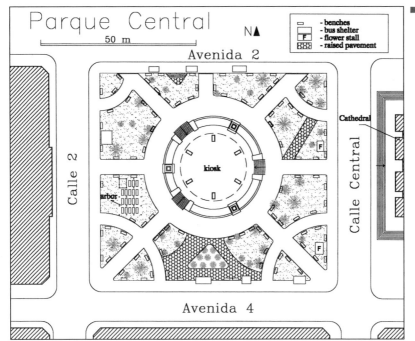

1. Plan of Parque Central

ued, manifesting itself most recently in the ongoing resistance to the replacement of the original 1890 kiosk. In 1944, a giant cement kiosk, which housed first a disco nightclub and then a children's library, was donated by Anastazio Somoza. By now, daily users have incorporated the cement kiosk into their spatial pattern of activities. It makes a convenient stage and a place to continue business on a rainy day. Children play on its ledges, and it is large enough to hold the orchestra and audience for the weekly Sunday concert (see Map 1).

However, as recently as the spring of 1992 there was a movement by a group of citizens to tear down this cement structure and reconstruct the original Victorian one; the conflict was so controversial that it provoked a series of well-attended town meetings. The cement kiosk and its current uses do not fit many Josefinos' idea of the appropriate architecture for the ceremonial and civic center of the city. Yet the citizens who are attempting to reconstitute Parque Central in its elite turn-of-the-century image are not the daily users or the municipal designers, but are professional and middle-class Josefinos who yearn for an idealized past. Thus the conflict over the architectural form of the kiosk reveals a struggle over the social construction of the symbolic meaning and appropriate use of public space. This struggle is the basis of the analysis of public space and protest in Chapter 8. The symbolic contrasts of Victorian/modern, wooden/cement, elite/working-class provide architectural metaphors for class-based taste cultures, a forum for public conflict over appropriate modes of symbolic representation, and a convenient cover for broader class-based social meanings and conflicts.

Daily life in the Parque Central has changed over time, and these changes can be seen in the architectural furnishings, the social class and gender composition of the users, the range of occupations and work sites, the nature of the policing and social control, as well as what people say about their experience of being in the plaza. Most of these changes are the end result of global economic and political forces, which have led to declining socioeconomic conditions and increasing cultural and social diversity. Most upper-class families have left the central city and moved to the western sector of the city or to the suburbs, abandoning the central city, and thus Parque Central, to the poor and working classes. The symbols of a new kind of global economy based on debt and world banking controls, and dependent on foreign capital—national and international banks, movie theaters playing English-language movies, soda shops, and small businesses—now surround Parque Central, replacing the civic and residential context of earlier plaza life. By 1985, the Latin American debt crisis had increased Costa Rica's dependence on United States AID funds (Shallat 1989), and the International Monetary Fund (IMF) had intervened to monitor Costa Rica's economy to ensure timely debt payments (Edelman and Kenen 1989).

The increase in unemployment because of the decline in the value of agricultural exports has encouraged the growth of an informal economy, which is very visible in Parque Central. The plaza is used as an urban workplace of exchange and coexistence: shoeshine men control the northeast corner, ambulatory vendors use the sidewalks and pathways, salesmen use the benches as office space, construction workers wait for pick-up jobs under the arbor, sex workers stand in the kiosk or sit on benches, and men move through the crowd gambling and selling stolen goods. The influx of refugees from Nicaragua, El Salvador, and Guatemala has increased both the number of vendors and the competition among them, as well as contributing to an increased presence of homeless adults and street children.

Middle-class businessmen and nonusers, however, have generated political pressure to increase the number of police in order to remove "undesirables." Concerned about the increase in crime and vagrancy, which they associate with the ongoing economic crisis, these citizens perceive the resulting rise in the number of people working in the plaza and of homeless people who hang out there, as well as their associated activities, as reflections of their fears. The state therefore is attempting to constrain these uses in several ways. The police maintain open surveillance from the top of the cement kiosk, thus repeating and reiterating Parque Central's colonial history as a public space originally produced as a spatial representation of state domination and social control (see Photograph 39). In addition, there are plainclothes policemen looking for drug dealing and the selling of stolen goods. A young couple moving through the plaza who stopped by to ask what I was doing turned out to be plainclothes police. There are also municipal agents, representing a different kind of state control, who require vendors to pay for the right to sell on city streets and in the plazas. If vendors do not have the money to pay for a license—a frequent occurrence—they forfeit their proceeds for the day.

Many of the older men in the park are Costa Rican pensioners who come to spend the day on their regular benches with a group of cronies.

39. Police surveillance in Parque Central

One pensioner, Don Carlos, says that he is eighty-six years old. He comes to the plaza every day about ten in the morning, after having his coffee, bread, and cheese—"something to nourish one"—at home. He sits with his friends on the southwest corner until the afternoon, and then returns home to eat a late meal. When he was younger, he was employed by the civil police and at one time had worked as a guard in the plaza. He opened the gates at six in the morning and closed them at ten at night. When I asked how the plaza had changed, he replied: "The plaza was more strict before; they locked the gates at night. People of all kinds can come here now, but not before. It was a very polite place then, and not everyone was allowed in." So, access to the plaza is apparently controlled less openly and more subversively than it used to be.

Another example of symbolic contestation in Parque Central lies in the number of evangelical healers and preachers who hold prayer meetings in the shady arbor and healing services on the northwest corner. These evangelical healers and preachers are the result of the influx of North American missionaries who have come to San José to convert Catholic Costa Ricans to various Christian sects. Protestant practitioners and their adherents can be interpreted as symbolically contesting the religious hegemony of the Catholic cathedral that flanks the eastern side of the plaza. Although the original Parque Central was designed as the "front garden" of the Catholic church (Richardson 1978), the diversity of religious beliefs and practices has now reconstituted the space as one of broadly defined religious heterodoxy. The presence of various religious sects, from Hare Krishna followers to born-again Christians, in front of the city's major Catholic institution challenges the professed state Catholicism of the plaza's spatial symbolism.

The experience of the plaza users who say that they enjoy the spectacle of the healing ceremonies—to which successful cures draw large crowds of believers—also contests the hegemony of state Catholicism. One of the more successful healers—a man called the "Christian" who dresses in a robe of rough sackcloth tied with animal skins—appears about noon each day on the northwest corner of the plaza. A crowd of passersby quickly gathers around the raised plant bed where he stands. As the circle forms, he calls out: "Who wants to receive Christ and be healed?" (Photograph 40).

There is no unified experience of being in Parque Central, but fragments of its social production are reproduced in the everyday practices

40. Christian healer in Parque Central

and feelings of its users. Many of the older men express considerable affection for and attachment to the plaza; often the sense of being comfortable is based on memories of being in the park at an earlier time or in different circumstances. One elderly man expressed his feelings when he began to cry upon seeing a giant palm cut down and reminisced about how it felt to sit in the shade of that tree.

Women, however, often express a sense of unease and are rarely found sitting for very long, especially during the week. A woman who sat down next to me gave me her explanation when I asked her if she came there often. She replied: "No, but I am resting because my package is heavy." She said that she lived in an outlying suburb and was on her way home. "I normally only come to the plaza on Sunday," she commented. I asked her why. "Because there are a lot of unemployed men here and women are usually working, or if they are not working, they are in the house. Sunday is when women come to Parque Central with their children."

Younger adult men are often found working in the plaza. One man was running his real estate business from a bench: "With the high price of rent, the electricity, water, and everything else, it is difficult to stay in business. Here my clients can find me, and I do not have all these other expenses." Other regular plaza workers include the food, candy, flower, lottery ticket, and newspaper vendors; shoeshine men; gamblers; sex workers; and day laborers waiting for pick-up work in the morning. These working users are territorial about their spaces and defend them both from new workers trying to find a workplace and from casual passersby. When asked about their work, they express satisfaction with their working conditions, and in the case of the shoeshine men, intend to hand down their work location to their children or friends.

Other plaza users come to participate in the illicit world of gambling and the trading and selling of stolen goods. One rainy day, while standing on the kiosk, I watched a well-dressed young man sit down, take off his watch, and show it to the man currently running the "shell game." The man gave him some money while taking the watch. They proceeded to play until the young man finally lost the game, handing the money back to the gambler, who now had both the watch and the cash. As the young man walked away I went up to him and asked him what had happened. He said not much, that he had traded his watch for cash to gamble, but had lost everything. He said that he knew that he would be more successful next time (see Photograph 41).

According to some plaza users, more sex workers now work in Parque Central. One afternoon I was working on a map sitting next to a man who asked me what I was doing. After I told him, I asked him who the women were in front of us. He replied: "Prostitutes, young prostitutes. They come every evening. There seem to be more [of them] than ever now out of economic necessity." I also asked him about why there are so few women in the plaza. He replied that there is increasing unemployment and that the unemployed men in the plaza make women uneasy: "It is the government's fault. Have you heard that they want to build 80,000 houses? You could not even do it physically! And the price supports for farmers and manufacturers just do not work."

Even the clowns who work in Parque Central are concerned about the economic conditions of people who use it. In an interview with two clowns, I commented that they had cut their performance short the day

41. Gambling in Parque Central

before. The older clown responded by saying that they do not make much money in Parque Central and do better at the Plaza de la Cultura: "Because the people of the Plaza de la Cultura are of a higher social class, and are richer . . . there are more tourists and foreigners. Here in Parque Central they do not have the resources." An older man who had overheard us walked up and said: "I am a pensioner, and I enjoy the clowns and would like to give money, but I do not have enough to even support myself. That is how we are."

The experience of being in the plaza is sensory as well as social. When I returned to study the plaza during the dry season, I noticed that a group of pensioners had moved from the benches on the southwest corner, where I had always seen them, to the inner ring of benches near the kiosk. Until that point the territories of different groups of people had been quite stable in terms of both location and time of day. When I asked them if I had been mistaken to assume that their preferred bench was on the southwest corner, they told me they had sat on that corner for the past five years, but that the noise and fumes from increased bus traffic had become intolerable. The inner ring had benches where it was quieter and smelled better. I also noticed subtle sensory changes in the environment throughout the day: the bird songs early in the morning and at sunset, the bells of the cathedral at noon, and the smell of roasting candied peanuts and meats that announced the vendors who catered to the evening movie-theater crowd. These sensory perceptions are part of the cultural landscape that is valued, yet these sensations are also being changed.

Thus, the ethnographic evidence for the transformation of Parque Central into a workplace and a place mainly for pensioners and unemployed men during the weekdays shows how the space is being contested by the conflicts over the nature of social and spatial representation in the urban center. The struggle over the design of the kiosk, the number of police and the kinds of state control, the increasing territoriality of the vendors and shoeshine men, the discomfort of women and children, and the heterodoxy of religious practitioners illustrate how individuals and groups resist and counterresist the consequences of the larger sociopolitical, economic, and historical forces.

Plaza de la Cultura

The second case study, the newly built Plaza de la Cultura, sheds further light on these processes by allowing us to observe how a new public urban space was created and defined, only to be appropriated by a group of users different from those for whom it was intended.

The Plaza de la Cultura is a modern paved plaza reminiscent of the futurist design of the Pompidou Center in Paris (see Photograph 42). Beneath the plaza are subterranean museums, exposition spaces, and the Costa Rican tourist center, entered from the northern edge by a series of grassy, sloping steps. The plaza is bordered on the south by the National Theater; on the west by the Gran Hotel; and on the north and east by busy shopping streets lined with McDonald's, Burger King, Pizza Hut, Sears, photographic supply stores, bookstores, as well as other local businesses (see Photograph 43). The few trees are in planters lining the western edge alongside the hotel shops, which include a newspaper stand carrying the *Miami Herald,* a clothing store, and a shop that sells the renowned Costa Rican ice cream, Pops.

The building of the Plaza de la Cultura, introduced in Chapter 3, was an inspiration of the Minister of Culture. At one time, Costa Rica's world-famous collection of Precolumbian gold artifacts was stored in the Central Bank of Costa Rica. In 1975 the head of the Central Bank convinced the Legislative Assembly to allocate funds to build a Gold

42. *Pompidou Center in Paris, France*

43. *McDonald's next to Plaza de la Cultura*

Museum in order to display the collection as a celebration of indigenous Costa Rican culture. The plan was supported by the "Liberationists," members of the political party in power at the time. The National Liberation Party (Partido Liberación Nacional; PLN) represents a politically liberal coalition of professional, middle-class, and working-class Costa Ricans, in contrast to the Social Christians' Unity Party (Partido Unidad Social de Cristianos), a more conservative party that grew out of earlier political coalitions, including the landed gentry and coffee-growing elite.

The Minister of Planning and the head of the Central Bank selected the land around the National Theater, already partly owned by the Central Bank, as an appropriate site for a cultural center that would accommodate tourists and visitors to the new Gold Museum. Of the thirteen lots needed for the project, three were owned by the Central Bank, two by the National Theater, and the remaining lots were registered to individual citizens or their heirs. According to Edgar Vargas, the architect/planner heading the project, the state purchased the corner lots for 6,500 colones per square meter, and the rest for 5,000 colones per square meter. They tore down the old, turn-of-the-century houses and retained the *balcones* (balconies) for use in the shopping structure known as "the arcades." Then they cleaned up the area and put a fence around it. Some structures would remain: the new plaza would incorporate the already existing *parquecito* (little park) Juan Mora Fernández in front of the Gran Hotel and the shopping structure (Coto 1982). Everything else was demolished, including Librería López (a bookstore), Optica Rivera (an optician's office), Casino Española (a gambling spot), and other small businesses as well as the homes of a few older residents.

This initial design was radically changed and expanded. According to Minister of Culture Guido Sáenz, when he went to the site to survey the progress of the demolition, he saw the National Theater sitting in an open space created by the destruction of the surrounding buildings. In an instant, he said, he realized that it would be a much more powerful plan to have an open public plaza, with the Gold Museum underground, so that there was an unobstructed view of the National Theater. Thus, the architectural plans for the original Gold Museum were scrapped, and a new phase of planning and design began.

The planning, design, and building of the Plaza de la Cultura began in 1976 and was finished with its opening in 1982. Although some of the buildings selected for demolition, such as the turn-of-the-century houses mentioned above, were deemed of historic significance, the plan moved forward despite local protest. More vigorous protests were expressed in the media, which criticized the government for spending money to put the Gold Museum underground (an expensive and difficult feat of engineering) when a particularly harsh rainy season prevented the project from moving ahead on schedule.

Both the location choice and the design program were produced by a combination of local sociopolitical forces and global, particularly North American, capital. When the plaza was conceived in 1976, global capital was already fueling the Costa Rican economy and the IMF restrictions would soon be in place. Foreign as well as local interests influenced the siting of the plaza—placing it next to the major tourist hotel and the National Theater and in the center of North American businesses such as McDonald's, Burger King, and Sears, where there was the greatest tourist activity. The design, on the other hand, was influenced by the political ideology of the National Liberation Party, which was under the leadership of a new professional class that desired a representation of Costa Rican culture as both modern, drawing upon contemporary European idioms of design, and indigenous, based on the Precolumbian past.

The spatial form and design, however, were ultimately determined by a team of three architects who had won the design competition for the original plan, the above-ground Gold Museum. The architects themselves, although all Costa Rican, represented Costa Rican, European, and North American design training blended to create what they defined as a new Costa Rican design idiom. From my interviews with them, it seems that each had a different vision of the plaza. Further, they produced design features best appreciated from a male point of view (see Map 2).

One architect imagined it to be a plaza where men could watch women walk by, and he designed a vast paved open space, providing the longest sight line in the city for watching women (see Photograph 44). Another architect saw the plaza as a meeting place, symbolically linked to other plazas in the city by a second grid, with pedestrian walkways and trees. He imagined young men leaning on the outside rails of the perimeter piping and put a foot rail just where a man's foot might rest. The third architect was concerned that the new plaza be a significant open space: "Costa Ricans have their gardens and their parks, and they have their special places, but they do not have a center for jugglers, music, political

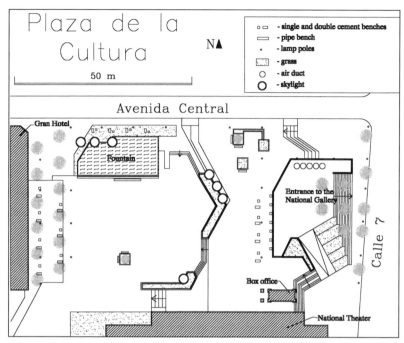

2. *Plan of Plaza de la Cultura*

meetings, and large gatherings like in New York." He wanted an open space for public performances: "But we did not want a huge dry space, so we put in trees along the edges."

These different social imaginings and representations of space were integrated to create a rather eclectic space with a modernist style—a design idiom that many Costa Ricans did not like or understand. When the plaza first opened there were spontaneous demonstrations by people who came and tore out the plantings, started fires in the trash cans, and tried to destroy as much of the furnishings as possible. There is even conflict over the meaning of these demonstrations: it is not entirely clear, either from the media reports or from firsthand accounts, who the demonstrators were or what exactly they were protesting, but the media interpreted them as protest against the plaza's stark modernity.

Nonetheless, the plaza appears to be successful in terms of the objectives of the architects: the unusual modern and empty urban space produced by these sociopolitical and economic forces and professional imaginings has been rapidly appropriated by groups of users. The vast open space is used by street performers, religious singing groups, political speakers, and teenagers break-dancing or playing soccer (to the delight of the third architect). These are all users who did not have a public place before this plaza was constructed, since these activities are not well accommodated by the parklike atmosphere of Parque Central.

In addition, the small plazas created by the designers in front of the National Theater and the Gran Hotel are used by officially licensed vendors with semipermanent stands from which they sell local crafts to tourists. The Gran Hotel generates a seemingly endless stream of tourists who sit on the edges of the plaza watching people from the safety of the hotel's sidewalk café. Women and families bring their children, who run after pigeons and play in the fountain during the afternoon, while in the late evening the plaza becomes a "cruising area" and social meeting place internationally known through guidebooks such as the *Spartacus Guide for Gay Men*.

But, from interviews with key informants and conversations with users and friends, one learns that this tranquillity is disrupted by a number of illicit activities that make people perceive the Plaza de la Cultura as

44. Sight line for women-watching in Plaza de la Cultura

an unsafe and unpleasant place to be. This perception is reinforced in a number of ways: the newspapers regularly run articles reporting frequent mishaps and transgressions and criticizing the municipal government's management. The hotel bouncer remains posted at the edge of the plaza, ready to protect his customers from the sight of beggars or poor people looking for a place to rest. Official uniformed police stand outside the National Theater and refuse entrance to anyone who looks as if they might cause trouble or incite a disturbance, and when a young man ran by and grabbed a gold chain from the neck of a girl, the police were everywhere within seconds. The intensity of social and spatial control appears even greater than in the Parque Central, more visible, more intensely contested, and as yet unresolved.

The experience of being in the Plaza de la Cultura produced by these conflicting forces is characterized by considerable ambivalence. Nonusers uniformly describe the plaza as dangerous, scary, and uncomfortable. The media seem to have influenced many potential users in ways that I find hard to understand, since the bright, sunlit plaza seemed unthreatening to me. Mothers and children do come to this plaza to play with the pigeons or to splash in the low fountain. Many more young men and women, often students, stop by to meet one another or to have lunch or an ice cream cone in the afternoon sun than can be seen in the Parque Central. Tourists seem quite secure and comfortable.

Yet many of my students at the Universidad de Costa Rica were uncomfortable and unwilling to go there, even for a field visit. The one female student who finally did visit was afraid the entire time that a thief was waiting to take her purse. Friends told me that there was drug dealing and that it was a terrible place to be. Most nonusers cited examples of robberies, pickpocketing, or uninvited sexual proposals that someone they knew had experienced there. For people who were not familiar with the Plaza de la Cultura, it was not a place to visit, and certainly not a plaza that represents the positive aspects of Costa Rican culture.

Frequent users also had criticisms of the space, even though they admitted to spending a considerable amount of time there. For instance, an artist who said that he spends too much time in the plaza told me that he thinks it is poorly designed: "It should have had a roof—a roof where artists could work and things could happen. This plaza is useless when the weather is forbidding, and it is usually forbidding. We might as well have had a football stadium here."

Another frequent user—a young man—when asked how he liked the plaza, said that he preferred the Parque Morazán, a small park a few blocks northeast. He said that just young people come to the Plaza de la Cultura and they make a lot of noise and commotion. "Like what?" I asked: "They have radios blaring, shout, and make a scene," he replied. He prefers the other park, where it is quiet.

Another man, who was sitting with his girlfriend, complained: "The plaza should be for cultured things, not for rudeness, drugs, or radios." He went on to recount all the performers who had come to the plaza: "The ball man who bounces a ball with his body. The doll, an old woman, who sells violets. A 'crazy' man who acts like a truck—these are special. But a plaza is for sitting, watching, talking . . . for music, meetings, and groups, but not for the rest of this stuff." He went on to say, "If you have a bar and let the wrong kind of person in, even one, then more will come and it will be too late."

People who work in the Plaza de la Cultura express some of the same ambivalence about working there. While the clowns prefer the crowd because they can collect more money, the vendors complain that they are charged a high fee for putting up a stall in the tourist area. These stalls are carefully regulated by the municipal government and have expanded in numbers over time. During most of the time that I observed the vendors, they sat around, talked, and smoked cigarettes while waiting for the busy Saturday craft market held in front of the National Theater. During my visit in December 1993, however, the plaza was crammed with stalls and vendors, most of whom were illegally selling clothes and souvenirs from other Central American countries. It seems that a Guatemalan vendor, who was fined for selling without a permit, sued the city and is bringing his case to court. He is arguing that the plaza should be a "free market" with no charge for selling in this "democratic" country. So even the vendors are resisting the control of the city to regulate their means of making a living. The Plaza de la Cultura also has a few child workers—young shoeshine boys in front of the Gran Hotel and children who sell gum and candy—who are illegal under Costa Rican law. These young boys—about seven to nine years old— are not found working in Parque Central.

However, there are those who are happy with the plaza, often for very specific reasons. For example, two North American men whom I interviewed in the café next to the plaza said that they like the plaza for one simple reason: it has the best girl-watching view anywhere in San

José. One offered this observation: "You can watch them all the way across the plaza on the left to the end of the hotel plaza. It is a long walk—and the girls are the best here, mostly upper and upper middle class . . . I mean the best for watching. I prefer the lower-class and country girls. They are friendlier, warmer, and it comes from the heart— not stuck-up like the upper-class girls." The two men talked on, complaining that the benches in the Plaza de la Cultura were not comfortable and that there were no good places to sit, but saying that they meet there every day as part of their daily routine. Another retired North American commented that although the plaza pipe benches were uncomfortable, he liked how friendly the young girls were, and he knew he would find young people there. The Plaza de la Cultura is also near the McDonald's, which is another teenage hangout: "Imagine a middle-aged guy like me hanging out in a McDonald's in Kansas City to meet girls. I would be arrested."

Probably the happiest group are the teenagers who hang out in the evenings along the pipe railing. One young man said he found the spaciousness appealing. "Here," he said, "we feel at home." When I asked two young men what they were doing in the plaza, they replied: "Passing the time, shooting the breeze. What do young people do in the U.S.?" Before the creation of this plaza, the teenagers were not a visible part of any park or plaza. You could see them walking down the streets or in couples kissing or quietly talking in Parque España or Parque Morazán. But now they have their own space, designed in a way to create a stage for their nightly performances. And they have successfully appropriated this public space for their activities in the evenings. But, as in Parque Central, the visible presence of the Gran Hotel bouncer and the Guardia Civil (civil police), who question the youths and in some cases stop or detain them, contests their symbolic dominance.

Compared to Parque Central, this recently designed urban space represents and accommodates more modern spatial practices based on youth, foreign capital, tourism, and an ideology of liberal modernism—framed by the localized discourse about the safety and comfort of the plaza. The Plaza de la Cultura is more about the "consumption of culture" than the working landscape of Parque Central. Most important, the forces that produced this new plaza are reflected in its design and social use as well as in the ambivalence about being there. The teenagers and tourists are comfortable, while other Costa Ricans either fear the plaza or wish that it was quieter, calmer, more shaded and sedate.

But in both cases, Parque Central and the Plaza de la Cultura, there is a relationship between what is experienced and socially constructed by the users, and the circumstances that socially produced the space and its current physical form and design. For example, the North American tourists and pensioners gravitate to and feel comfortable in the open plaza that was designed as a Costa Rican advertisement for foreigners, and teenagers identifying with North American rap culture make it their hangout. On the other hand, both tourists and "cool" teenagers avoid the shady Parque Central that in 1992 still retained the parklike design created by the 1890 Costa Rican elite, who reflected an earlier version of Costa Rican culture. The architectural design and furnishings of these plazas are subject to interpretation and manipulation by the users in such a way that the designs and material conditions of these two worlds become cultural representations to the users themselves. Thus, the contestation of the design, furnishings, use, and atmosphere of a plaza becomes a visible public forum for the expression of ongoing cultural conflict and social change. The increasing social differentiation and distance between classes, the widening values gap between age groups, and the changing definitions of gender roles are all captured in the discussions and disagreements over plaza behavior and use. These social changes are investigated further as microgeographies of culture, class, age, and gender in Chapter 7.

Conclusion

In these two examples of Costa Rican plazas, I illustrate how an anthropological approach to the study of urban space would work ethnographically. I have focused on the historical emergence, sociopolitical and economic development, patterns of social use, and experiential meanings of plaza life and design as a means of empirically working out the implications of the broader perspectives of social production of space and social construction of space. The ethnographic illustrations highlight sociopolitical forces, spatial practices, symbolic meanings, and efforts at social control that provide insight into the conflicts that arise as different groups attempt to claim and define these urban spaces. Further, these processes elucidate how the forces and limits of the social production of space and social construction of space are engaged and contested in public space.

To summarize how these complementary perspectives work analytically, I return to the example of the recent conflict over the design and style of the kiosk in Parque Central. As I mentioned, from 1990 through 1992 the city held a series of town meetings to discuss replacing the 1944 modernist cement kiosk with a replica of the previous Victorian wooden one. Many Josefinos argued that the Victorian kiosk was a better representation of Costa Rican cultural values because it evoked a nostalgic image of bourgeois decorum and *cultura* (culture; see Low 1997b; Richardson 1982, and Chapter 7 of this work). Others, however, argued that the 1944 cement kiosk was part of the city's patrimony and should not be torn down, but instead preserved and improved.

Ultimately the forces for historic preservation won, and the cement kiosk has been restored as the central design element in a redesigned plaza that opened in 1994. This vignette illustrates several key points: (1) the cultural importance of the design of the kiosk, as shown by the fact that citizens staged demonstrations and the government responded with a series of open town meetings; (2) how these two images of a kiosk were materially produced in different historical and political periods and retained symbolic meanings from the periods of their material production; (3) how these spatial representations have taken on new social meanings in the recent struggle between modernization and historic preservation forces in San José; and (4) how this conflict highlights the importance of spatializing culture and human experience as a strategy for understanding people's negotiation of cultural values and representations of those values. Thus, the conflict about and local resistance to change in plaza design tells us about the social divisions and cultural disjunctures in Costa Rican society, and illustrates how the politics of public space attempts to manage these divisions and disruptions and their symbolic expression.

Another important aspect of this sociospatial analysis is the highlighting of the "visible" and "invisible" in public space. Many of the illegal activities that occurred in Parque Central—the prostitution, the drug dealing, and the gambling—were apparently tolerated within the confines of this plaza. The dense foliage and tree cover provided places for clandestine activities that were in some sense "invisible" to the cultural gaze. But with the development of the Plaza de la Cultura as the new ceremonial and cultural center, these same activities were "exposed" by the modern landscape architecture, open design, and increased social scrutiny. The increased visibility of these activities creates an atmosphere characterized by ambivalence, fear, and increasing social sanctions. When faced with the invisible made visible in public space, the state reacts with increased social controls, and if this strategy does not work, it abandons the public space, building a new one where "culture" can be represented in a more pristine form. This effort at social control through design is explored further in Chapter 8.

These insights leave me with a number of questions. Will the public spaces in San José become like those in New York City, with police and guard dogs to keep out homeless persons and drug dealers or designed with benches that do not allow sleeping and ledges with spikes so that you can not sit? Will the plazas of San José become emblematic of social conflict over the presence of disenfranchised people like People's Park in Berkeley, California (Mitchell 1995), or Tompkins Square in New York City (N. Smith 1996)? Or will the public spaces of San José become centers of so much conflict that they become uncomfortable places to be even in a participatory democracy?

CHAPTER 7

Constructing Difference

The Social and Spatial Boundaries of Everyday Life

■

Introduction

The concept of spatial boundary often elicits an image of a physical or social barrier, a metaphorical fence or wall that separates and defines space and its use. It seems equally possible, however, that boundaries as such do not really exist and that what we are describing are locales where difference (different people, different ideas, different activities, different land uses) is evident. Gregory Bateson (1972) argues that humans focus on perceived difference as a way to make sense of the world, and that it is difference that creates edges, borders, boundaries, and peripheries. Difference, in fact, gives shape and form to the world by providing the differentiation and features that permit labeling and classification.

This reconceptualization of spatial boundaries implies that territories of influence, such as the workplace of the shoeshine men in Parque Central or the sitting areas of the teenagers in the Plaza de la Cultura, are perceived to be bounded or distinct because the activities and people within the territory are distinct from the people and activities outside of it. The boundary is nothing more than the marked transition from one sphere of control to that of another. This kind of boundary, the locale where differences come together and create something that can be perceived or felt, may take many forms, as it is only there in the sense of a contrast that marks the interface of the spaces. It is the contrast, the difference, that makes the distinction possible. For instance, imagine a plaza where people and social activities were evenly sprinkled throughout space and time. Would one then experience or observe any spatial boundaries? Thus, boundaries are said to exist only where there is difference and contrast.

Boundaries are inherently arbitrary based on cultural rules of difference and differentiation. They are extremely useful, however, in that they allow symbol-dependent humans to order and make sense of the world. Many anthropologists have argued that this ordering is an essential part of human culture and that boundaries and boundary-maintaining systems constitute the most basic forms of social organization and social structure.

Boundaries, however, are also political devices for social control and discipline. In situations of social or political inequality, boundaries may provide the logic for inclusion or exclusion, with tragic consequence for those without power. The history of the genocide of selected groups throughout the world is an adequate reminder of the political consequences of boundary systems used as weapons of repression and war. In the context of geopolitical forces, boundaries are frequently set as a consequence of major conflicts and then become the focus of nationalist and ethnic conflicts for future generations. Moreover, increasing segmentation of populations by nationality, race, class, and gender is essential to the functioning of the global capitalist system, and "as people define themselves nationally and regionally, they are also vociferously defining out other groups" (Mullings 1997, 23). Therefore, how we construct our boundaries has significant impact on both the production of social space and the politics of our daily lives.

To explore the implications of this reconceptualization of spatial boundaries as locales where different people, activities, and ideas come into contact with one another, this chapter examines the microgeographies of everyday life in Parque Central and Plaza de la Cultura. These locales are created by the individual temporal and spatial attributes of plaza users whose daily movements and activities define these spaces. As Alan Pred has explained:

> Since each of the actions and events consecutively making up
> the existence of an individual has both temporal and spatial
> attributes, time-geography allows that the biography of a person
> may be conceptualized and diagrammed at daily or lengthier

scales of observation as an unbroken continuous path through time-space subject to times of constraint. In time-geographic terms a project consists of the entire sequence of simple or complex tasks necessary to the completion of any intention-inspired or goal-oriented behavior. (1984, 256)

The paths and projects of individual plaza users are presented as a series of population counts, movement maps, and behavioral maps organized by time and day for each plaza. The overlap of the movement and behavior maps combined with ethnographic description identify a series of distinct locales that are defined by class, age, and gender.

The growing differences of these locales in terms of the users' class, gender, and age, and their corresponding social activities are reinforced by differences in local interpretations of the concept of *cultura*. These social, behavioral, and ideological differences have created spatial boundaries such that people do not cross from one locale to the other, the users do not overlap, and their representations of cultural life are seen as competitive and mutually exclusive.

Based on the ethnographic evidence, I suggest that this differentiation is a constructed spatial representation that symbolizes the changing nature of Costa Rican ideology and culture. The contrasting and often conflicting images of the two plazas reflect important differences in class orientation, gender participation, and generational values that separate contemporary Costa Ricans socially and politically. These differences can be understood through the use of Miles Richardson's concept of *cultura* in the plaza and Costa Ricans' ongoing public discourse about culture.

In his study of the plaza in Cartago, Costa Rica, Richardson (1978, 1980) is able to link phenomenologically different places by contrasting the cultural importance of being "proper" in the plaza with being "smart" in the marketplace.

The terms *cultura* (culture) and *progreso* (progress), which appear frequently in the conversations of people talking about the qualities of life in small Spanish-American towns, come close to expressing the contrast. *Cultura* is the victory of Spanish-American civilization over nature and over the bestial aspects of human behavior. The plaza, by its very greenery and by its behavior, leisurely strolling under the trees, epitomizes *cultura*." (1980, 226)

He resolves the different images of public life as being separated, yet integrated, by space and experience. Richardson does not discuss specific spatial boundaries, but he is concerned with how we know how to behave and experience places differently while maintaining a sense of continuity of the experiential world.

This chapter expands Richardson's analysis of the plaza as a place of *cultura* by comparing the two central plazas, located a block away from one another, as different and competing expressions of *cultura* in San José. The ethnographic examples illustrate the way in which differences in users, social activities, built environment, and symbolic intentions reinforce the contrast between the two places. I argue that it is the difference between the plazas and between the users and their activities that constructs the perceived boundaries between the two places, and that these spatial boundaries mark social and political locales that become concretized over time. Even though they are located almost next to one another, these two plazas represent distinct facets of Costa Rican culture—the traditional, Spanish, hierarchical, predominantly older male, Catholic culture of the past; contrasted to the modern, younger, male and female, North American culture of the present. And though symbolic elements of each force their way into both plazas, the hegemony of the traditional or the modern ideology of *cultura* remains. Yet the class and culture tensions, and fears about social contact and public expression, continue unresolved, highlighting the political nature of these cultural expressions.

In San José, *cultura* is often discussed as a value from the past, a cultural ideal that is desired but that conflicts with aspects of modern life. In order to discuss how *cultura* remains a cultural theme in the urban plaza, the everyday life and social behaviors of Parque Central and Plaza de la Cultura are compared. In this comparison, time, space, and social activity change the meaning and interpretation of *cultura,* reinforcing the contrasting metaphors expressed in the physical design of each.

Rhythms of Everyday Life

Three specific kinds of data were collected and analyzed to describe everyday plaza life: population counts by gender on a typical (not a holiday or rainy day) weekday and Sunday, movement maps by gender at two-hour intervals on a typical day, and behavioral maps of group activities by time and place. These counts and maps provide quantitative data and physical evidence of plaza users' activities, supplementing interpretations made based on qualitative sector observations, participant observation, and unstructured interviewing. Taken together, these data identify the locales, paths, and projects that mediate the actions of individual plaza users with the social structural differences and spatial boundaries observed between the two plazas. Thus, individuals produce these social and spatial boundaries by their everyday plaza routines and practices.

Population Counts

The plaza populations were counted in fifteen-minute intervals alternating between fifteen minutes before and fifteen minutes after the hour in each. Counts were recorded on a clipboard, transferred to a summary sheet, and then added together by category to complete the analysis. Two people counted at a time whenever possible, one recording women and the other recording men. The results are presented in the following series of population count charts and compared by day of the week and by plaza.

In Parque Central there is so much activity on Sunday that it is hard to see any pattern other than differences in the number and location of men and women, who are spatially separated into distinct concentric rings, with women usually seated and men standing. On Sundays at 10:00 A.M. the band starts playing, drawing a large crowd of men, women, and children who stand on the kiosk or sit on benches to listen. Sunday morning is the only time when there are many people in the park, yet compared to the crowd at 4:00 P.M., there are still fewer women, children, and teenagers present: 30 percent women at 10:00 A.M. compared to 34 percent women at 4:00 P.M., and 16 percent children and teenagers (0–19) in the morning compared to 23 percent children and teenagers (0–19) at 4:00 P.M. (see Table 1).

The total number of people in Parque Central on this Sunday exceeds the weekday by 70 percent, and the composition of the crowd is primarily families and couples rather than single males: 35 percent women on Sunday as compared to 19 percent women during the week (see Tables 1 and 2). Children (ages 0–12) make up 10 percent of the population on Sunday, compared to 3.5 percent during the week, while teenagers and children together (ages 0–19) make up 23 percent of the Sunday population, and only 7 percent on a weekday. The Sunday crowd also fluctuates widely depending on the presence or absence of local entertainment—such as the band playing or the "soccer" man bouncing a ball with his head—that attracts spectators (see Table 1 at 10.00 A.M.). On Sunday there are women in the park throughout the day, making up as much as 42 percent of the total population at 2:00 P.M. (see Table 1). During the week, on the other hand, most women are at home or work in the morning, and do not go out until after the main noon meal is served. There is a steady increase in the proportion of women users throughout the day, with the largest number of women (33%) present at 6:00 P.M. (see Table 2).

Plaza de la Cultura is spatially organized quite differently from the concentric circles of separated men and women in Parque Central. Instead, people arrange themselves in a series of tiers from the most visually exposed to the least visually exposed: the most exposed is the highest tier next to the National Theater and the Gran Hotel, the second is the transitional space between the main plaza and the lower level, and the third is the grassy area in front of the lower area where the tourist office, art gallery, and gold museum are located. The first tier is made up of families, single men and women, and couples; the second, of middle-aged and older men; and the third, of young single men. Edge zones are particularly important and desirable, especially along the railings and on the pipe benches. The edge along Central Avenue is dominated by teenagers at night, but during the day the composition of the group occupying it often changes.

There is also a clear pattern of sun and shade distribution among users and spectators. On sunny days, girls and women eat their lunches sitting in the shade of the fringe of trees alongside the National Theater, while men stand under the trees in the area in front of the National Theater. Students in uniforms, both male and female, and some men reading papers occupy the small bench seats in the shade of the fig trees along the shopping arcade. Only young men sit on the sunny benches along the back ledge watching others cross the plaza.

On Sundays, Plaza de la Cultura is used by more women than men (52% women overall), even in the early morning (see Table 3). Children under twelve years of age make up 25 percent of the total population, and teenagers from ages thirteen to nineteen make up another 33 percent. This unusual population pattern of 52 percent women and 53 percent teenagers and children on Sundays, compared to 35 percent women

Table 1. *Population Count of Parque Central, Sunday, August 3, 1986*

AGE	0–12		13–19		20–39		40–59		60–79+		Totals	
GENDER	M	F	M	F	M	F	M	F	M	F	M	F
8:00 A.M.	2	4	5	16	14	8	35	7	15	7	71	42
10:00 A.M.	18	24	7	19	36	50	149	32	92	7	302	132
12:00 A.M.	4	10	8	18	23	17	37	4	25	1	97	50
2:00 P.M.	14	9	27	42	49	30	49	19	7	4	146	104
4:00 P.M.	24	27	27	28	165	69	70	31	20	1	306	156
6:00 P.M.	5	12	4	12	36	34	46	15	13	0	104	73

TOTALS BY SEX   M 1,026   F 557   TOTAL BOTH SEXES   1,583

Table 2. *Population Count of Parque Central, Thursday, July 31, 1986*

AGE	0–12		13–19		20–39		40–59		60–79+		Totals	
GENDER	M	F	M	F	M	F	M	F	M	F	M	F
8:00 A.M.	0	0	1	0	22	3	35	0	36	1	94	4
10:00 A.M.	3	3	0	1	31	9	43	3	53	0	130	16
12:00 A.M.	2	1	1	2	34	12	85	11	41	4	163	30
2:00 P.M.	4	4	5	4	21	8	79	15	26	5	135	36
4:00 P.M.	4	5	3	8	12	15	75	9	32	1	126	38
6:00 P.M.	1	6	3	0	60	29	27	13	14	4	105	52

TOTALS BY SEX   M 753   F 176   TOTAL BOTH SEXES   929

and 32 percent teenagers and children on weekdays, provides further evidence that the plaza is perceived as an appropriate and comfortable place for families and, even more important, for mothers and children to relax and play when they have leisure time (see Tables 3 and 4).

On weekdays the most dramatic change in population composition is the appearance of mothers and children in the afternoon (see Table 4). Mothers are free after lunch and their young children are out of school, so they bring them to play in the fountain, chase the pigeons, and then sit on the shaded benches and planter ledges. By 6:00 P.M. on a beautiful evening, Plaza de la Cultura is full of people. On the lowest tier next to the tourist office, couples sit and hold hands, while a young-adult crowd fills the second and intermediate level. On the main plaza, teenagers gather along the planter edge: boys play soccer, interrupted by flirting with girls, or sing accompanied by a blaring radio. Other young people fill the fountain edges, and a few older men and couples remain seated under the fig trees. The population counts reflect these changes: the

Table 3. *Population Count of Plaza de la Cultura, Sunday, August 3, 1986*

AGE	0–12		13–19		20–39		40–59		60–79+		Totals	
GENDER	M	F	M	F	M	F	M	F	M	F	M	F
8:00 A.M.	1	2	2	3	2	5	0	2	0	1	5	13
10:00 A.M.	3	4	2	7	7	6	2	0	2	0	16	17
12:00 A.M.	11	15	4	7	5	18	4	4	0	0	24	44
2:00 P.M.	8	13	12	12	17	12	7	2	2	0	46	39
4:00 P.M.	13	14	26	26	30	19	3	8	3	1	75	68
6:00 P.M.	21	19	30	36	16	14	5	10	4	1	76	80

TOTALS BY SEX   M 242   F 261   TOTAL BOTH SEXES   503

Table 4. *Population Count of Plaza de la Cultura, Thursday, July 31, 1986*

AGE	0–12		13–19		20–39		40–59		60–79+		Totals	
GENDER	M	F	M	F	M	F	M	F	M	F	M	F
8:00 A.M.	0	2	0	0	10	2	9	0	2	1	21	5
10:00 A.M.	0	4	9	7	9	2	13	4	10	1	41	18
12:00 A.M.	0	3	0	2	51	19	16	3	4	0	71	27
2:00 P.M.	8	12	4	5	25	15	7	7	6	3	50	42
4:00 P.M.	8	8	11	7	18	9	10	5	2	0	49	29
6:00 P.M.	6	7	27	17	32	15	4	3	2	0	71	42

TOTALS BY SEX   M 303   F 163   TOTAL BOTH SEXES   466

largest percentage of women (46%) can be found at 2:00 P.M., but the plaza crowd remains 37 percent female even at 6:00 P.M., and the largest percentage of teenagers (39%) is found at 6:00 P.M.

The population patterns found in Plaza de la Cultura are not unlike those of Parque Central except that there are many more women, teenagers, and children on a weekday afternoon and on Sunday. In Parque Central, the percentage of women and children increases on Sunday, but not to the degree in Plaza de la Cultura, since the former is still perceived as the domain of men and workers. The total population of Plaza de la Cultura is also much smaller, only a third of the number of people counted at Parque Central on Sunday (503 compared to 1,583), and half of the number of people counted in Parque Central on a weekday (466 compared to 929).

Overall, then, Parque Central retains the largest number of people, both on Sundays and on weekdays, while Plaza de la Cultura has the highest percentage of women, teenagers, and children, both during the week and on the weekend. Based solely on the population counts, gender and age distributions by day and time differentiate the two public spaces.

Movement Maps

Pedestrian movement in the two plazas is another way to describe the rhythms of everyday life. Movement maps were created by recording the pathway of each pedestrian during a fifteen-minute or thirty-minute observation period. Vicky Risner, a dance ethnologist at the Library of Congress, worked with me to develop a simplified system of notation based on her extensive research experience recording dance in its cultural context. She worked out a system that recorded pathways used, as well as gender and estimated ages of the observed pedestrians. The entrances were rotated throughout the observation period, and notes were made as to who was sitting in the plaza at the time and other significant behavioral details (e.g., the pedestrian shakes another man's hand as he walks through).

Movement maps were collected from 8:00 A.M. to 6:00 P.M. in both plazas. Maps 3, 4, and 5 record observations in Parque Central on Thursday, July 31, 1986, a day that started out cloudy and damp, but became sunny in the afternoon. At 8:00 A.M. a few men are moving from northwest to east, and from east to west and southwest, while only two women, a young woman and an elderly woman in a pair, journey in a southward route across the park. By 10:00 A.M. more people are crossing and circling, moving from the northwestern to the eastern pathway that faces the cathedral. There are still more men than women, and mostly men are exiting at the southwestern corner (see Map 3). By noon the direction of movement shifts significantly as the majority of people exit at the southwestern corner: these seem to be men and a few women catching the buses that stop along Fourth Avenue (see Map 4). The afternoon is the busiest time, with many more women moving through, mostly in an eastern to southwestern direction. Between 4:00 P.M. and 6:00 P.M. the flow of people reversing their morning journey reaches its peak. People exit both east and west, but the western exit is used predominately by young men going to the bars located on the west-northwestern edge of the park (see Map 5).

The movement maps from Wednesday, June 18, 1986, on the Plaza de la Cultura (Maps 6, 7, and 8) record a similar pattern with an increase in activity from the morning to the early afternoon. One popular pedestrian pathway, from the southwest corner near the entrances to the Gran Hotel and the National Theater to the northeast corner on Central Avenue, is used as a shortcut by people moving in either direction (see Map 6). At 4:00 P.M., however, there is a lull when a sudden rainstorm temporarily stops all activity. Only four young men venture out into the rain during the half-hour observation period (see Map 7). But by 6:00 P.M. activity has picked up again. A secondary pathway, from northwest to southeast, emerges, with men walking in both directions from Pops ice cream store on Central Avenue (northwestern corner) to the lower level of the plaza and Second Avenue, where there is a bus stop that services the eastern part of the city (see Map 8).

Comparing the movement maps of Parque Central and Plaza de la Cultura adds another dimension to the way in which the spaces are used and experienced differently. The maps describe "rivers" of movement that make up time-geography paths, segregated for the most part into male and female spheres. When integrated with participant-observation field notes and photographs of people walking, the movement maps indicate that there are two major types of people in each plaza: those who are traveling through the space, and those who have taken up residence by sitting on a bench or leaning on a wall. Many people move from one category to another, of course, but overall there seems to be a residential and a transient population on both plazas.

What is noteworthy, however, is the manner in which the two groups interact with each other, which is different in each plaza. In Plaza de la Cultura, people take up residency in large part to watch the nonresidents and other residents move through the rivers and along the paths. In Parque Central, however, the residents are much less interested in the nonresidents who move through the space. This difference in group interaction illustrates a kind of "closed-society" versus "open-society" behavioral ecology (Wulff and Low 1987). Parque Central, with its internally focused groups of men talking and reading and not necessarily interacting with passersby, could be characterized as a closed society, socially and spatially bounded by cultural rules and notions of tradition and *costumbre* (custom). Plaza de la Cultura, on the other hand, consists of outwardly focused groups of men and women who are constantly looking around, talking to passersby, and frequently breaking out of the group to meet someone or to join another group.

The design of the Plaza de la Cultura certainly reinforces this openness and increases the possibilities of interacting across groups, while

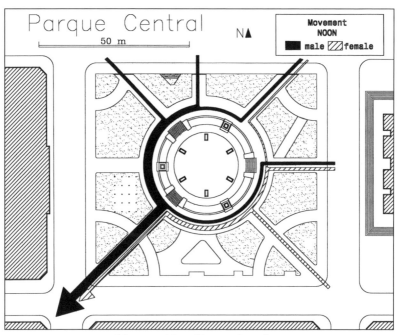

3. *Movement Map of Parque Central,* 10:00 *A.M.*

4. *Movement Map of Parque Central,* NOON

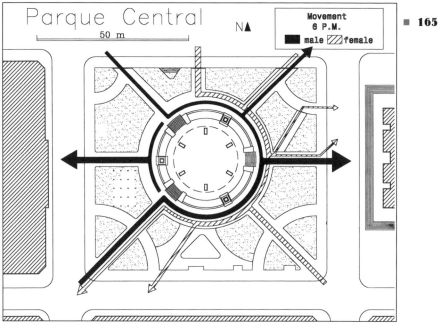

Parque Central

50 m

N▲

Movement
6 P.M.

■ male ▨ female

■ 165

5. *Movement Map of Parque Central, 6:00 P.M.*

the shaded, enclosed corners of the pre-1994 Parque Central provide more privacy and seclusion. But the differences observed in the interaction and movement patterns express more than just the design of the space; they represent an example of landscape architecture and the cultural rules reinforcing each type of pattern, and it is difficult to separate out the extent to which each influence plays a determinant role.

The March 25, 1994, opening of the redesigned Parque Central provides additional evidence (see Map 9). The new design required the removal of many trees, paved over most of the grassy areas, replaced and relocated three-person benches with two-person ones, and added wide expanses of pedestrian walkways. A series of telephone booths plus the police station and art gallery appropriated spaces for municipal use. The remaining hard landscape is much more open and does not offer residents the same sense of privacy.

Nonetheless, some of the Costa Rican pensioners are still there, along with the photographers, only one shoeshine man, and a few sex workers. At the same time, though, real changes have occurred: young Nicaraguan domestic workers predominate on Sundays, and they spend most of their time looking for friends and joining other groups. The socioeconomic changes created by the economic crisis and the influx of Nica-

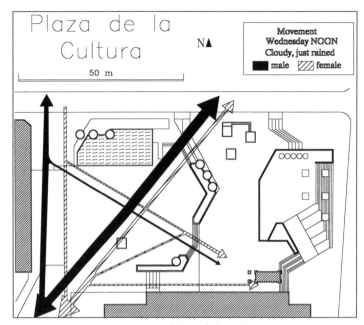

6. Movement Map of Plaza de la Cultura, NOON

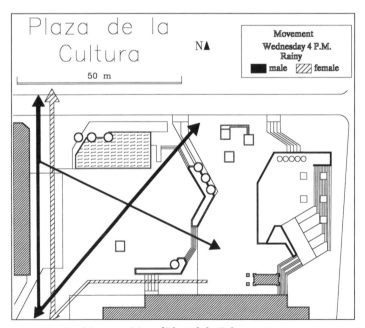

7. Movement Map of Plaza de la Cultura, 4:00 P.M.

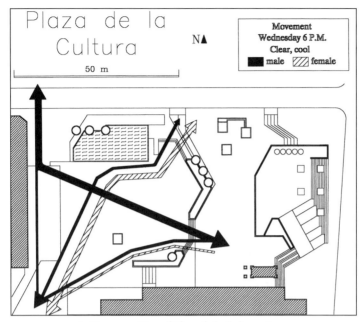

8. Movement Map of Plaza de la Cultura, 6:00 P.M.

raguan refugees discussed in Chapter 3 can be seen in the spatial appropriation of the redesigned Parque Central on Sunday. Furthermore, juvenile gangs take possession of Parque Central at 5:00 P.M. now that the shoeshine men have been cleared out. It seems that the redesigned spaces afford new social "niches." Thus, it appears that the reclaiming of Parque Central by its traditional groups of Costa Rican men has been only minimally successful, while the modern curved benches of the new design accommodate the newest residents. The "closed society" of Parque Central has been partially transformed by its new design, yet it retains elements of its original movement and interaction patterns in the remaining shaded spaces that allow for sitting and talking.

Behavioral Maps

Although the plazas are very different in history, design, and representation, the daily activities that occur there are similar. Yet the people who perform these activities are again quite different. These different groups of people define the public space of the plaza in terms of their distinct social worlds. This difference is significant in that these users—and their

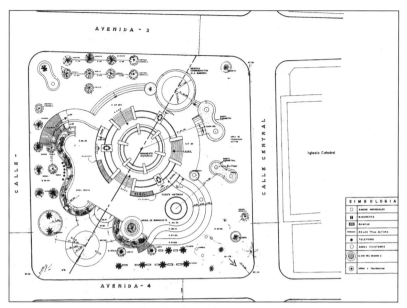

9. Plan of Redesigned Parque Central

distinct social worlds—socially construct an "out-of-awareness" (nondiscursive) boundary-maintaining system. For instance, older men and women, female prostitutes, shoeshine men, and gamblers are almost exclusively found in Parque Central. On the other hand, tourists, young women and children, students in uniforms, teenagers with boom boxes, and North American pensioners are almost exclusively found on the Plaza de la Cultura.

The following description of a sunny weekday in January 1987 illustrates the similarities and differences. Observations were made continuously and in timed samples recorded on behavioral maps from 8:00 A.M. until 10:00 P.M., although the majority of activity occurred during the late morning, afternoon, and early evening. A few of the behavioral maps are included to illustrate the points made; however, the bulk of the maps were used as the database for this summary. The maps were drawn on 8 1/2-by-11-inch plaza plans using black ink and colored pencils to record various ongoing behaviors and locations of individuals. Since the colored-pencil data could not be reproduced here, circles and written descriptions are used in an attempt to convey the richer data of the originals.

Parque Central

In Parque Central, morning is a time for men to sit and read the newspaper. By 10:00 A.M. almost every bench is filled with an adult man reading his paper (see Map 10). The shoeshine business in the northeast corner is slow, and vendors of fruit and lottery tickets are not doing much business. The passersby are mainly on their way to the bus or shopping. The most active person is the municipal employee who sweeps the sidewalks and picks up fallen leaves and trash.

By noon the tempo has picked up (see Map 11). The men on their benches are joined by friends who talk animatedly as the walkways fill with men and women meeting for lunch or catching the bus home. The healer starts his routine in the northwest corner, and the missionaries set up under the arbor. One group of elderly men leave Parque Central at this time to go home for lunch and their siesta and do not return. Others leave but will return after their lunch. As one seventy-year-old man said: "The plaza is my place of employment now that I no longer work. I am underfoot at home. The house is my wife's domain, and I feel better being out of the house during the day."

In the afternoon, a few older women appear, bringing their children to the library, shopping with friends, or resting from a busy morning in town (see Map 12). The shoeshine business is at its peak as middle-class men stop to get their shoes shined on their way back to work. Sometimes during the midafternoon a clown and his assistant begin their routine telling jokes on the kiosk platform. Vendors of ice cream, peanuts, candy, and snow cones circulate along the edge of the crowd. The police walk by in pairs, stop and watch for a while, and then continue on their patrol of the street.

By 4:00 P.M. most of the older men have left, and young and middle-aged couples meet in Parque Central for coffee or to take the bus home. The number of women is the highest at this time, still only making up about 20 to 30 percent of the population, but very different from the all-male reading period of the morning. At 6:00 P.M. the light begins to fade and the air is cooler (see Map 13). A new group of vendors with carts of hot corn or skewered beef appear on the edge of the sidewalk. As couples circumambulate around the kiosk, they stop to buy food and talk to the vendors, drawn by the smell of the sizzling grilled beef.

At 7:00 P.M. it becomes quiet. The shoeshine men have left for the day, and only a few couples, some single young men, and the vendors

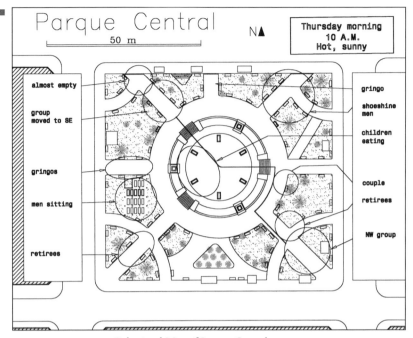

10. Behavioral Map of Parque Central, 10:00 A.M.

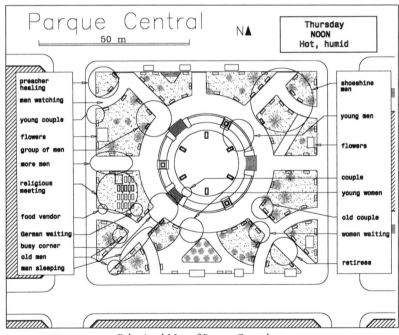

11. Behavioral Map of Parque Central, NOON

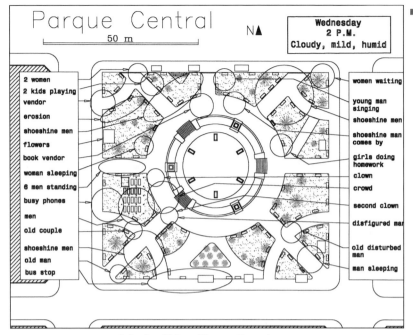

12. Behavioral Map of Parque Central, 2:00 P.M.

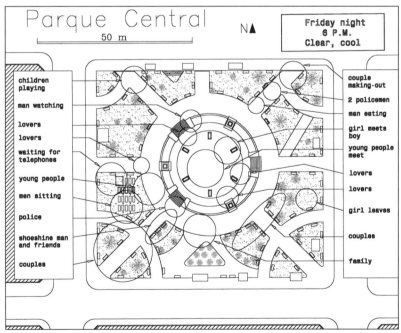

13. Behavioral Map of Parque Central, 6:00 P.M.

remain. If it is a nice evening, more people will wander by on their way to the Rex Cinema or to have a drink in the Soda Palace. A small group of street kids run by trying to beg money from a passing gringo, and tired young prostitutes sit under the arbor waiting for business. By now the lines of the buses are not as long, and tired workers wait in groups talking about the day or buying lottery tickets from the corner vendors. Later in the evening, between 9:00 P.M. and 10:00 P.M., Parque Central is almost completely deserted except for one or two solitary men sitting on the benches or walking slowly down the paths. Even later, men from the countryside, drunk and sleepy, may find their way from the cheap bars surrounding the central market to sleep relatively undisturbed on the park benches until morning.

One footnote must be added to this description. The redesign of Parque Central instituted a new set of municipal laws about what could be sold and who could be there. As of January 1997, only one shoeshine man was working on the plaza, while a few remained across the street, and the number of vendors was restricted. From my observations, it still looked as if people were selling candy as well as the ubiquitous lottery tickets. The uniformed police did not stop the vendors that I saw; however, overall there were many fewer vendors than in 1987.

Plaza de la Cultura

In the Plaza de la Cultura the day also starts slowly. During the morning there are very few people, usually just a couple of men or male tourists reading a newspaper in the sun, and a group of green-uniformed plaza employees who sweep and empty the trash cans. Sunday is a little busier, with the artisan market for the tourists, but even then there is little activity.

About noon the older North Americans, known as *gringos verdes,* or "green" Yankees, appear in their baseball hats, sunburns, and smiles (see Map 14). They will stay for most of the afternoon waiting for girls or watching those that walk by. These men are a mixture of regular tourists who come each winter to enjoy the weather and *pensionados,* North Americans who have elected to retire to Costa Rica full-time. Attracted by tax advantages and other benefits from the Costa Rican government, they live off their guaranteed monthly pensions from the United States or Canada. Students, young office workers, and friends sometimes stop to have their lunch in the plaza or to buy ice cream at the nearby Pops and sit a moment to finish eating. Tourists are in the café having lunch or wandering in front of the National Theater buying souvenirs or taking pictures.

By 2:00 P.M. the pace quickens as more and more office workers return to work walking through the plaza on their way from the bus stop. Young mothers and children stop to look at the fountain or to play with the pigeons during a shopping outing. Students, finished with classes, stop to meet friends while they are still in their school uniforms. On some afternoons a clown and his wife/assistant or a Peruvian musical group may come by. The clown performs almost in the center of the plaza, attracting children and their parents as well as the downtown office crowd. The Peruvian singers play in the tourist area and draw a crowd of tourists and young adult Costa Ricans. Later, an evangelical group with guitars, singing popular songs in praise of Jesus, might entertain a bored teenage crowd (see Photograph 45).

At 4:00 P.M. the gringos leave for their afternoon coffee and rest, and many of the families start on their way home (see Map 15). By 5:00 P.M. or so, teenagers in blue jeans begin to appear (see Map 16). They play music on portable radios or tape decks, dance, and even start soccer games on the far end of the main open space. They are the major occupants until the National Theater opens at 8:00 P.M. Sometimes there are special evening events, such as a tribute to local high school bands or a radio interview of teenagers who are there. If there is no performance at the National Theater, the plaza becomes quiet by 8:00 P.M. as the teenagers leave to go on to their evening destinations. Later in the evening, after 9:00 P.M., single men gather on the lower plaza near the theater ticket window to meet and talk. Groups of young men often wander by or stop to smoke marijuana. In a few cases, policemen passed by and arrested one of the young men, either for drinking or having drugs on him. The encounters were brief, however, and carried out in hushed tones. The atmosphere in the lower plaza seemed to me to be more relaxed than frightening as the men shared their thoughts and waited to meet friends.

It is apparent from these two descriptions that the activities of reading, talking, eating, and meeting friends are the same. Both plazas are dominated by men and their related activities of reading, sitting, watching, and talking in the morning, and accommodate women, families and children, and couples in the afternoon. They both have vendors who sell flowers, food, and trinkets; people who provide personal ser-

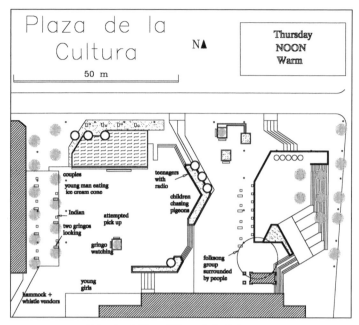

14. Behavioral Map of Plaza de la Cultura, NOON

vices; entertainers who sing or clown; and preachers of various denominations. They are both surrounded by cafés where users can go to get inside from the rain or sun or where nonusers can simply survey the scene. They both have a small number of people who want to lay claim to the space but who are considered by some to be undesirable occupants, such as people begging, prostitutes, homeless people, drug dealers, and gamblers. Police who patrol and maintenance people who clean up the trash are also there representing the municipal social order.

What seems more important, however, is not that the activities are the same—although this sameness may indicate some common cultural response to the use of public space—but that the activities take on such different forms and meanings and are performed by such different people. For example, the cafés of Parque Central are populated only by men—when an unaccompanied woman enters one of these cafés, it causes a minor stir. The cafés on the Plaza de la Cultura, on the other hand, are frequented by both men and women, usually tourists and upper- or middle-class Costa Ricans. The prostitutes in Parque Central are young female Costa Ricans who are professionals and who solicit men of all ages and nationalities. The young women who meet men in the Plaza

45. Religious singers in Plaza de la Cultura

de la Cultura, however, call themselves *tourras,* which I was told means that they engage in sex in exchange for a nice meal or clothes, but not for money or as a professional occupation. The *tourras* are involved mostly with older men, often North American pensioners or tourists who come to Costa Rica searching for very young women and for a sexual, and sometimes loving, relationship. The expectations of both the older men and the young women vary from romantic to mercenary, and the reality of the relationships vary as well. Vilma Loría's story of a Costa Rican returning home who is robbed and "rolled" by a woman he meets in the Plaza de la Cultura portrays some of the ambiguity of the situation (see Chapter 3 for the complete short story).

Other examples of the contrast in the expression of social activities include what is sold: tourist items, popcorn, and balloons in the Plaza de la Cultura versus lottery tickets, food, and newspapers in Parque Central; the difference in the green-uniformed maintenance men in the plaza and the municipal maintenance man's rag shirt in Parque Central; the presence of a large number of foreigners in the Plaza de la Cultura and the absence of many foreigners in Parque Central. The contrast can be summarized as the emerging social divisions between young and old,

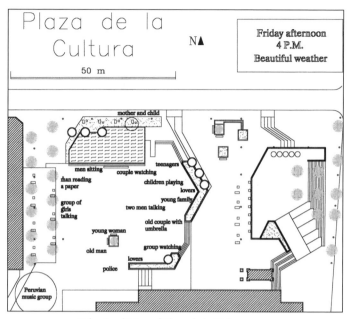

15. Behavioral Map of Plaza de la Cultura, 4:00 P.M.

16. Behavioral Map of Plaza de la Cultura, 6:00 P.M.

foreign and local, lower and middle class, and male and female that are now spatially and temporally distributed across the two plazas.

These differences in expression reiterate the historical and physical comparison, that is, the separation between an identification with modern North American or international culture in the Plaza de la Cultura and the maintenance of a more traditional Costa Rican identity in Parque Central. Taken together, yet separated and bounded by their difference, the two plazas express the contemporary dimensions, contradictions, and tensions of Costa Rican culture.

The new plaza, built only one block northeast of Parque Central, was to be a reflection of contemporary culture based on different values and by its difference, created a "symbolic space," a "spatial boundary" between the images of Costa Rican *cultura* produced in these two places. The social boundary that separates these two worlds is one that is constructed more by the contrast than by any physical or social barrier that exists between the two plazas. In fact, one would think that the shoeshine men, the pensioners, the couples, and the vendors would travel between the two plazas, depending on weather, business, and amount of crime or disturbance that might exist in either place. Yet the residents of Parque Central remain firmly in place and regard the new plaza as suspect. They say that the new plaza is an uncomfortable place where the "wrong" people hang out, while the residents of the Plaza de la Cultura describe Parque Central as dark and dangerous. One explanation for this separation of the two places is that the new plaza has, in fact, been successful in reconstituting Costa Rican culture with a different image, and has succeeded in disenfranchising the older, more traditional representation of social life presented in Parque Central.

Thus, the contrast between the two plazas is significant; their histories, design, and users are in many ways distinct. Within Parque Central there is very little contested space because a long-term pattern of users and activities has built up over the years. New activities such as the Christian healing are accommodated either at the edges of the plaza or through the reallocation of space in time. The Plaza de la Cultura, however, is still a highly contested arena; tourism and the Costa Rican image of *cultura* conflict with the nightly appropriation by "cruising." The separation between the two plazas is a cultural gulf, with older retired and working men dominating one scene, and students, young women, women and children, tourists, and teenagers enjoying the other. Both are Costa Rican representations of *cultura*, but they represent different versions of that cultural goal. There is an invisible boundary between them, yet their commonalities link them. Culture is not some homogeneous set of rules for life, but is made up of conflicting and fluctuating images and aspirations.

Conclusion

The behavioral maps complete the time-space descriptions begun with the population counts and movement maps. While the movement maps describe paths that link walking individuals with gender segregation in Parque Central, the behavioral maps record individual projects such as men shining shoes, elderly pensioners meeting to talk, or teenagers playing soccer. The accretion of multiple paths and projects located in space and time links the individual activities to age, gender, and class differences found in the two plazas. Over time these differences become naturalized, as has been argued by Pierre Bourdieu (1977), and perceived as social reality. Thus, individual paths and projects are transformed into cultural norms for behavior reenacted in daily social practices.

These microgeographies demonstrate how plaza meanings are socially constructed through historically constituted social practices, political ideologies, users' behaviors, group activities, and urban design to represent and reproduce distinct aspects of Costa Rican culture. This social construction occurs through the historical and sociopolitical forces that created each plaza (discussed in Chapter 6) and through the paths and projects that create the distinct social worlds presented here. These differences are reinforced by the social practices of the people who inhabit these spaces.

The social and spatial boundaries that separate these two spheres, which are so physically close yet so culturally different, are social constructions that are meaningful at the level of lived experience of everyday life. They provide clues as to the significant schisms in what otherwise seems like a very homogeneous culture.

For example, culturally ideal gender roles in which the woman/housewife stays at home and the man/provider goes out to work and into the public realm of the plaza are breaking down as women are needing or wanting to work in response to changes in the political economy. The cultural norms of Parque Central restricted women's attendance to Sundays and late afternoons and to being accompanied by their partners or children, leaving them without a public space. Thus, the Plaza de la Cultura has become an important alternative space and a means of expressing this new cultural definition of gender roles.

In a similar vein, the social status of being a teenager has become more important with the influx of North American capital and culture that includes age-specific modes of dress, music, and behavior. Before the 1970s most teenagers were working adults. I remember interviewing adolescents from 1972 through 1974 who said that after the sixth grade (age 12 or 13) they were expected to go to work. In the countryside and in very poor urban households, this expectation may still hold, but in the city most San José teenagers go to school and many hang out to meet their friends. The Plaza de la Cultura provides the new public space necessary for this change in culturally proscribed behavior, and its open design allows for the possibility of dancing and playing soccer in the urban center.

The increasing social divisions and socioeconomic inequality resulting from the impact of global market forces, the influx of North American capital, local economic crises, and shifts in modes of production have also resulted in the segmentation and redefinition of the Costa Rican class system. This segmentation can be seen in the differences in cultural ideals reflected in the notion of *cultura*. The traditional myth that "Costa Rica es diferente," that Costa Rica was historically a country of small farmers that produced an egalitarian class structure, has been disrupted by obvious differences in wealth, increasing segregation of residential neighborhoods, increasing unemployment and underemployment, and the dismantling of the legislated safety net of social security, basic food subsidies, and other social welfare programs. Older Costa Ricans will still tell you that "we are all middle class" if you ask about class structure, but increasingly young people and the disenfranchised point out that things are changing, and that while everyone may be the same politically, they no longer are in terms of wealth. These changes in class are also expressed in the discourse concerning behavior and activities in the plazas and are captured in the cultural metaphor and social sanction of *cultura*. Thus, class, gender, and age differences separate these two socially and spatially bounded domains, as well as the cultural notion of *cultura*.

This exploration of spatial boundaries also reveals a secondary theme of how imperfectly concepts of culture are realized. The introduction of a new cultural image was intended to be a sociopolitical statement resolving the problems of socioeconomic change that were altering the sense of *cultura* in Parque Central. But social problems have reappeared on the Plaza de la Cultura, and the design, instead of representing *cultura*, exposes other cultural goals and reflects the underlying structural changes in Costa Rican society.

CHAPTER 8

Public Space and Protest

The Plaza as Art and Commodity

■

Introduction

This chapter tackles the problem of the relationship of landscape architecture and visual culture to unstable cultural meanings by examining the design and designing of urban plazas. The examination of public space as art and commodity provides a glimpse of the contradictions between the artistic and often idealized representational purposes of the urban plaza and its political and economic base. Bringing these contradictions to light helps to demystify visual culture and highlights the ways in which landscape architecture and urban design are deeply ideological, both in artistic style and in political purpose.

Further, by reconsidering a designed public space as a commodity, its planning, design, construction, or refurbishing takes on new economic meaning. A public space that is valued ostensibly as a place for people to sit, read, and gather becomes a way to maintain real estate values, a financial strategy for revitalizing a declining city center, and a means of attracting new investments and venture capital.

Landscape design and the reorganization of space are part of the creative destruction of forms of society, replacing traditional forms with new capitalist relationships (Harvey 1990). Global economic forces influence both the production and construction of these new spaces. At the same time, spatial forms such as public plazas are systems of representation and social products whose style is a confirmation rather than a cause of social differentiation. So the designs produced are at some level simply reflections of social changes that have already occurred, and their analysis highlights the cultural conflict and contestation that are ongoing as economic forces restructure the public space of the city.

One of the best ways to analyze a visual and cultural artifact is as a moment in a particular historical time and cultural place. The analysis should consist of visual and spatial as well as social strategies (Zukin 1995), including an analysis of architectural form, urban location, symbolism, and role in social relations. Yet even in the clearest of place narratives, it is difficult to separate design from commodification. The interpenetration of artistic, political, and economic intent and interpretation is part of the process by which art and architecture serve ideological and economic rather than simply artistic ends. Certainly the position of the viewer—socially, politically, and physically—influences what can be and is seen.

The notion that a plaza can be analyzed as a commodity as well as an artistic artifact is drawn from the work of Sylvia Rodríguez (1989), who is concerned with the way that painting mystifies the economic or political objectives of its production. The design and building of public plazas serve these same purposes; even more so in that citizens perceive the plaza as a cultural mirror by which they can see themselves—and sometimes they do not want to look. In this sense, the mystification process may begin with the design of public space, but local residents, plaza users, city administrators, and the media actively participate in the obfuscation of certain political meanings.

Thus, a landscape design, like a painting, can be seen as a case study in mystification. Urban public spaces that planners and administrators say are designed for the common good are often designed to accommodate activities that will exclude some people and benefit others. Further, the economic motives for the design of urban public space often have more to do with increasing the value and attractiveness of the surrounding property than with increasing the comfort of the daily inhabitants, except where the social amenities are written into the zoning and economic equation.

Rodríguez (1997, 1998) presents a classic example of this transition from local plaza to the commodified version in her study of the main plaza in Taos, New Mexico, where the traditional plaza of grass, flagstones, and exposed dirt was redesigned to become a "plaza-mall" in 1976. The new design attracts tourists and tourist-related shops and services, further alienating the local population. By the 1980s the "day-to-day presence of native Hispano-Mexicano people on the plaza diminished, and it became a place most natives and locals now prefer to avoid" (Rodríguez 1997, 50). However, Rodríguez's ethnohistory of the realignment of ethnic, religious, and class relations involved in the production of the Taos fiesta ritually located on the plaza suggests that there is some resistance to this spatial appropriation. Even though the plaza is now a gentrified tourist space abandoned by locals in their everyday life, the fiesta has increasingly become a vehicle for the nativistic expression of Hispanic pride and the domain of the Hispano middle class. Rodríguez demonstrates how complex the interrelations of space, social stratification, and ritual can become by demonstrating how the cultural meaning of the Taos fiesta contests the symbolic furnishings of the redesigned plaza.

In another example of the transition in public-space design from a local cultural form to a more commodified, middle-class version is found in a study of the central public spaces of Los Angeles, California. Don Parson (1993) argues that three successive central spaces—the Plaza, Pershing Square, and the California Plaza—represent and symbolize Los Angeles's cultural core, and that it is in the sequence of each space becoming the symbolic center of the city that the underlying social transformations of race and class can be seen. These three centers "reflect both the history and the actuality of the spatial recomposition of race and class in Los Angeles" (Parson 1993, 236). The Plaza was the focus of the historically Hispanic and now the Latino city; Pershing Square was the center of Anglo downtown; and the new California Plaza, next to the Los Angeles Music Center and the luxury condominiums of Bunker Hill, is the contemporary center of corporate exclusivity.

In the case of the two Costa Rican plazas presented here, the actions and conversations of local users contest the redesigned public spaces, as in the Taos plaza example, but there is no clear example of a civic event that ritually inverts their new meanings. And, like the moving center of Los Angeles, the plazas of San José represent the changing class composition of the city and the increasing corporate and commodified nature of public space through the expansion and renovation of plazas throughout the downtown area and through the redesign of the original Plaza Principal.

Ethnographic analyses of plaza design as art and commodity thus allow for some degree of demystification of the ideological, political, and economic bases of public urban design. To illustrate this contention, I will discuss a contemporary conflict concerning the image of the plaza and design of the kiosk and the results of remodeling this traditional space. For the Plaza de la Cultura, I explore in greater detail how the artistic and economic goals of its creators do not meet the needs of traditional plaza users, but instead accommodate the needs of the growing tourist trade. In this discussion, the images of the plaza producers and concerns of the users are contrasted with the intentions of the designers and government officials to highlight how the conflict between representational and use value is worked out in a specific context.

Public Space and Public Protest

Another aspect of this analysis concerns the power of public space to communicate civic sentiments and social resistance through its design and commodification. Public space is often about public protest, but the form of that protest is not always the same. I am particularly interested in three kinds of protest: *manifest* protest such as public demonstrations or the appropriation of space by marginal or outcast groups, *latent* protest such as the symbolic struggle for architectural and cultural representation within the built environment, and *ritual* protest such as fiestas, parades, and carnivals that temporarily invert the everyday social structure and hegemonic meanings of the public space.

Manifest protest is the most apparent and obvious. It includes strikes, demonstrations, and other gatherings organized to express discontent and disagreement. Spatial appropriation is another form of manifest protest. Although it is not as transparent as a demonstration, spatial appropriation can be seen by all participants and is clearly identifiable by outsiders. Spatial appropriation by groups such as drug dealers or homeless individuals, as in Tompkins Square in New York City (N. Smith 1996) or People's Park in Berkeley, California (Mitchell 1995), or shoeshine men, prostitutes, and alcoholics in Costa Rica, is frequently cited as a "problem" by municipal officials and acted upon by the state.

Latent protest is usually framed as an ongoing public contestation of the symbolic furnishings, design, and surrounding businesses and buildings of the public space. It is latent in that it requires decoding by the social analyst to illuminate the underlying sociopolitical struggle, as is demonstrated by the Costa Rican plaza examples.

Ritual protest, on the other hand, also resists hegemonic definitions of public space and it is visible. However, unlike the examples of manifest protest, resistance takes the form of the temporary control of the space, a symbolic inversion of its meaning, and then a return to normalcy. It does not materially change the furnishings or constitute a reason to redesign or close the space, as illustrated in the case of the Taos plaza in New Mexico (Rodríguez 1998).

There are at least four basic outcomes of public protest. When manifest protest by demonstration is too successful—that is, it threatens the state—the public space is closed, sometimes gated, and policed. When manifest protest by spatial appropriation is successful, the public space is briefly closed down and redesigned in such a way as to discourage its continued use by the groups that are deemed undesirable, and then it is policed when it is reopened.

When latent protest by means of symbolic representation is successful, the public space becomes a contested arena for the control of meaning in the built environment. Conflicts about design and use become part of an ongoing public discourse expressed in newspaper articles, television discussions, and interviews, and in some cases, a public plebiscite (DePalma 1998).

When ritual protest by means of a popular fiesta or parade is successful, the public space is reclaimed by the protesting group for a limited period of time, but is then returned to the domain of hegemonic forces. There are numerous examples of ritual protest in the form of parades, such as the Mummers' Parade in Philadelphia (Davis 1986) or the Halloween Parade in Greenwich Village, New York (Kugelmass 1994), and in the form of fiestas, as in Taos and Santa Fe, New Mexico (Rodríguez 1998; Wilson 1997), and carnival in Brazil (Da Matta 1984; Linger 1992). In each of these examples, the symbolic protest is limited in time and space, expressing unresolved social relations but not necessarily changing the physical environment.

Only some public spaces become arenas for working out social and cultural conflict. I discovered, based on my research on the history of the Spanish American plaza, that planned central public spaces—sacred spaces or civic plazas—take on layers of historical meaning that are retained through the mnemonics of environmental memory (see Chapters 4 and 5). Spaces such as the Zócalo in Mexico City, Tiananmen Square in Beijing, Plaza de Mayo in Buenos Aires, or Parque Central in San José have layers of past meanings semiotically encoded in the spatial relations, furnishings, and architecture of the place. These meanings, embodied in the space itself, become a subtext for the protest that occurs there, and by placing protest in the symbolic center of the society, it captures national attention.

Probably the best example of the outcome of manifest protest is the closing down of Tiananmen Square in Beijing—the sacred center of the Chinese Empire in front of the Forbidden City. When the student demonstrations of 1989 challenged the oppressive regime of Deng Xiao Peng, the students were fired upon by troops under the control of China's Minister of Defense, General Chi Haotian, and the square was closed down. Even a year later when I was there, the space was heavily policed to discourage any activities other than those sanctioned by the state.

Another example of a space of manifest protest being closed down is the Aguascalientes built by the Maya Zapatista rebels in Chiapas. The name Aguascalientes commemorates the abortive meeting held in the town of Aguascalientes, Mexico, between Emiliano Zapata and Pancho Villa to chart the future of the Mexican Revolution in 1914. The first Aguascalientes was hastily built in July 1994 of posts and canopies on the edge of the Lacandón jungle to house the First National Democratic Congress. The Zapatistas invited a host of national and international media representatives and political candidates of the opposition parties to witness their first "revolutionary forum" (Gossen 1996). By 1995, however, the Mexican army had destroyed and occupied the site of the 1994 Aguascalientes convention.

In response, "New Aguascalientes" were constructed to resemble the plazas of ancient Maya ceremonial centers in four sites outside of existing municipal centers. These public spaces were "complete with raised platform mounds crowned by posts covered with multicolored, plastic-laminated sheets" (Gossen 1996, 529), and the four pavilions have become potent political statements, acting as new social and cultural centers for the media and the public. Yet even the New Aguascalientes have become threatening; the Mexican government has blocked access to the dispersed sites from public roads so that no gatherings can occur there. Nonetheless, these centers remain a permanent public forum and symbolic center of the contemporary Zapatista movement. In this illustration, the success of using public space as a form of protest has been blocked, policed, and occupied, while the symbolism of the sites is retained.

An example of manifest protest by spatial appropriation with the resulting outcome of the space being redesigned is Parque Central in San José, Costa Rica. By 1987, this public space was heavily populated with drug dealers, people selling illegal goods, shoeshine men gambling, day laborers waiting for pick-up work, and prostitutes—socially mar-

ginal individuals who challenged some Josefinos' and municipal officials' cultural image of themselves. Their vision of San José as an attractive tourist site was not reflected in the presence of underemployed and
unemployed workers or of workers whose occupations had taken over
the plaza. The government responded first by building the Plaza de la
Cultura to represent their new cultural ideals. But when this new plaza
also became a stage for activities that middle-class citizens and government officials did not want visible, the municipality closed Parque Central in 1993 and redesigned it without its cover of trees, secluded arbor,
and private benches. The redesigned Parque Central opened in 1994.
With increased policing and the addition of new laws to prohibit vend-
ing and shoe shining, there was a dramatic reduction in these activities.
Nonetheless, there has also been a corresponding increase in the presence of teenage gangs who gather in the late afternoon to plan their
evening of mugging tourists and pickpocketing shoppers.

An example of latent protest through architecture, and of the outcome of the space becoming contested terrain, is the Zócalo in Mexico
City (see Photograph 46). The indigenous symbolism of the archaeological remains of Tenochtitlan and the Templo Mayor contests the architectural dominance of the colonial grid, the cathedral, and surviving
colonial buildings, as discussed in Chapter 5. In this setting, two representations of the state retain an uneasy relationship to one another
through the politics of historic preservation and archaeological excavation of the built environment. Another example is the stark modernity
of Plaza de la Cultura in San José, Costa Rica, and the continuing criticism of the plaza by the local press as well as the public's destruction of
some of its features upon its opening, as discussed in Chapter 6.

This chapter reanalyzes the two Costa Rican plazas and considers
data collected during the final field visits in 1993 and 1997 in order to
answer how public space embodies civil protest and social resistance
while at the same time semiotically encoding the artistic desires of its
designers and the economic and investments goals of its founders and
administrators.

The Plaza as Art and Commodity

The building of a new plaza is usually heralded as an artistic achievement, and both the Plaza de la Cultura and Parque Central were introduced as significant contributions to the aesthetics of downtown San
José. The Plaza Principal began as a municipal market, a site of the war

46. Zócalo in Mexico City

for independence from Spain, a source of water for city residents, and the place where the monthly lottery was drawn. It was not until 1885 that the Plaza Principal was converted into a garden, and a municipal market was established as a separate entity where businesses could be concentrated. By 1890, Parque Central emerged with its greenery, wooden kiosk, fountain, and garden gates as part of a comprehensive landscape design (La pila del Parque Central 1944). During the subsequent decade, Parque Central was thought to represent the highest achievement in landscape design, incorporating indigenous plants and flowers into a park where the public could go to refresh themselves in the shade of the large and venerable fig trees (La capital de antaño 1928).

The political intentions of this dramatic transformation from marketplace to ceremonial plaza and park are difficult to decipher from the writings and news clippings of the past, but if the present is any guide, the artistic aspirations of park design were just as political as recent decisions about Parque Central's renovation and restoration. I will begin with the analysis of the conflict of the early 1990s over the historic preservation of the modern kiosk and the park remodeling, discussed briefly in Chapter 6 but now focusing on these changes as artistic endeavors that would beautify the comfortable but decaying Parque Central. Following this analysis I will discuss the corresponding commodification of this traditional public space into a site that planning and design professionals and the governing elite considered more appropriate for global tourism, middle-class values, and social control.

Parque Central: Historic Preservation or Social Control?
The contestation of the turn-of-the-century image of Parque Central as an elite plaza or as a contemporary heterogeneous urban center was sparked by a public debate about replacing the modern cement kiosk with a model of the original wooden one. In the spring of 1992, a group of citizens brought a petition to the municipality to tear down the cement structure and reconstruct the Victorian bandstand. I was not in San José at that time, but the newspapers describe the conflict in great detail. The number of articles and the extent of the debate confirms my contention that this space is one of the most charged battlegrounds for the symbolic control of the Costa Rican cultural landscape.

Concern over the deteriorating condition of Parque Central was editorialized as early as August 8, 1988, when Jorge Coto E., a columnist for *La Nación,* commented that Parque Central was to be a site of urban redevelopment. He notes that the Minister of Culture, Youth, and Sports (Minister of Culture) had initiated the renovation to give the plaza more visibility, but that he was concerned that Parque Central, the true symbol of Costa Rican identity, might lose what little personality it had left.

By December 1, 1991, a plan to remodel Parque Central was announced as part of a joint program of the municipality and the Minister of Culture to renovate the parks and plazas of the capital. An interinstitutional commission was set up as the planning and decision-making body. They hoped that the work would begin in February 1992.

But by February 10, 1992, Jorge Solórzano, a reporter for *La Nación,* wrote that there was a lack of consensus concerning the demolition of the kiosk. The executive officer of the municipality, the engineer Johnny Araya, stated that there was some doubt within the interinstitutional commission as to whether the kiosk donated by Anatasio Somoza García should be replaced by a model of the 1905 Japanese-style one (*sic*). Mr. Araya stated that the present structure did not add anything aesthetically to the park and that it took up a great deal of space. However, Aída de Fishman, the Minister of Culture, argued that the integrity of the park must be respected. The commission suggested that a questionnaire be distributed to the public to vote on the destiny of the kiosk.

On March 10, 1992, the Council of the Municipality of San José was asked to hold a town meeting (*cabildo*) so the public could participate in this difficult decision. The public would be presented with sketches of the alternative projects: one of the park restored with the actual kiosk, and the other based on the original image with the wooden kiosk, fountain, and iron fences. Johnny Araya reported that in a questionnaire undertaken by the municipality, more than 75 percent of the respondents wanted the elimination of the kiosk and the restoration of Parque Central as it was at the turn of the century. The previous Ministers of Culture, Guido Sáenz—who was instrumental in the creation of the Plaza de la Cultura—and Francisco Echeverría, also attacked the aesthetics of the current "temple" (a nickname for the kiosk). On the other hand, the architect Jorge Grané argued that no one was sure why they wanted to tear it down or to what end. The columnist José David Guevara M. of *La Nación* commented on March 24, 1992, that the sixty shoeshine men and their clients, the "crazies" (*locos*), and the elderly (*viejillos verdes*) who inhabit the park were not being asked their opinion. He concluded that "the long and the short" of the question is whether the renovation will conserve the park's identity as the heart of the capital.

The vote took place on April 4, 1992, at 2:00 P.M. at the Liceo de Costa Rica. The government presented three initiatives: demolishing, improving, or leaving the kiosk intact. Seven thousand people were expected to participate in the first town meeting ever held in San José.

The day after the plebiscite Jorge Solórzano reported that a majority of the people voted to demolish the actual kiosk. Only 1,153 people voted: 487 for the destruction of the structure, 372 for leaving it intact, and 292 to conserve it with modifications. The results of the vote further divided the members of the commission. Those who were opposed to the demolition thought that the two options that received fewer votes should be added together to produce a majority of votes to save the kiosk. Other members, such as Johnny Araya, thought that the commission should respect the winning option, which was to eliminate the actual kiosk and reconstruct the original park. Mr. Solórzano commented that Dr. Arias, ex-president of Costa Rica and builder of many parks and plazas, had suggested that the decision should be delayed until the economic situation in the country improved.

The public's vote to tear down the kiosk and its reinterpretation by the commission was met with professional alarm. The Colegio de Arquitectos (similar to the A.I.A. in the United States) put a full-page ad in *La Nación* stating that the vote did not represent an adequate sample of Josefinos and announcing their opposition to the plan. Nonetheless, on April 21, 1992, the Municipal Council of San José approved the demolition of the kiosk by a vote of nine to four. But on April 23, 1991, the Minister of Culture, Youth and Sports, Aída de Fishman, disapproved the destruction of the kiosk based on Law 5397, the Historical Patrimony Law, which states that no public building or property can be destroyed, remodeled, or modified without her approval. Thus, the battle ended with the assertion of the Minister of Culture's legal power to resolve the conflict.

The citizens who were attempting to reconstitute the Parque Central in its elite, turn-of-the-century image were not the daily users, but professional and middle-class Josefinos. The conflict over the architectural form of the kiosk was a struggle about control of the artistic style of the Parque Central in which the architectural furnishings represented broader social and class-based meanings. The final resolution was a compromise in which the kiosk was remodeled and a replica fountain added; at the same time, the green spaces, many of the trees, the arbor, the working spaces, and generous stone benches were removed to correspond to an image of modern middle-class civility and contemporary urbanity, and to discourage the activities of its traditional residents.

The conflict over the design of the kiosk led to a much broader reconception of Parque Central. In a series of interviews with Rudolfo Sancho Quesada, the municipality's chief engineer in charge of the renovation, I learned that the final reconstruction was based on the original plans for the plaza that surfaced during the uproar about the kiosk. After 1940, it seems that the municipal engineers decided that the plaza was complete; the fountain was removed to make room for the new kiosk, but there was no further maintenance or restoration. The engineers at that time, in fact, threw away many of the beautiful details of the kiosk, including a statue of Venus that was to crown the cupola. The carved details on the side fountains were never repaired or repainted, and trees were cut down and not replaced.

From the municipality's point of view, the redesign of Parque Central accomplished three artistic objectives and resolved the design flaws of the original plan. The overwhelming monumentality of the kiosk was ameliorated by raising the level of the park and creating a more balanced sense of scale and proportion. By reducing the amount of seating and number of benches, the plaza became more of a ceremonial center than a residential park. And Parque Central became a celebration of the city, a place for presidents to speak after mass, and with the addition of paving, a *paseo* (walkway) rather than a park.

The new design included an art gallery for national artists to exhibit in the space below the kiosk where the children's library used to be, twenty-four telephone booths along the eastern edge of the park, and a municipal police station to protect the public from escalating juvenile crime. Mr. Sancho reported that at first the public was dismayed that the library was removed, but later appreciated that children's books could now be found in their neighborhood libraries. The shoeshine men and flower stalls were moved to an area in front of the post office, a few blocks away.

Blanca Suñol, an architect with the municipality, developed new regulations and design guidelines for Parque Central to keep it cleaner and safer. When it was reopened, these rules went into effect: Ambulatory vendors would no longer be allowed; all subsequent construction would be restricted to the height of the original buildings (seven meters); and bus stops were replaced by taxi stands. She also identified other changes that contributed to a reduction of crime in the area: The Soda Palace, a center for black-market money changing and other illegal activities, had been separated from the street by a high wall and windows to protect the café's clients; the new users of the park, Nicaraguans, were very poor and therefore did not attract criminals looking for wealthy tourists; and the park's renovation increased visual surveillance because of the open design.

The design objective of Mr. Sancho and Ms. Suñol was to reclaim the public space by displacing the juvenile delinquents and criminals, replacing them with other people, "regular people," who want to be there. Moving the vendors and adding the police would help to keep it cleaner and safer, while height restrictions and extensive paving have changed the character of the park.

Aída de Fishman, the Minister of Culture who commissioned the renovation and reopened Parque Central on March 19, 1994, expressed her design objectives in other terms:

> Parque Central is a great big headache. It is the heart of the city,
> but has been eaten away at the edges. The wooden kiosk, the

fountain, and the fence are gone, and we were left with this great albatross of cement. We wanted to turn it back into a park that could welcome the large masses of people who would come. So we made it into a *plazolita* [little plaza] with a replica of the fountain, because we could not move the original, and retained the Nicaraguan kiosk. I feel satisfied that we have conserved this place and rescued a bit of the city center.

She commented on the conflict over whether to keep the kiosk by explaining that they spent months discussing what the park should be. In the end, the local government took the side of preserving the kiosk, and in order to do so, declared it a part of the national patrimony. She added: "Who is to say what will be considered beautiful in the future? I did not want to be responsible for discarding the past."

Local Josefinos are well informed about the renovation and reopening of Parque Central. I asked a taxi driver what he knew about the renovation of the park, and he replied that Aída de Fishman had renovated all of the parks:

Not only did she beautify the park, which is good, but she restored a place for people to reflect and think. People are sometimes in the city and need to stop to think and reflect. She has created an environment where one can do this. It is important to have such places in the city.

But not everyone agrees that the new design is attractive or that crime has been reduced. Many local users read the artistic intentions of the redesign as a means for excluding them from what they perceived as their place. Older users, such as the three pensioners who moved away from the traffic in 1987, are discouraged and do not understand why the municipality removed the trees, grass, and greenery they loved. I asked one of the men what he thought of the changes. He replied that he liked more green. All the men sitting there agreed that there was too much cement and disagreed among themselves as to whether the absence of vendors made it any cleaner.

"Do you feel safer?" I inquired. One man replied that there may be fewer illegal activities because it is more open, but added:

You still must be careful because of the gangs [*chapulines*]. They are everywhere, and gather here each evening at 5:00 P.M. The open vistas of the new park do not accommodate some illegal transactions that have now moved inside the Soda Palace, but it is even easier for the pickpockets and juvenile gangs to assault tourists and wealthy citizens.

A young man who has been coming to sit and reflect for more than eight years responded to my question of whether he liked the new design by saying: "No, it is too modern. I liked it the old way, green and more 'ancient.'" Another man overheard our conversation and added: "Because of the new design, it is harder to hide from the police, but even so, there is more prostitution than before." He went on to explain that it is because of all the Nicaraguans: "Costa Rica is not the same with all the foreigners."

Some of the regular users have actively resisted the mandated changes. I spoke to one of the older shoeshine men who was standing on the corner of the park (see Photograph 47). He was busily working on the black boots of a man who smiled hello. I asked him where everyone was. He replied: "Four of the older guys are in front of the post office and there are three more on the Boulevard. And there are some across the street next to the cathedral. They asked for permission to be there."

I asked him how he could continue to work there. He smiled and said, "I have special permission from the municipality." He laughed and so did his client. He added: "I have taken my story to the public." The client then commented: "He is famous, he was on Teletica, Channel 7 television, protesting that this was his workplace."

The design objectives of the municipality have created a new kind of public space, one that excludes many of the traditional users because of the regulations that restrict commercial activities and the lack of shady, comfortable places to sit. The new design with its open vistas certainly looks safer and appears more modern and European with its reconstructed fountain, paved walkways, and promenades. Yet the artistic and symbolic goals of the designers have been only partially realized because of the changing social environment of San José: an increasing number of Nicaraguan refugees have made the park a place to meet family and friends, and gangs of teenagers find it an excellent hangout, close to the Soda Palace where stolen goods and credit cards can be sold or traded, and close to the downtown stores where Costa Rican shoppers and tourists with money can be found.

The artistic expression of the redesign of Parque Central masks the

47. Remaining shoeshine man in Parque Central, 1997

producers' desire to "clean up" (implying clean up socially as well as physically) this central public space by removing the architectural affordances—activity-enabling furnishings such as the arbor, the trees, and the benches—that previously invited older pensioners to spend the day. The cleanup also included restricting commercial activities to other areas of the city, removing the vendors and shoeshine men who had worked there for more than forty years. With these restrictive regulations, new forms of crime and criminals have appropriated the space and taken over the local ecology. It is ironic, to say the least, that the removal of the vendors and shoeshine men, which was intended to increase safety, may in fact have decreased it because of the loss of the local surveillance and sociability they provided. William Whyte (1980), the small public spaces guru, argues for the addition of food vendors and well-placed benches to increase public security in plazas and parks. The example of the redesign of Parque Central does not contradict his findings, even in this Latin American setting.

The conflict over the redesign of Parque Central was just the beginning of an attempt to commodify this site. Parque Central had not been the social or cultural center of the city since the early 1950s, and in 1976, the government responded by building the Plaza de la Cultura to represent the new interests and political affiliations of the Costa Rican state. Tourism, not coffee, was now driving the Costa Rican economy, and the Plaza de la Cultura was designed to reflect the state's corresponding cultural as well as social aspirations: an indigenous archaeological heritage, a history of public education, and a national program for the arts. But the Plaza de la Cultura failed to fulfill these dreams and instead became a tourist shopping center and a hangout for teenagers and North American pensioners.

With the failure of the Plaza de la Cultura, and continuing complaints from tourists and middle-class Josefinos about the run-down state of Parque Central, the municipality turned back to the problem of the redesign of the oldest and most illustrious central plaza. By 1993 many of the parks and plazas in San José had been renovated. Aída de Fishman's tenure as Minister of Culture coincided with the tenure of her husband, Luis Fishman, as Minister of Public Security, and the two of them working together were able to accomplish an extensive overhaul of downtown public areas.

Mrs. Fishman's objective was to rescue San José based on the lessons of other large cities, and she selected the worse part of downtown to begin her project. Her plan included changing municipal laws to make landlords responsible for their buildings and the sidewalks in front of their properties. She cleaned the city, moved the street vendors, and, beginning with streets that connected the public spaces, created walkways and promenades that linked the various plazas.

Rudolfo Sancho reports that businessmen claim their sales have doubled in areas near the renovations and that this increase in business has provided even more money to continue their work. Even the land surrounding Parque Central is valued at almost twice its prerenovation price. The municipality now has a plan to expand and reclaim parks throughout the city based on the evidence that doing so will attract business and people as well as increase land and housing prices. Currently 50–60 percent of the funds used to renovate parks and plazas come from private sources—from business organizations, industry groups, and business districts interested in improving their facades and streetscapes—and the municipality now contributes a larger percent of tax revenues to the maintenance budget. According to Mr. Sancho in 1997: "It is much easier to get money than three years ago because of the success of Parque Central and Parque Morazán."

The response of the general public and users to these changes has been mixed at best. On July 22, 1991, before the park renovations had been approved, there was a violent protest by street vendors who had been removed from the sidewalk in front of the Municipal Building at Eighth Street and Second Avenue, a block from Parque Central. Eight people were injured and forty-three were detained. This protest was the first in a series of confrontations between the vendors and the municipal officials who were trying to clear the sidewalk for pedestrians and shoppers. Businesses surrounding Parque Central (and Plaza de la Cultura) were complaining that street vendors were blocking their entrances and unfairly competing by selling lower-priced goods.

This same conflict has also erupted in other cities; for instance, there is an ongoing legal battle between the Times Square and 42nd Street Business Improvement District (BID) and an organization of sidewalk vendors who held an open-air market on Fridays in front of Bryant Park in New York City. The struggle is over whether the vendors can continue to hold their market after the renovations and private reorganization of Bryant Park are completed. The vendors and the shoeshine men removed from Parque Central also protested, and, as in the case of the shoeshine man mentioned above, took their case to the public through television and newspaper interviews.

Individual users also responded negatively to the "cleanup" aspect of Mrs. Fishman's campaign. An older man gave me a typical answer to my question of what he thought of the new park:

> It is fine, but the trees are missing and there is no place to sit. There are no cultural activities, and no permanent program for these activities. The band no longer plays here, and even though there is an art gallery there are not enough exhibits. The gallery is usually closed, and the art that they show is too elitist for most people.

He went on to say that there is not as much religious activity now, and that all the protesters, sinners, and community activists are no longer here. He added: "This is what is missing."

Another part of the cleanup is reflected in the observation that many of the Costa Rican pensioners have moved to the Boulevard, an area a few blocks north of Parque Central where trees and benches have been added. They say that they miss the arbor with the drunks and evangelists, the music in the kiosk, and the dances where even those without money could go to celebrate the New Year. "It is important to have a place to see your friends and family who you would otherwise not see," one man added, and went on to say that it is sad that this no longer occurs in Parque Central. They say that they no longer feel comfortable there and have moved their socializing away from the ceremonial center of the city. There are some groups who still meet in the park: young Nicaraguan domestic workers gather on Sunday to visit with family and friends, and juvenile gangs gather in the late afternoon, but the traditional users—regulars, pensioners, vendors, and workers—no longer feel at home and are certainly no longer accommodated there.

Thus, some users are subliminally aware of the increasing commodification of their public spaces and remember with growing nostalgia when plazas were places for people to meet. The meeting place of the past has become the marketplace of the future, where the goods that are exchanged are representations of the nation and city, and the creation of public space has become part of the imagineering of a city.

Plaza de la Cultura: Art Space or Tourist Market?

As discussed in Chapters 3 and 6, the idea to build the Plaza de la Cultura is said to have been the inspiration of the Minister of Culture, Guido Sáenz, in 1976. The head of the Central Bank of Costa Rica had gotten the national Legislative Assembly to allocate the funds to build a museum to display their world-famous collection of Precolumbian gold artifacts that were housed on the second floor of the Central Bank. The museum would represent pride in indigenous Costa Rican culture and was supported by the National Liberation Party. The land around the National Theater was selected by the Minister of Planning, Oscar Arias, and the head of the Central Bank as the site that would easily accommodate tourists and would represent a new center of culture in San José.

The outcome was a modern space that most Costa Ricans did not understand or like. The Central Bank's goal was described thus in the plaza's inaugural brochure:

> This Plaza de la Cultura that we inaugurate today unites the forces of Costa Ricans interested in humanizing the city, embellishing it, preserving the National Theater, and giving it the space required. To work on culture is a tradition of the Costa Rican people. . . . Economy and culture are closely bound, and

their union is represented in this plaza that will become the center of our city (Naranjo Coto 1976, 1; my translation).

The architects' design objectives were more diverse but focused on creating a space "like they have in New York": a large open space where meetings can be held and demonstrations can occur. Ironically, the open plazas of New York City are often underutilized and become filled with illegal activities that drive other kinds of users away. This Costa Rican open-plan plaza has, in fact, attracted illegal activities and vendors, as well as teenage soccer games, tourist shopping, and various kinds of sexual cruising. The attempt to bring culture to the center of the city through the artistic expression of landscape architecture has not produced anything near an ideal representation of civic space. And as of my last visit in January 1997, the plaza was closed and fenced off awaiting the completion of a technical renovation.

In terms of the commodification of public space, the Plaza de la Cultura is an even clearer example of the kind of imagineering that is taking place and illustrates the role of landscape design in the creative destruction of forms of society (Rutheiser 1996; Sorkin 1989). A residential, small-scale commercial neighborhood was transformed into an advertisement for Costa Rican culture. At the same time, this transformation generated new investment opportunities for foreign capitalists to expand their interests in tourism and tourist-related activities. The disguise for this commodification of a public space was the sociopolitical ideology of the National Liberation Party. The leadership of the new professional class wanted to represent Costa Rican culture as modern, drawing upon modern European idioms of design, but also as indigenous, based on the Precolumbian past. North American capital influenced the siting of the plaza next to the major tourist hotel and in the center of North American businesses (i.e., McDonald's, Sears) and tourist activity. Thus, the siting, spatial form, and ultimately the design of the Plaza de la Cultura came from a combination of ideological and economic forces rather than solely from the artistic intent of the designers.

The most intense representation of the commodification of the Plaza de la Cultura is its takeover by foreign vendors. The plaza was opened in 1982, and during my first three field trips in 1985, 1986, and 1987, the only vendors on the plaza were part of a tourist market jointly approved by the municipality and the Gran Hotel located on the small plaza in front of the National Theater. These vendors paid for permission to sell on the plaza at the price of 50 colones per day (see Photograph 48).

By 1991, however, the plaza was jammed with sidewalk vendors. On February 24, 1991, Juan Fernando Cordero of *La Nación* wrote a feature article on the surprises of the Plaza de la Cultura, pointing out that vendors speak English, cash travelers' checks, accept international credit cards, and bank in dollars. He further comments that no one would have thought that the plaza would become 5,000 square meters of commerce and spectacle, rather than a place of rest and escape from work. By October 18, 1992, the "plaza of surprises" was described as the "plaza of chaos." The editorial points out that the plaza represents such an enormous investment financially and politically that the vendors, criminals, drug dealers, and undocumented workers should not be allowed to appropriate the space.

By November 3, 1992, the vendors were forced to leave by the joint efforts of the municipality and the Minister of Public Security, Luis Fishman. They dislodged the vendors by immediately expelling those who did not have proper papers and by allowing those who were members of the National Independent Artisans Association (ANAI) to remain until they could find a place to relocate. The president of the ANAI,

48. Foreign vendors on Plaza de la Cultura

Marco Vinicio Balmaceda, protested that these expulsions would leave five hundred families homeless. Luis Fishman, however, stated that the majority of the illegal vendors came from two South American countries, implying that they were not Costa Rica's responsibility and should return to their native countries. Only a few vendors remained, and those had permission from the municipality to do so. But when I returned to San José in 1993, the plaza was again packed with vendors. It seems that the ANAI had succeeded in getting an injunction for associated vendors to remain on the plaza until the issue was adjudicated.

The story ends with the Central Bank's proposal to put a fence around the entire plaza, with gates that would be closed in the evening. On January 18, 1995, there was an open meeting to discuss issues of security on the Plaza de la Cultura. Representatives of the National Theater, the foundation that administers the plaza, the Colegio de Arquitectos, and the International Council of Monuments and Sites (ICOMOS), an international historic preservation organization, were available to present their proposals to the public. The fence was proposed as only one possible solution to the daily invasion of hundreds of vendors and delinquents who vandalize the place. Vanessa Bravo of *La Nación,* however, reports in her January 19, 1995, feature article that there was opposition to fencing the plaza, and that other solutions would be found to improve security. By 1996, the Plaza de la Cultura was closed for renovations, and it had not reopened by January of 1997 when I was last there. I am sure that its lengthy closing, its refurbishing, and increased policing upon reopening are the result of this local conflict. Commodification in this case is commercialization, that is, the transformation of an art space and meeting place into an open marketplace—and back again, if the current renovation and closure are successful.

Conclusion

Returning to the analysis of public space as a site of protest, it is possible to illustrate all three outcomes through the examples of Parque Central and Plaza de la Cultura. When manifest protest by demonstration threatens the state, public space is closed—sometimes gated—and policed, as exemplified by the attempt to fence in the Plaza de la Cultura. Even though the plaza administrators decided not to fence the open plaza in 1995, I would anticipate that some part of the plaza, perhaps near the National Theater and Gran Hotel, will ultimately be fenced and gated, as well as policed, to protect the middle-class residents and tourists.

49. Remodeled Parque Morazán

In Parque Central, when manifest spatial appropriation by socially marginal groups was successful, the park was briefly closed down and redesigned in such a way as to discourage its continued use by "undesirables." And many of the conflicts in Parque Central and Plaza de la Cultura illustrate how latent protest by means of symbolic representation transforms the public space into a contested arena. Thus, culturally significant public spaces are forums for working out political, economic, and social conflicts that can not be resolved by more direct verbal means and, as such, provide rich material for ethnographic analysis and cultural interpretation.

The renovation of Parque Central is only one of a series of park restorations that took place between 1990 and 1997. According to Rudolfo Sancho, the renovation of Parque Morazán in front of the Holiday Inn changed the way the municipal government thought about the politics of public space—even though the Holiday Inn did not participate because its administrators wanted a parking lot, not a park (see Photograph 49). The response from the public was tremendous and generated money to renovate La Merced in front of Hospital San Juan de Dios as well as Parque Central and the neighboring park, Plaza Víquez. The money for these renovations came from the municipal government, from industry and business contributions, and from Venezuela. Public monies previously had been spent on public spaces in the suburbs; now they were being invested in the city. And according to Mr. Sancho, users have expressed their satisfaction with the renovations by respecting the new plantings and by writing letters to the newspapers about how pleased they are with the changes.

Presidents are also learning to use public space to document their achievements and concretize their contributions through the medium of plaza design. President Daniel Oduber initiated building the Plaza de la Cultura, while President Rodrigo Carazo took the credit for its opening in 1982. President Oscar Arias created the Plaza de la Democracia in front of the National Museum to fulfill a promise made during his political campaign (see Photograph 50). And President Rafael Calderón claimed responsibility for the renovation of Parque Central. These new

50. Plaza de la Democracia, 1997

51. Oscar Arias

plazas and plaza renovations were presented as gifts to the capital city to enhance citizens' enjoyment of everyday life. They were designed specifically to bring culture and art (Plaza de la Cultura) as well as democracy (Plaza de la Democracia) and social equality (La Merced, Parque Central) to the central city, and to represent these ideals in the urban landscape.

But these public plazas also communicate the political objectives of their sponsors. Plaza de la Cultura represents the political aspirations of a maturing professional elite that incorporated foreign capital investment and tourism as the basis for a healthy economy. Plaza de la Democracia underscores President Oscar Arias's political investment in the Central American peace process, for which he received the Nobel Peace prize and international acclaim (see Photograph 51). And the renovation of Parque Central responds to President Rafael Calderón's neoliberal mandate to clean up San José in order to become a world-class tourist city that enhances rather than detracts from Costa Rica's image as an ecotourist mecca.

Thus, plazas are politically motivated artistic expressions designed to represent the donors' and contributors' objectives and social ideals. At the same time, they are commodities given in exchange for political or economic power and support. This exchange is intended to reinforce middle-class values as part of an unstated, ongoing "bargain" between urban citizens and the state, even if these values exclude many traditional public-space users. If the plazas do not conform to these political objectives, or are not valuable as political currency, then, as I have documented, they are redesigned or public access is threatened.

This story is not unique to the plazas of San José, Costa Rica; examples such as the plaza in Taos, New Mexico (Rodríguez 1998), or Santa Fe, New Mexico (Wilson 1997), and Tompkins Square in New York City (N. Smith 1996) demonstrate some of these same dynamics. And it is not surprising, given that public works have always been the domain of politics. What is significant, however, is that public spaces are important arenas for public discourse and expressions of discontent. If they are closed or redesigned in response to protest or spatial appropriation that does not fit within the narrow cultural guidelines of "modern," "middle-class" or "appropriate" behavior, then where will this protest be located? Further, what are the consequences of erasing from public space its disorder and disorderly populations? Is this erasure and re-design of spatial form an additional kind of "historical amnesia" (Wilson 1997, 313) that accompanies the myth making of tourist and historic-preservation forces? Central public spaces of most cities are becoming increasingly homogenized, middle-class, and state-controlled representations because of similar amnesiac and sociopolitical forces.

PART FOUR   Conversations

Parts II and III have presented historical and ethnographic perspectives on the Spanish American plaza based on archival research and participant observation. These understandings, however, no matter how well worked out and substantiated, are shaped by the ever present voice of the ethnographer and author. In the Introduction, I commented on how important multivocality and multilocality are in any portrayal of culture, yet the textual medium of an ethnography or scientific monograph constrains the author's ability to represent this diversity of voices and experience of places. Individuals besides the ethnographer experience parks and plazas as specific places that have particular meaning and resonance for them, but in this text, the individuals experiencing the plaza are largely silent.

In an effort to provide greater multivocality and breadth and a more unmediated experience of being in the plaza than is possible in an ethnography, I include narratives other than social science and historical analyses in my portrayal of plaza life. Part IV, Conversations, is made up of literary and personal accounts of Parque Central, Plaza de la Cultura, and other Costa Rican plazas, as well as conversations with informants about their plaza experiences. Chapter 9 consists of Costa Rican literary accounts that describe or place a conversation in a park or plaza. Chapter 10 is composed of transcribed and translated conversations with individuals who lived next to Parque Central or who were regular users of the park. Chapter 11 is a conclusion presented as a conversation with the reader about the significance of the Latin American plaza as a site of democratic politics and urban civility.

CHAPTER 9

The Park and the Plaza
in Costa Rican Literature

Imagined Places

Introduction

Parks and plazas have been imagined, remembered, and represented in a variety of Costa Rican literary narratives, including autobiographical memoirs, short stories, novels, and poetry. Some of these literary descriptions provide a glimpse of what it was like to be in the plaza around the turn of the century, while other depictions evoke the precise character, language, and habits of contemporary scenes and inhabitants. A few of the selections present politically manipulated and idealistic portrayals; other authors create a more realistic, hence complex, vision of everyday plaza life.

Not surprisingly, the literary examples reiterate some of the same themes of the ethnographic and historical analyses: nostalgia for a past in which Parque Central played an important role in everyday life; Parque Central as the appropriate setting for all civic celebrations and social interaction; and Plaza de la Cultura as well as Parque Central as places of romance, politics, crime, and deception. Although some authors offer a more realistic, and others a more impressionistic, representation, all of the narratives explore how Costa Rican authors have imagined these important public spaces across time. They offer the reader a variety of Costa Rican perspectives on how it looks, smells, sounds, and feels to be in the plaza that can be juxtaposed with the ethnographic descriptions.

In a way, the authors are also ethnographers who are trying to capture the culture of the plaza in their narratives, but they use their imagination and memory to create their stories, filling in gaps that the ethnographies can not always fill. The literary narratives present a clearly located point of view identified by life history of the author, literary period, and genre. In these narratives, the plazas and parks become emblematic of the specific ambiance, time, and place as they were imagined rather than observed. And I find that in some of these narratives the descriptions appear more compelling than the fragments of ethnographic field notes I present because the "sense of place" is intentionally and completely constructed.

Alan Pred takes as a point of departure that "people produce history and places at the same time that people are produced by history and places" (1984, 251). This process of structuration is illustrated in the time-space geographies presented in Chapter 7, but this same statement holds true for literary accounts and conversations. People, in this case authors, are producing the history and place of the plaza by writing about it. Literary narratives are relatively effective in producing places and history because "imagined places" become "real" each time the author's description is added to a reader's own social construction of the place. Thus, fictional accounts have an impact on the social construction of the material world. These imagined places influence the meanings of the parks and places by enhancing the reader's own imagination and perceptions in the same way that I hope your view of the plaza will be embellished as you read these accounts.

In this chapter, then, I present a series of literary narratives that have had material consequences in their social construction and interpretation of the Costa Rican plaza. In Chapter 10, I then reverse this analysis by illustrating, through interviews with Costa Ricans whose lives were influenced by growing up near Parque Central, how people are produced by history and places.

Memoirs

The first literary narratives I encountered when searching for references to parks and plazas were autobiographical memoirs that described Costa Rica during the early part of the century. Mario Sancho, a writer best known for his critical treatise on Costa Rican norms and customs, *Costa Rica: Suiza centroamericana* (Costa Rica: The Central American Switzerland), published in 1935, writes about Cartago's Parque Central with irony and barbed humor. His description depicts Parque Central as a center of social activity: a combination adventure playground, social club, and commercial center.

Mario Sancho's memories of the plaza are based on his experiences growing up in Cartago, the original capital of Costa Rica. During Costa Rica's struggle for independence, Cartago became identified with conservative monarchist forces and the city's own Spanish colonial beginnings, an image that contributed to the capital being transferred to San José, a city identified with the new republicanism. Don Mario's memoirs reflect his nostalgia for the plaza of the past—an unpaved and unstructured open space—as a place where he could play with his friends in the center of town. This theme of the plaza as a playground is also fondly remembered in the conversations, presented in Chapter 10, with San José residents who lived near Parque Central.

CARTAGO MEMORIES

When I was boy, there was no other carriage in Cartago except for the one that belonged to Juan de Dios Troyo, since the one that Doña Juana Jiménez de García used to go to her small piece of land in the countryside had been parked in the yard of the house for a long time without offering any service other than the ones we discovered in our childhood games. Of course, carts [decorated carts from the countryside] would arrive in the city, but these did not run, they only walked at the processional pace of the oxen [that pulled them].

In the middle of town was the plaza, planted with trees, where, before my time, festivals were held on Thursdays and Sundays, or so our grandfathers used to say. To the north loomed the Town Hall—which in my time was called the Municipal Palace—and to the east was the structure designated for the parish church that, after the earthquake of 1910, was converted into ruins, without ever having been finished or having fulfilled the religious purpose for which it was being built. If it were not for that catastrophe, this immense mound of stone could have been an honorable cathedral. But instead fate condemned it to be a perennial symbol of a failed time.

Ever since I can remember the town had a building for a food market, and it is lucky that I can remember the plaza before it was converted into a park, even though not as urbanized as it is now. It already had the gates and flower beds, but it still had a dirt floor and the fig trees that my grandfather Don Carlos Sancho Alvarado planted and in whose branches lived many sloths.

Since then, the park has changed a lot. First the sloths disappeared, victims of a press campaign that called attention to the mishap that they might bring on the unsuspecting stroller or sedentary dreamer; then the corpulent fig trees fell under the ax because it was said that their roots broke up the sidewalk; later the fountain was taken away and a kiosk was put in its place, illuminated first by gas lamps that came from the beer factory of José Traube. In the coming years, the government decided to pave the streets, and finally the gates, a present from President Rodríguez, were removed.

I did not go to the park much as a child, because the sign "No climbing in flower beds," in combination with the alert vigilance of the policemen, made me lose my desire to run and jump around. Only on an occasional afternoon during the *recreo* [recreation or recess, that is, the period of time each afternoon when the band would play] would I sit to hear the musical band, directed by Rosendo Freer, perform selections from Rigoleto and Traviata. More often I would prefer going with my friends to play tag around the walls of the parish church, which were then quite low and abandoned, and that's how they stayed for a long time until my uncle Francisco Jiménez decided to continue the construction and, through stubbornness and force of will, succeeded in seeing the walls raised so high that by the date of the earthquake they were almost to the height required to place the roof. We, the little ones of Cartago, ran over the walls of the parish church, jumping over the enormous holes that were supposed to be windows with our dangerous leaps. The reason why dozens of boys did not break their bones must be attributed to the miracle of one of the saints, probably Santiago, the patron saint of the primitive church of Cartago.

At the same time when games like baseball and football began to get organized—games that were imported to Cartago by Carlos Peralta and some other guys arrived from the United States—young men started to hang around the church plaza. Some afternoons we would play, and other days we would just hang around.   —SANCHO [1935] 1984, 516–517

Novels

The contemporary Costa Rican novel has its roots in regionalism, *costumbrismo,* realism, and modernist literary movements. The two selections included here, however, draw upon what has been called the "new Central American narrative" (Ramírez 1973), prose that reveals a struggle to go beyond regionalism and realism to incorporate broader political and transnational issues as well as urban realities and settings. These novels employ parks and plazas to locate new conceptions of civic society. The authors' depictions of these public spaces can be as traditional as Fernando Durán's satirization of the political and philosophical undercurrents of Costa Rican everyday life in Parque Central in Alajuela or as atmospheric as the park sketches of Gerardo César Hurtado.

Gerardo César Hurtado established himself as an experimental writer early in his career, upon graduating from the University of Costa Rica. He has been active in developing a number of literary magazines and wrote a column in the university weekly for many years. At this writing, he teaches literature and writing at the University of Costa Rica.

I visited him at his home in Barrio Luján in San José, where I was warmly greeted by his wife and daughters and treated to coffee and snacks. We discussed the difficulty of translating this section of *Los parques* without the context of the novel's story and intent. But I had been struck by the veracity of his descriptions of Parque Central, Parque Morazán, Parque de la Merced, Parque Nacional, and Parque España, which encapsulated the essence of each as I experienced them from 1972 through 1974. These parks are located throughout the central section of the city; each has its own distinct ambience and clientele that Hurtado weaves into the fabric of his novel about two lovers. The parks, however, are only temporary settings; Hurtado moves the reader back and forth through time and space by juxtaposing dialogue with place, and place with memory.

THE PARKS

Central

Ahead, the solid building of the cathedral; trees, public announcements. Somebody screams, someone is called, the name becomes lost in the odor of burnt gasoline. Buses, pedestrians; women holding children's hands, at the center the kiosk with its granite arches; palm trees, some empty benches, others with men reading newspapers, women and children; prostitutes, if it is six in the evening. Faces, faces lost in the great shadows of gray among the smoky light of the sunset. Lorena walks at a slow pace; crosses the street to reach the north side. She takes the bus that goes to San Pedro. She looks at no one.

"What did you think?"

"Me, nothing, Lorena . . . Only that it was over."

"Don't you miss her, Tino?"

"No, it is the way it had to be. One never knows what you have until destiny demands it of you. I felt I had no freedom."

La Merced

It is the same hour. Blind people, street vendors. Vagabonds, children playing around a giant stone ball [Precolumbian artifact] that sits on a grassy hill. The sun illuminates the trees that filter its rays, playing with the shadows hiding faces. A dusting of powder covers the branches of the bushes. Garbage is scattered about. A woman standing alongside the statue waits for someone. Far away, people walk hurriedly by, heading to San Juan de Dios Hospital. A filthy smell reaches even the impenetrable faces of visitors. One of them takes pictures with a Kodak camera; he steps back to take a better picture, verifies the visual quality, and shoots with a "click." Juan Rodrigo hears it while walking slowly, pensively, his face in a worried expression. The sound of a siren is heard. A song, soon forgotten in the yellowish space of the park.

"Who is Juan Rodrigo?"

"I didn't know, Sebastian."

"Wait, Tino, when did you know?"

"The day that Teresa mentioned it. She described it to me in great detail. One time I saw him; he was driving a white Volkswagen. I saw him from behind. He was just as I imagined him to be."

"Did you know what you were doing?"

"Of course I did, Sebastian. It tormented me for many a night."

Morazán

Tall buildings surround the vegetation, the flower beds well taken care of. A policeman strolls by looking at his watch (3:45 in the afternoon); he wants to smoke but he is on duty and dares not do it. The landscape is quiet and silent. Not a single child. Suddenly, from the school on the north side, a group of screaming children burst forth. They go directly to the playground where they jump, go up the slide, giggle about nothing, bang together the iron chains of the swings. A nanny comes with a baby carriage. A dove begins to fly behind the entanglement of fuchsias. Another boy comes from the enclosure and runs into the Japanese garden, jumps around, and as he starts running again, he trips, and his hands dip into the water that surges from a hidden fountain. The swans look at him curiously as they stride elegantly by. A turtle also notices him. Across the way the noise grows into an uproar. Sebastian walks briskly through the park, not looking in any direction. He walks deep in thought and suddenly disappears from sight.

"Did you ever tell what happened to you in the jungle of Limón?"

"Never. A snake bit me and I almost died."

"Do you remember Tino?"

"Yes. I have not seen him again."

"How long has it been since you last saw him?"

"A month, I think. He is still with that woman."

"With Teresa?"

"Yes. She is his downfall."

"I don't know, maybe she wants to redeem him. But I think she lacks the courage."

"You don't think so? Cowardice is a woman's weapon."

"Poor Tino."

National

Statues with golden edges: sunlight everywhere. Dust, fallen leaves on the ground, students stroll by unperturbed, some talking among themselves. Looming from the north side is the National Library, its clean windows and its stately presence. The smell of paint. The smell of fresh-cut grass. The scent of a woman. A noise stands out among the clamor coming from the west side of the park. Silence, the statues sleep. The stone benches are wet from the recent shower, but now the sun erases the water stains, its rays reflected in the puddles. The sky is clear, in spite of some dark clouds in the distance. A supersonic plane flies by at incredible speed over the Monument to the Heroes. A bird unleashes its excrement over the bronze heads. Teresa lingers in the middle of the park. Somewhere there is a forgotten memory, perhaps she dreamt that once upon a time she came to sit and wait for Tino, but he did not come. She took it for what it was, a lie; he had gone for a walk with Ileana, a very sweet and sexy little friend. Teresa sits down. The afternoon quiet, there is no breeze. A man stares at her insistently, he looks at her beauty, later strolls away, as if he had never seen her.

"Who is Tino, Teresa?"

"I do not know, Roxana, I don't know. I don't want to talk about it. It was nothing important."

"Is that how you classify it? All your friends, we already know about it. You had a lover who was younger than you."

"Do you care?"

"Very much, Teresa, because I would have loved to have one too, just like Tino."

"How much do you know about him?"

"He talked to me the other day. He took me by surprise; he is very sweet. I started asking him little by little if he knew you, if you were old friends, and he said yes, yes, and as if your husband didn't exist, he told me, I like her, she must be good at love making, it's wonderful just to see her."

España

The park has a monument dedicated to Spain, hidden somewhere, in some corner. Nobody notices it. In front of it a new building under construction. The poppies, begonias, and lilies abound everywhere. Everything well cared for. There is bamboo on the south side. To the west, the same children's park adjacent to the Morazán. Couples come together in any corner, and the sunlight always reaches them, a light that firms them up, lazy light, outlining the lawn. The sound of crickets hidden in the thicket. This is where they would meet, in the beginning, Teresa and Tino, they would talk among whizzing bees, among inopportune visitors and some abandoned dog for whom they would invent a name.

"Is this the place that you were telling me about, Tino?"

"Yes, Teresa, it is a motel. The employees say there is no water or lights. But now that we're here . . ."

"It is the first time, Tino, the first time; this means a lot to me."

"For me too (laughing)."

"We are going so we can talk, O.K. ?"

"Yes, Teresa, just to talk."   —HURTADO 1975, III–II5

Fernando Durán Ayanegui was the rector of the University of Costa Rica during my 1985–1986 field trip to Costa Rica. I was in the University bookstore looking for works on parks and plazas when he walked by and told me about his humorous novel on everyday life and conversations in Alajuela's Parque Central. Alajuela is the second-largest city in Costa Rica, just a short ride from San José, and it is a place where Costa Rican traditions and institutions appear relatively unchanged. According to Fernando Durán, each park regular has a designated seat on a stone bench and participates in a dense community of gossip and information exchange. The social life of park users as re-created in Fernando Durán's novel *Mi pequeño bazar* is not unlike the daily conversations, intrigues, disputes, and humorous repartee of the pensioners and older men that I found in Parque Central in San José.

MANGO UNIVERSITY

We don't understand why Alajuela is trying for a university because underneath the shade of the mango trees, in Parque Central, there is one. Of course, each mention of that forum brings an incredulous smile to the faces of our interlocutors, but to that we can only answer that it is not a myth. Parque Central, more so than any newspaper, magazine, school, or university, is the most consistent resource—formative as well informative—in all of Costa Rica. There, in the most simple, direct way, through concise and efficient witticisms and joking, you are aware of all the information and hear all the commentaries; there, every day, fresh blood circulates through the only authentic national philosophical vein and, in fact, had it not been for the harshly intellectual flow that emerges with bitter potency from the Alajuelan stone benches, Costa Rica would have emerged since 1832 as a well-governed country. And "well governed," Latin America style, is something that you all know about.

In order to furnish proof that the motor of Costa Rica runs on mango juice, we sent an informant into Alajuela's Parque Central on Friday, June 23, with instructions to collect, in a couple of hours, the intellectual product of the block that, in Costa Rica, contains more grams of gray matter per square meter than anywhere else. Here is the report:

In the almost innocent world of sports, as far as soccer goes, it was said that Alajuela would never be on the play-off charts unless the charts were done alphabetically; even if that were to happen, Abangares would end up at the finals. The wise men at the park have discovered, from watching the Argentine World Cup, that the Alajuela Sports League only needs an extreme left, an extreme right, nine players, and the resignation of the president of the board of directors.

On the other hand, the city of mangoes has been baptized "Slouchy Socks City" because it has a loose garter.

And on a more complicated topic, the bench sitters commented that the idea of charging a dollar tax per kilo of merchandise exported by "El Coco" [name of the Costa Rican airport] was misunderstood; the promoters were referring to the island, not to the airport. That explains the rush Don Rodrigo Carazo was in to install customs in our overseas territory. Nevertheless, they say that the Colegio Universitario de Alajuela would have made it if there was a dollar tax for every goal that was kicked in.

Again on the subject of soccer, someone proposed that if the Holland team calls itself "the mechanical orange," the Alajuela team should be called "the air mango." Saprissa should then be called "the tight rope," and Limón should be "the breadfruit of petroleum," Puntarenas should be "the bionic mussel," and the University should be the "logometric fruit."

Under circumstances that our informant does not make clear, a city dweller told, in front of the Milan theater, the story of the "doctors of Baghdad" who informed the Caliph that the big thieves were invariably intelligent, this being the reason why the Caliph released the Vizier and replaced him with the most imbecile of Arabs.

Now openly political, the park academics commented that if Don Daniel Oduber [ex-president of Costa Rica] had coined the term "halt to corruption," Don Rodrigo Carazo [president of Costa Rica at the time of writing] should hurry to coin the phrase "halt to the operetta." One recommended that the Minister of Human Rights should be called "Foundation Evita Perón," and another, who speaks English, followed by saying that the Minister of Interior Affairs should be named after John Locke, to honor the British philosopher. One of the younger ones pointed out that the soap (Irish Spring) and the Carazo government have a great resemblance, and, when asked what he meant, he answered that both had streaks of green and white [the colors of Carazo's political party]. They renamed the Minister of Education "the triangle of exchanges," as suggested by a young teacher. The recent problems of the INA [National Institute of Apprenticeship] are attributed to the fact that Don Rodrigo Carazo, after watching an episode of *Simplemente Simplicia* [Simply Simplicity, a popular soap opera], was finally able to catch the Maggi soup commercial, "chicken, pure chicken." To add to all this, we already know that Don Rodrigo [Carazo] works from 6:00 in the morning to 12:00 at night because he wants to complete his government by 1980.

Continuing with the nicknaming chapter, which that day failed to shine, we found that a stranger who had just arrived, who was over six feet tall, was awarded the following nickname: "mother's love." Justification: there is nothing higher than a mother's love.

On the subject of television, it was unanimously decided that the television show *The Rest Are Left Over* is the worst program of all. It was said in a grave manner that "the rest are left over" are more than left over, and if the show were canceled, nobody would much care.

Finally, in an incomprehensible territory, someone pointed out that the slogan for the traffic inspectors should be "the one who slices and gives away [*parte* and *reparte*], retains the best piece." [*Parte* in Spanish means a traffic ticket, and the verb *repartir* also means to give away.]

As you can see, not bad for two hours of idle joking on a Friday afternoon. We assume that the affair has proceeded because, as of today, Monday, it was already decreed that the winner of the tournament was not Argentina: it was Perugina. This was offered by a Brazilian fanatic who could not forgive Peru. July 1, 1978. —DURÁN AYANEGUI 1989, 11–13

These conversations on the plaza are fictional creations that illuminate real experiences of everyday gossip and dialogue in public space. These places are imagined, yet they influence our perceptions of the material world. The romance of Hurtado's park and plaza scenes and the political commentaries of Durán resonate with my experiences and with the experiences of other Costa Ricans who spend their days passing through these places. Even those who only think about the plazas and parks are influenced by these descriptions because through the author's writing, the reader can imagine experiencing these conversations as if they had occurred in real life.

In addition to conversations that literally take place *on* the plaza, "conversations on the plaza" also refer to conversations *about* the plaza and can include an individual's personal memories, dreams, opinions, and prejudices. Chapter 10 captures some of the conversations I have had "on the plaza," referring to this second meaning of the phrase.

Conversations on the Plaza

Remembered Places

Introduction

This chapter presents personal accounts of what it was like to be in the plaza through the recollections of Costa Rican friends and colleagues. I distinguish my voice and the voices of my informants by presenting their unstructured, open-ended interviews as transcribed, translated dialogues that reflect the give-and-take of our social interaction. The conversations record warm, nostalgic, humorous remembrances of Parque Central and the role it played during the interviewees' childhoods and in their everyday lives. These memories provide a more nuanced understanding of being in the plaza, since the historical details take on new meaning in the context of individual lives.

In the previous chapter, I argue that people—such as authors—produce places and history through their imagination. In these interviews, however, we can see how history and places produce people: the historical period and the social, political, and physical setting of the plaza provided opportunities for children's games, to meet new people, and to learn about the social world outside the home. Certainly the influence goes in both directions, but in these memories, reconstructed from fragments of a person's past and present knowledge of the plaza, the impact of the place and time seems quite clear. One example is how World War II changed Marlene Castro's life when her father started taking her to the movies to see newsreels about the war. The movies brought new romance and mystery but also disrupted her earlier plaza routine.

There are five conversations: two with sisters who grew up next to the park, two with a couple who enjoyed the park during their adolescence, and one with a man who has used the park for over thirty years. An introduction to each conversation sets the stage and circumstances of each, but the transcriptions are meant to stand alone. These reminiscences resonate with the ethnographic and historical analyses previously presented, but they also add poetry and personality, as well as historical detail and personal documentation, to otherwise rather academic historical descriptions of plaza life.

Conversation One

An interview with Marlene Castro Odio in her garden
Marlene Castro grew up next to Parque Central—only a few steps from the southwest corner—and lived there from 1933 until she was married at the age of seventeen. I interviewed Marlene both in Spanish and in English, but without a tape recorder, I was forced to rely on taking notes. As I worked on the project, I became convinced that the interview should be in her words, not mine, so when I returned in 1997, I scheduled a long Sunday afternoon to tape-record her childhood memories.

M: What is it that I'm supposed to talk about . . .

S: What I really want are your experiences of growing up next to Parque Central, and I think it would be best if we could try to do it in order. Where were you born?

M: Right there in the house! I was born in the house. I was baptized in the house . . . and everything happened there . . . (she laughs).

S: Tell me where the house was . . .

M: It was ten or fifteen yards from the park . . . from the corner of the park.

S: And who did you live with there?

M: With my parents and Alfredo, my half brother.

S: What is your first memory of Parque Central?

M: Parque Central was part of my life. I mean, I grew up there. We didn't have any garden. This was a city home. We didn't have any place to play or run or get dirty, so I was taken to the park every single day. And the park was part of my home. It was like home to me. I never felt odd in the park.

S: Did you go alone?

M: No, never. I always went with someone, with a companion, an older person, of course. I didn't have brothers and sisters. I was an only child for eleven years. So, the only place where I could see children was the park.

S: Did you play with other children in the park?

M: Always. Children just like me, children who lived nearby and whose houses were fairly old buildings with no gardens. They also had to be taken there. We were sent to take the sun . . . I don't know . . . maybe it was healthy for us to go to the park. I never realized that.

S: Did you play games in the park?

M: Yes.

S: What kinds of games did you play?

M: I suppose hide-and-seek was the game.

S: Where would you hide in the park?

M: Behind the palm trees. They were huge . . . several of us could hide behind just one (laughs) . . . there were no shrubs.

S: Was there grass or just cement?

M: Well, grass and also dirt. And there were some evergreens, the kind of evergreen, *araucaria,* that sheds feathery leaves. We would gather these leaves and take them home.

S: Were there other people there?

M: It was always crowded. Of course, compared to now, it probably was very empty then, but I thought it was crowded, and there were always policemen and children with nannies and older men sitting on the benches whom we never talked to.

S: Why?

M: I don't think we were allowed to talk to strangers. There were poor children also. I remember barefoot children and the pool, *¿cómo se dice?* [how do you say?]

S: *¿La fuente?* [The fountain?]

M: *La fuente* was there. And it had red fish, big red fish; that was just wonderful. And the poor children would even get into the fountain. We didn't. I don't remember playing with the poor children. They came by themselves in little gangs, but they were very young. They were as young as we were . . .

S: How old do you think you are at this point?

M: Oh, before school probably, four or five. And I had a boy-friend . . .

s: *¡No!*

m: *Sí, por supuesto* [yes, of course], and I have pictures of him.

s: You had a boyfriend at four or five?

m: Yeah, maybe even younger than that.

s: Did you meet him in the park?

m: Yeah (laughs). He was the Minister of Tourism a few years ago. . . . He probably is my age or maybe a year younger, I don't know . . . He was fat and short and chubby.

s: And did you see him every day? Did you talk with him?

m: Of course. We played together. He was an only child . . . he was very shy.

s: And were you shy also?

m: I don't think I was shy at that age. I became shy much later. I was very intrepid . . . is that a word?

s: Yes, it is. Did you do any intrepid things in the plaza, though?

m: No.

s: No? There wasn't anything dangerous to do? Nothing to jump off of?

m: . . . No. The *kiosco* [kiosk] was very old . . .

s: Was it the wood *kiosco* [the Victorian kiosk]?

m: It was the wood *kiosco* . . . it had some steps. Have you seen the kiosk in Heredia [third-largest city in Costa Rica, near San José]?

s: Yes, I have.

m: It was very similar to that, maybe larger, with latticework on top . . .

s: Were you upset when they took down the kiosk?

m: I remember people being very upset, because they had to destroy 50 percent of the park to build this huge monument. It was a fascistic thing [the kiosk], like a railroad station or something. I don't think I was upset.

s: When you start going to school there must be some change. You don't go every day with your nanny anymore?

m: No . . . but I have to go through the park to go to school. So, I cross the park twice a day regularly. At seven in the morning. At eleven going back home. And by eleven there is a special program, and this is during the war. There is a special program about the war that is being transmitted via loudspeakers, so I could hear what was going on every time when I came back from school. And people would gather there to hear the news. And my father used to have this huge map where we would follow the war. The war was part of my childhood, very much so.

s: But Costa Rica wasn't part of the war.

m: Yes. We declared war . . .

s: You did? . . .

m: Second to . . . I think second to nobody . . . to . . . we declared war on Germany.

s: Did you have an army?

m: *Sí, seguro que sí* [Yes, of course we did]. I guess an army meant two hundred people, or I don't know. We never had parades or anything; declaring war didn't mean sending people to fight . . . it was a moral thing.

s: Did your father go with you to the park ever?

m: No, I don't think so. Although we went to the movies very often . . . to the Cine Palace.

s: When did you start going to the Cine Palace?

m: In school. Very early. And he would take me to see any movie. I had no censorship ever . . . neither for the movies nor for books. This is something I don't quite understand. I was allowed to read anything. I was allowed to read many things, books, medical books with naked people. That was fascinating . . . I would read forbidden books that I did not know were forbidden. I couldn't understand a thing, but I read them anyhow . . . and I kept lots of books under my mattress so that I could take them out at night and nobody would notice.

s: (laughs) I also read a lot. I read everything in my parents' library. They did not say I couldn't, and I didn't understand half of what I read, but I'd read it anyhow.

m: It probably was very boring. . . . Of course, there were many things I didn't appreciate, and many things I didn't understand, and maybe twenty years later I thought: "Oh, this is what it meant!"

s: Ahuh! (laughs)

M: (laughs)

S: Did you go to the movies just with your dad? Not with your mother?

M: *Sí.* We would have dinner and then he would say, okay, let's go and watch the news. That was what he wanted to see . . .

S: . . . during the week . . . Would this be . . . ?

M: . . . during the week . . . any day. So we would start whenever the siren came on, which meant we would still have two minutes to get to the movies. It was the way of calling people. It was like bells in churches. And by the time we got there, we could watch the newsreels and then we would stay; we wouldn't stay to watch the whole movie always. Only if we liked it. If I liked it very much, I would tell him to stay. And we had our seats. I mean, it was part of the everyday life, going to the movies, and by the time I was nine and my parents went to the United States . . . that was, when did Pearl Harbor happen? That was 1941?

S: *¿Sí?*

M: Okay. I didn't want to go because I was afraid of the war. They were going by boat and I was afraid of being sunk. So I stayed home with an aunt . . . she was my father's sister . . . she was a very strict woman. I had to wear slippers all the time because she didn't like noise. And of course I didn't like it. I was not very happy. And my older brother would take me to the movies every day. But he didn't take me to Cine Palace. He took me to Cine Moderno. Cine Moderno was a block from our house to the south. It was a very popular movie house. It showed different kinds of stuff, like Doc Savage [a character popular in books in the 1940s and 1950s] and things like that. . . . It was a whole different experience. And I put up with it because I wanted to go to the movies. I didn't like them very much. And I didn't like the place; it was smelly, and the crowd was noisy. People participated in the movie. They yelled and . . . but . . . I guess . . . going to the movie was very important for me.

S: What about neighbors? Did you have any close neighbors there on the street? Children that you are still friends with?

M: No.

s: Were there other families living right there?

m: Um . . . The little boy who was my boyfriend, he lived two blocks from the park to the west, so I didn't consider that neighbors. I would never see him except when he went to the park. And I never went to his house, although my mother knew his family. And my father was very close to his grandmother.

s: What about birthday parties? Where might you have a birthday party?

m: I had my birthday parties at home. But children were brought there, . . . and I don't know where they lived. I have no idea where they lived.

s: Okay, let's move on. So, the inauguration of the new kiosk takes place when you are eleven?

m: . . . for the . . . um . . . inauguration . . .

s: Yeah, how did that all happen?

m: I think the new kiosk had six or seven pillars, probably six pillars . . . huge pillars. And for the inauguration they decided to ornament the whole thing with girls dressed up as the six republics in Central America. And I was one of the republics, and I don't know which one because we all wore the same white tunics with the flag draped around us.

s: In that year they must have totally redone everything. That's when they took out the fountain and the kiosk at the same time? . . .

m: Yes, of course, because there was no place to put the fountain. The kiosk took all of that space. The veranda [iron fence] had already come down.

s: I met a man who thought that the veranda came down in 1924. So you would never have seen it.

m: No, I never saw it . . .

s: Tell me . . . many people have told me that Parque Central is a park of romance more than anything else. As you get older—eleven, twelve, thirteen—getting to be a young woman . . . do you remember what it was like? Did you go to the park, and what were your activities then?

m: On Sunday, that was the place.

s: Tell me all about it in great detail.

M: I suppose it was after the *tanda de siete* . . . it was around 8:30 in the evening . . . 8:30 to 9:30, or to 10:00. . . .

S: . . . What's a *tanda*?

M: *Tanda* means "film." The film would start at 7:00 P.M., and it was on for one hour and a half, so it was before 9:00 we were out. And people had already gathered around the parq, and they were walking around the parq, and everybody did that.

S: Everybody?

M: The young people.

S: How young?

M: Teenagers.

S: (laughing) That's the *retreta* [the retreat]!

M: The traffic allowed you to ride around the park . . . so those who had cars, who were very few, would drive around the park . . . and those who didn't have cars, and that was the majority of people, would walk. The men would walk on the inside and the woman would walk on the outside so we could watch both the cars and the guys inside . . . and some of the cars were parked, and the young fellows would sit on top of the hood, on top of the motor; I don't know . . . I thought it was fun. And there was always music in the kiosk at that time . . . and it didn't rain, so I think it was during the summer . . . because I don't remember being . . . wearing an umbrella, or being soaking wet, or anything.

S: And this is the *retreta*? And what does the word mean? Everybody uses it. It is called a *paseo* [stroll] in some other countries.

M: People say that it has something to do with the band, that the band would play a retreat. There was also a *retreta* on Wednesday evenings, but the young people didn't show up very much.

S: And who was that for?

M: It was for the music for the . . . I suppose some people did come to hear the music . . .

S: Also that late at night, at 9:00?

M: No, maybe at 8:00.

S: And you think it was more for adults?

M: Probably. I don't remember ever going on Wednesday. . . .

I guess it wasn't fun because nobody was there. . . . The funny thing is that women were by themselves and men were by themselves . . . and how did they get together? [When Marlene's husband, Claudio Gutiérrez, reviewed this conversation, he was concerned that we did not explain how couples got together. He said that groups of boys and girls would walk in sets of three or four clockwise and counterclockwise, girls on the outside and boys on the inside, around the plaza. When a boy saw a girl he liked, he would move to the position that was closest to the girls and *darse cuerda* (stare lovingly). If the girl was interested, she would change her position to the one closest to the boy, and on the next revolution, he would join the girl and walk together as a pair for a while. If the girl was not interested, she would not change position, and the boy would move back to his original position in the group of boys.]

s: Did you have a boyfriend then?

m: No . . . I didn't. I was in love with a guy when I was fourteen, no . . . I think I was fifteen. I never talked to him . . . it was entirely platonic. . . . I remember in the movies arranging the . . . do you remember those things that you powder . . . powder . . . ?

s: Powder puff?

m: Yeah, something that flips together and it has a little mirror . . . ?

s: Yeah, ahuh, a compact.

m: Yeah, a compact . . . and with the mirror you could watch people.

s: Oh, I see, yes, and you would watch for the boys.

m: Yeah . . . we would blush, when we wanted to blush.

s: (laughs) Now on Sunday after the mass, after the *banda toca* [the band plays], did you ever participate in that?

m: Yes . . . but the band played very early. The band played at 8:30 A.M. To begin with, the band came to church and played in church, and then after the mass, they stayed in the park for a while, maybe for an hour. I remember exactly the music they played because it was very dramatic (laughs at herself). It was very fun . . . I went to that mass sometimes. But most of the time I went to either the 11:00 A.M. or 12:00 noon mass. People dressed up to go to the 12:00 mass.

s: So, then you get married.

m: (laughs) . . . I get married, and then the park is no longer part of my life . . .

s: Do you ever go back to it?

m: Never, ever . . .

s: That's interesting, huh? You moved to what neighborhood? You get married at what age?

m: Seventeen. And I moved to Matina [on the Caribbean coast of Costa Rica].

s: They must have torn the house down by now?

m: No.

s: Is it still there?

m: It is still there, except that the front has been converted into shops, so the house itself is behind what you can see unless you go into a nightclub; there's a nightclub there now, I think it is called the Flamingo.

s: Aha . . . Flamingo is the name.

m: . . . and if you go into the nightclub, you will see some of my old house. Maybe it is a brothel, I don't know. Probably so . . .

s: Well, I'll go by and take a picture of the place anyhow . . .

m: . . . (laughs)

s: I want to go back to some comments you made in an earlier interview. The noise seems to have made a big impression. You said that the park was even noisier than it is now.

m: Noisy. I mean there was this loudspeaker, the sirens, the *banda*. Nobody complained, though, because the noise was structured, and it meant something. Sirens went off at a certain hour meaning that you could go to the movies, and the *banda* came at a certain hour. It was not . . . on the spur of the moment . . . it was organized.

s: It gave a kind of rhythm to the day.

m: Yeah, yeah . . . I didn't need a clock . . .

s: One of the things you began to mention before, and that I assume you saw up until you left, were [religious] processions . . . Do you want to talk a little about the processions?

m: That's very important, because Holy Week was a very important part of my life. I was very religious. But my father never allowed me in crowds. I always stood on the balcony; everything took place for me at the balcony. I would watch boys, and the processions and funerals.

s: And were you ever an angel [referring to young children dressing up as angels and shepherds on Corpus Christi Day]?

M: Never!

s: Not a shepherd either?

M: My father never allowed me in crowds. I was very isolated, I guess because he feared germs. So, I never went to big gatherings . . . I never went to *turnos* or *ferias* or Plaza Víquez. Nothing! I would watch from the balcony at a distance, so I was safer there, I suppose, from germs. Germs were very much in the air . . . no, no . . . I mean my father was very concerned about germs.

s: Now, the other thing you told me about the park is that you said your sister decided that the garden by the cathedral was not taken care of properly. When was this?

M: By the time my sister was born I was eleven. I don't remember taking her to the park. I suppose that I was in school. And she probably was taken by a nanny, just like me. And she probably has some stories about the park herself. She was born at the Clínica Bíblica, she was not born in the house . . . but we lived in the same house . . . and by the time she was seven, I was married already.

s: But she stayed.

M: She stayed. And then she became very active. She has always been a leader. And by the time she was fourteen she thought that the park by the church was in very poor condition, and she was able to find people to help her fix the place. I don't know where she got those people from or who they were . . . I don't think they were schoolmates, because nobody lived there. But you should talk to her . . . she probably has different stories.

Conversation Two

*Conversation with Ana Cristina Castro Odio
in her car driving to the country on January 29, 1997*

Ana Cristina told me as I got into the car that she had not prepared notes or thought about the subject before so it would be fresh. Surprisingly, her relationship to Parque Central was quite different from Marlene's, and in ways that I do not feel can be attributed solely to the period of time (1945–1955) during which she used it. Ana Cristina is more interested in the people who inhabit Parque Central and in reconstructing her past, while Marlene thought about the park as a physical setting for play and other social activities.

s: I would like to start with where you were born, where you grew up, and what were your earliest memories of Parque Central?

a: I was born in 1944, right on the corner of Parque Central. I believe I was born at home. I have very early memories from the park . . . huge trees that were not big, but I remember them as huge . . . and lots of kids running around and playing with balls and kicking them and having fun and lots of older people just sitting on the benches. There were a lot of shoeshine boys. There was a section of the park [for them]. And my dream was to be a shoeshine boy. For Christmas, I think it was my fifth year or something like that, I got the box, and I got all of the shoe creams, different colors and brushes for each color and flannel pieces, and I went around shining shoes. I didn't go to the park. I don't know if it is because they didn't let me. But my dad was a doctor, and he had a huge waiting room, and so I'd come through the outside door and ask the people if they wanted their shoes shined. And I charged, I think it was twenty-five cents. I really enjoyed it . . . and I'd kick the box when one shoe was ready, and I'd spit on the tip of the shoe to make it shine better, and I'd do all those things. I really enjoyed it. I remember there was a big fence around the park, and then there was no fence. I don't remember when they tore it down [this memory is probably her reconstruction of the past based on what Marlene and others have said]. I knew there were nice afternoons in the park with older boys and girls, but I never did that. I don't remember that. I just remember hearing about it. My dad, after dinner, went around the park twenty times every single night. Rain or shine, he would go twenty times around the park. He was fit as he could be. And many times I went with him. That is one of my memories, a very strong memory. And then there were several movie houses around the park, and at nine o'clock all the people came out of the movies, and I remember there were lots of people . . . it seemed to be like lots of people. And that's about the only part that I remember. In the *kiosco,* that's the central building of the park, the construction in the middle of the park . . . there was some sort of slide, stone slides. We'd go down there, and I tore up my pants on those slides [children still slide down the vertical supports of the kiosk]. That was fun. And there were the taxi drivers. There was one section of the park where all the taxi drivers would park their cars . . . and . . . I remember many faces . . . and talking with them . . . just having a chat. My dad was much older than all of the other dads. And my brother could have been my father. So, when I went to the park, they had lots of friends, so I thought they were my friends too, otherwise they wouldn't be talking with a little girl around.

s: When you were starting school, does your relationship to the park change?

A: Yes. Yes. I don't remember . . . I don't remember ever playing again in the park. I never thought of this . . . never ever again did I play in the park.

s: About what age do you think?

A: After starting school . . .

s: Did you cross the park to go to school?

A: Yes, I had to, but I don't remember. I walked to school, and there was another big park . . . Oh! . . . There was another big park right in front of school. And that was Parque Morazán, and we used to play a lot in that park!

s: Ahuh . . .

A: Yeah, before I said I didn't play in any other park! Okay, I played a lot in that park . . . we played ball and bat . . . creole baseball.

s: But when you went home from school . . . ?

A: . . . when I went home from school, okay, . . . then my dreams changed. I wanted to be a cowboy. We had a saddle at home and I rode my riding horse. But there was no wooden horse either . . . just the handrail of a stairway. And I set the saddle there, and I rode and rode and rode. I remember I rode for hours . . . whistling and singing and doing my homework . . . practicing things. Then I had a friend, a very close friend. Her grandmother lived in a boardinghouse a block away from our house. And she'd always bring her over to play with me. We always played in the house. There was an open space, not a real garden, but an open space, and my mom would let us do whatever we thought of doing . . . we'd camp in the house. I'd change into my cowboy jeans and long-sleeve shirt and a handkerchief around my neck and a straw hat and boots and my toy machete around my waist. I wore that every afternoon after school.

s: Well, did you ever play cowboy in the park?

A: No. Never . . . probably my dad didn't let me go there . . . because there were too many boys and men in the park . . .

s: That's what I was wondering, did something happen?

A: No. No. I have no bad memories whatsoever. I only have a scary memory of a guy . . . my bedroom was right on the street; it had a window right to the street. I remember a guy that used to stand on the sidewalk and make faces and go like this [gesturing] with his thumb . . . scary . . . just so scary . . . I can feel it. But I never saw him any closer than that.

s: Well, when you start becoming a teenager, do you participate at all in the *retreta*?

A: No.

s: No, and you no longer talked to the shoeshine men? So that's really the end of your relationship to the park?

A: Yeah.

s: Isn't that interesting?

A: . . . Yeah . . .

Conversation Three
A conversation with Alvaro Wille Trejos on Saturday afternoon, January 25, 1997, at his home in the countryside

Alvaro Wille spent time in Parque Central as a young man in the 1930s and 1940s. He is particularly interested in the history of the park, and how it has changed. He is one of the few men I interviewed who remembers participating in the *retreta*.

A: Parque Central was not originally a park. Instead it was a place where vegetables and fruits were sold. It was one of the first parks that was built here; all small cities began this way. The central plaza was built first, then the church, and the plaza was left as an open marketplace. I do not remember when it was finally fenced in with large gates. But on Saturdays and Sundays everyone went to the agricultural fair [large open market] that they had there. In the previous century, it was mainly a market and the church, but with the appearance of supermarkets, it became more like a park. There was a fountain that was very famous, but it was finally moved to the University of Costa Rica, and then it was robbed.

S: What do you mean robbed? I thought it was inside the courtyard at the School of Agriculture at the University of Costa Rica.

A: I do not think so. It has been moved. . . . And at the same time as they added the fountain, they planted the large fig trees.

S: There are two old ones still left.

A: But now they are pouring cement over everything, making the park much uglier.

S: You think that it is uglier now?

A: Yes, the park was prettier when it had the fig trees. There were so many trees that it seemed like a forest. First they chopped up the roots to kill the trees, and then they planted pine trees. They built a rotunda for people to walk around—this must have been in the late 1930s or early 1940s that they erected it. And on Sunday afternoon young people would get together and walk around the park, with the girls on the inside and the boys where they could see them. It was a way to meet someone. I did it; yes, I went sometimes.

S: What year was this?

A: I do not remember exactly, but in the 1940s. I would have been at least fourteen years old in 1940.

S: And how was the experience? How did you feel about it?

A: Well, it interested me the first time—everyone told me that I had to do it because it was the custom. So I went after the 3:00 o'clock movie at Las Palmas. I went with my friends, and we would walk around. But this experience did not convert me into a regular (laughing). I did not have a single girlfriend to look at, and would not have one; there was plenty of reason to attend only if you had a girlfriend. Thus, it was a park of teenage romance. And afterward, I am sure, there were evening romances as we became more adult.

s: So this was in the afternoon?

A: In the afternoon, about 5:00. And we would stay until it got dark or a bit later. I went two, three, or four times; not much more than that.

s: Did you live near the park?

A: Not far away, on Paseo de los Estudiantes. But I did not go to the park to play. In those days there were few cars, and we could play on the street in front of our houses. We did not need to find a park to play. But Parque Central was not really a place to play, but a place for romances.

Conversation Four

An interview with María Eugenia Bozzoli de Wille on Saturday, January 25, 1997, while walking in town

s: When did you go to Parque Central?

M: For young people, the idea was to stroll down the avenue past the movie theater, make a circle of the park, and then continue on to Chelles. We would stop at the corner of Chelles because it was the bar with the best little pastries and *arreglados* [flaky pastry shells filled with meat, vegetables, or cheese; a popular *boca,* or "snack," in Costa Rica].

s: I like those . . .

M: The people who went to Chelles, however, were more adult, because it was a bar and people would go to drink. This trip to Chelles was part of the entire *paseo* in the early hours of the evening. Everyone would leave the movie theater about 5:00 P.M., make a circle before going down to Chelles. Some people would enter the movies at 7:00 P.M. and leave about 9:00 P.M., but even those that left at 9:00 P.M. spent a little time walking around. At other times, the parade was down the avenue, and the boys and men would stop at the corner as the girls and women walked by: boys watching the girls and men watching the women. Some girls would come alone, but normally a girl would not come with a boy. She would meet him at the corner. The other place that people stopped to watch each other was on the corner in front of the Balmoral Hotel, about one hundred meters up from the park. Do you know this place?

s: Yes, but I did not know it was a meeting place.

m: The majority of married couples stayed at the Balcón Europea eating . . .

s: Yes?

m: So the way it would go was that people would go to mass at 8:00 A.M. and afterward stay to hear the band. It was a military band that played marching songs. The police and the little soldiers that we had back then would parade around in their dress uniforms, and we would listen to the music. This was the first part of Sunday. Then the second part was to go to the movies at 5:00 P.M. or 7:00 P.M., and afterward to walk around the park, finishing up at Chelles. It was important if you lived in San José to spend your Sundays in Parque Central.

Conversation Five

*An interview with Alfredo Rodríguez on Friday afternoon,
January 24, 1997, while sitting in Parque Central*

Alfredo Rodríguez is a man who has spent over thirty years sitting and observing Parque Central. He is an expert on the subject and in this conversation shares some of his insights about the social and physical changes that have occurred over time. His observations and conclusions are by no means unique; many of the older Costa Rican men I spoke with shared his sentiments and point of view. I include this interview as representative of the types of conversations I frequently had while sitting in Parque Central.

s: . . . Well, what do you think of the park now?

a: Right now I do not like it.

s: Why?

a: Well, they took out everything; they changed the ecology and did not leave any nature. They left very little, and they cut down the trees. Before, it was prettier, with grassy areas and more vegetation. There was more shade.

S: Do you know why they made these changes?

A: They say that it is development and modernism, but the truth is that the parks that are attractive are the older ones, and they should leave them that way because it is what the people want. Now many people have forgotten how Parque Central was.

S: But you know how it was . . .

A: Well, here, in front of us, was a large arbor, do you remember? It was an immense arbor covered with plants and vines. Did you see it?

S: Yes, I have photographs of it.

A: And on top of the arbor lived people. This was home for the shoeshine men, and people would climb on top to make love. . . .Then there were many characters [*personajes*] that you no longer see.

S: Like who?

A: Characters, that is, people who do not live like us and who do not have a normal life, but they were typical characters around here. For instance, there was Víctor the preacher and another one, Ramón, and they had fights about religion. There was an alcoholic who you had to be careful with because she was a little demented, and she would hit you. She never bathed and was always here asking for money and usually getting it. People came because there were many characters here that they liked and could interact with. I have been coming to the park for thirty years, and I miss the characters who are now gone. I do not like it [that they are gone]. I also miss the dances.

S: Dances?

A: There were dances on Sundays. In the morning at 10:00 A.M. and also in the afternoon they played *la retreta*. Then on December 31 there was a dance to celebrate the new year. . . . That is how it was.

S: But are you safer now?

A: No. It used to be safer for people working here before, when the park had many levels and trees so the sellers had more opportunity to hide from the municipal police. But safer, no, there are more serious assaults now than there were before. Before there were no assaults and now there are. It all started when the teenagers arrived. They formed their first gang here, the one that is still active today. They meet everyday at 5:00 P.M. and organize what they are going to do that evening and plan their crimes. They get together in the kiosk, and then they go out.

s: But there are more women in the park now; what does that mean?

A: There are more women because many women come "to get what they are looking for." Do you understand? They come because they have a terrible economic crisis and solve the problems that they have at home with their bodies . . . prostitution.

s: And why are there so many Nicaraguan women?

A: Because the situation is very bad in Nicaragua, and they have come here to make some money.

s: Do you know the Plaza de la Cultura?

A: Yes, the Plaza de la Cultura is closed right now.

s: Do you like it?

A: Well, the Plaza de la Cultura was built for people's [the pueblo's, the city's] enjoyment. But it ultimately became a marketplace for foreign goods and has many assaults . . . and homosexual cruising.

Thus the plaza played many roles in these individual lives. It was a child's first playground and urban encounter, a place to meet friends and to find romance, and a stage that provided entertainment through the enactment of everyday lives. The cultural patterns and local politics of daily activities are enframed by the plaza, and its significance is embedded both in the physical environment and in these memories and contemporary narratives.

CHAPTER 11

Public Space, Politics, and Democracy

I would like to begin this concluding conversation by summarizing what I have learned from the plaza project, and why I think the survival of public space is so important to democratic societies. The linkage between public space and the globalizing political economy deserves closer scrutiny because societal mobilization about public space influences the shape of civil society and, by extension, democratic participation. This project's attention to the creation and use of the plaza reveals important political dimensions of the meaning of public space as a focus of contestation and as a place where disagreements and conflicts over cultural and political objectives become concrete.

I have found that public spaces have important personal meanings for individual users and urban residents. In the Costa Rican case study, these meanings are constructed from individual experience, social encounters, working conditions, political activities, memories and collective recollections, and from what is written and said about the plaza. Personal meanings are also created by published memoirs and historical accounts as well as literary imaginings about plaza life.

Public spaces retain cultural and political meanings symbolically encoded in their spatial relations and built environment. In the Latin American plaza, these meanings are historical as well as contemporary, produced by past sociopolitical and cultural forces and by current everyday behavior and sociopolitical conflicts. These plaza meanings are understood through individual interpretations and public exegesis of spatial relations, built forms, and furnishings and, especially, changes in the designed landscape. In this sense, the designed landscape acts as an environmental mnemonic for communicating past and present meanings to daily users and urban residents.

Understanding the social production and social construction of public space provides insights into how these meanings are encoded on and interpreted in the designed landscape. For instance, tracing the architectural and sociopolitical history of the building of the Spanish American plaza uncovers its indigenous architectural origins, enabling a more syncretic cultural interpretation of its design form. Likewise, examining the microgeography of Costa Rican plaza users' behavior, movements, and activities demonstrates how individual paths and projects create cultural norms and associated cultural meanings delimited by the specifics of plaza time and space.

These meanings are understood by public space users and urban residents in a variety of ways—from an emotional engagement with the place (place attachment) to a citywide struggle to define what the place should represent through its spatial relations and landscape architecture. In San José, Costa Rica, the forms of spatial engagement are both passive and active, ranging from everyday practices of sitting on benches and talking to friends, to organized street demonstrations, media campaigns, and town meetings. Costa Ricans have protested changes in plaza architectural representations through latent protests such as public discourse about what the plaza should look like and who should be there, and through manifest protest in which groups of people, such as foreign vendors or juvenile gangs, take over the park, restricting the use of the public space. These various forms of engagement and protest suggest that exclusionary practices based on socioeconomic differentiation are not the only responses to globalization and increasing reliance on tourism and North American capital, but that, conversely, models for demographic participation may also be generated by social practices derived from other interpretations of Costa Rican culture/*cultura*.

Spatial meanings are actively manipulated by the city and the state to represent diverse political and economic agendas. Over time, these agendas become embedded in the architecture and landscape design of public space, providing an arena for civic contestation and public involvement. By examining the Costa Rican plaza, it becomes apparent how these meanings have been actively manipulated by the government to facilitate political and social objectives—so much so that Costa Rican presidents use the creation of new public spaces and plazas to communicate their political messages and underwrite their political success. But this case study also demonstrates how the plaza becomes a center of protest and contestation by providing a place and a culturally charged symbol for expressing social conflict.

Therefore, public spaces, such as the Costa Rican plaza, are one of the last democratic forums for public dissent in a civil society. They are places where disagreements can be marked symbolically and politically or personally worked out. Without these significant central public spaces, social and cultural conflicts are not clearly visible, and individuals can not directly participate in their resolution.

In this sense, one aspect of the social production and social construction of public space is dialogic—that is, an ongoing, interactive, conversation-like process that changes through time, creating new ideas, social structures, and meaningful places. But it is also dialectical, that is, oppositional, often disruptive and contested, but ultimately politically transformative, uniting contrasting points of view and perspectives through new political and social alternatives. It is here that the need to make and remake public spaces, and to struggle relentlessly for the social and political availability of public space, can be seen as a precondition for any kind of democratic politics, and that the importance of the historical and ethnographic data on the Costa Rican plaza becomes particularly clear.

Even more important, however, is the evidence that these conclusions appear significant for urban public spaces cross-culturally. Drawing upon the few well-studied examples of public space—Tiananmen Square in Beijing; Plaza de Mayo in Buenos Aires; the Zócalo in Mexico City; Pershing Square in Los Angeles; People's Park in Berkeley; and Tompkins Park, Union Square, and Bryant Park in New York City—it seems that these central squares, parks, and plazas hold comparable cultural meanings and function as stages for demonstrations and public dissension. As in the cases of Parque Central and Plaza de la Cultura, their designs and built environments have been monitored and manipulated by the city, private businesses, and the state. For instance, they have been closed, redesigned, or policed in response to appropriation by "undesirables" or socially unacceptable conflicts and other visible displays. The strategies of social control documented in San José conform to an identifiable pattern that can be found in places far beyond the boundaries and influence of the Latin American plaza. Further, the practice of artistic mystification and commoditization through urban design and landscape architecture occurs throughout the world, spread by an increasingly global economy and communications system.

How do the plazas of New York City compare to those of San José? Stephan Carr, Mark Francis, Leanne Rivlin, and Andrew Stone (1992) provide an analytic framework for defining the "publicness" of spaces that includes five kinds of spatial rights: *access*—the right to enter and remain in a public space; *freedom of action*—the ability to carry on activities in the public space; *claim*—the ability to take over the space and resources in it; *change*—the ability to modify the environment; and *ownership*—the ultimate form of control. William Burton and I employed these spatial rights to evaluate the publicness of publicly owned and corporate plazas in New York City. We found that a variety of strategies were used to restrict spatial rights of all plazas users: from policing with guard dogs and guns to restricting behavior, and more subtle strategies were reflected in the pricing and nature of goods sold on or around the plaza (Burton 1993).

This lack of publicness was not unexpected in the private corporate plazas but was surprising in publicly owned spaces. We found the appearance of security guards to be an "intimidation factor" regardless of ownership and management style. The authorities directed their control-related policies and actions almost exclusively toward unwelcome users, most often defined as homeless people or people they called "bums" or, in the case of Lincoln Plaza, the residents of a nearby low-income housing project.

Direct methods of restricting access—by the erection of barricades or the use of guards—and indirect methods such as closing plazas for construction, repairs, and special events also occurred frequently. In some cases, the plaza closings were intended as a form of social control. Two publicly owned plazas—Lincoln Plaza and Bryant Park—were closed during the late night and early morning hours to discourage homeless people from spending the night. Other examples included observations that Lincoln Plaza was closed to prevent neighborhood public-housing residents from hanging out. Grace Plaza (near Times Square) was enclosed with a metal spike fence for six months in 1981–1982 to prevent its use by drug dealers. And Rockefeller Plaza was closed briefly to prevent a demonstration from spilling over from the street onto the plaza (Burton 1993).

Possibly the best-known example of the use of extreme measures of social control to close a public space is Tompkins Square, located in the Lower East Side of Manhattan. Neil Smith (1996) and Janet Abu-Lughod (1994) document the intense battle of local poor and working-class residents against the gentrification strategies of individuals, private developers, and New York City political interests. Tompkins Square had sustained an uneasy alliance between homeless people living in the park and a variety of very diverse neighborhood users until the pressures of gentrification and private vested interests resulted in a series of riots. The police response—practically a "scorched-earth" policy that included the razing of the tents and shacks of homeless individuals and the total closing down of the park—ultimately redefined as well as redesigned the public park. Smith (1996) argues that this show of force and the lack of middle-class protest against the use of such military tactics are part of his imagined "revanchist city"—a city that punishes minorities, women, and marginal peoples for not participating in American traditional values, a city of revenge against the poor and liberalism.

In Costa Rica, the use of private armed guards and dogs to police the plazas has not yet occurred. It seems that intimidation tactics are not yet necessary, as other forms of social control are still successful. Nevertheless, Josefinos share other restrictive trends—policing by new municipal police, more tourist-oriented shopping and expensive restaurants surrounding the plazas, and decreasing tolerance of people defined as "undesirables" and of other unwelcome users—with plaza managers and users in New York City. Restricted access is increasingly becoming a strategy for reappropriating space to attract more welcome users, that is, tourists and middle-class citizens, in both settings. Incidents such as the closing down and reconstruction of Parque Central in San José and of Tompkins Square in New York City, the temporary closings of New York City plazas at night and during special events and demonstrations, and the proposed closing off of Plaza de la Cultura with gates and fencing are all examples of the increasing similarities in the control tactics used in both places. Thus, many of the ethnographic findings and conclusions presented for the Costa Rican case are also applicable to urban public spaces in the United States.

What are the consequences when public space is closed,
redesigned, and restricted or the public realm becomes
redefined as a Web site in the informational city?

Public space becomes even more valuable in the network society imagined by Manuel Castells (1996). In *The Informational City* (1989), Castells outlines a new kind of dual city, one in which the "space of flows"—informational and production flows—supersedes the meaning of the "space of places"—neighborhoods and places where people actually work and live. This dual city is a shared space within which contradictory spheres of local society are constantly trying to differentiate their territories based on different logics. Space flows are organized on principles of information-processing activities, while the everyday spaces are organized by the logic of making a living, providing sustenance, and finding a place to live. The lack of connections between these spaces, and the resulting meaninglessness of everyday places and political institutions, is resented by people and resisted through a variety of individual and collective strategies. People attempt to reaffirm their cultural identity, often in territorial terms, by "mobilizing to achieve their demands, organizing their communities, and staking out their places to preserve meaning, to restore whatever limited control they can over work and residence" (Castells 1989, 350). He goes on to argue that

> at the cultural level, local societies, territorially defined, must
> preserve their identities, and build upon their historical roots,
> regardless of the economic and functional dependence upon the
> space of flows. The symbolic marking of places, the preservation
> of symbols of recognition, the expression of collective memory
> in actual practices of communication, are fundamental means
> by which places may continue to exist. (351)

These centers of local communication and resistance are located in urban public space.

In a subsequent paper on his vision of a network society, Castells presents a world in which control over knowledge and information decides who holds power in society. Communication technology and media control of images, representations, and public opinion, and the increasing ability of computer networks to allow the individual to create personal image representations as well, illustrate the growing tension between globalization and individualization (Castells 1996). People respond to this world of flows and resulting placelessness by representing their values and interests through the reassertion of primary community identities based on ethnicity, gender, or culture/biology self-definitions.

There are a number of examples of how the network society is not penetrating urban life and public space. In the movie *Pulp Fiction* (1990), Cass, one of the main characters, is identified as the place he is from, "Inglewood" (a neighborhood in Los Angeles), as if this one-word designation of place is enough to tell you all about him. At a viewing of the movie in Los Angeles there would be laughter in response to this designation, while in New York there was none. "Inglewood" encodes a complex set of social, class, and racial meanings that are understood only in the context of local spatial representations, and these place-identities play a major role in this parody of postmodern America.

Global cities such as New York, Los Angeles, and Philadelphia each consist of dozens of local cultural/spatial communities—Little Delhi in Jackson Heights, New York; Little Saigon in Philadelphia and Los Angeles; the Italian Market or Little Italy in New York, Philadelphia, Boston, and Baltimore; Chinatown in New York and Philadelphia; and Little Tokyo in Los Angeles. Social theorists such as Sharon Zukin (1991) or Saskia Sassen (1991) assert that these communities are simply extensions of the globalization process, remnants of a mobile labor force trapped by the long tentacles of flexible capital.

It is difficult to argue with this logic. Clearly, globalization of labor and capital has recast our urban landscape, but along with globalization comes a counter social force called *vernacularization*: the process by which the global is made local through the attribution of meaning. These local spatial/cultural spaces provide the emotional and symbolic bases for maintaining cultural identity. When interviewed in the streets and parks of these neighborhoods, people will tell you how good and happy they feel to be there, or even to visit there—to eat the food, smell the local smells, hear the sounds of their indigenous music, buy culture-specific products not found in other parts of the city, or simply to speak their native language. These neighborhoods provide the symbolic as well as the economic and practical sustenance for everyday life. The vernacularization of urban space, then, is a powerful and important corrective to globalization processes that contributes well-being and meaning to local lives.

Another example of the importance of the marking of social space in the physical environment is to examine what happens when peoples' histories are erased from the public space. As I drive Route 10 from

Palm Springs to West Los Angeles in California, my personal history passes by inscribed in the landscape through places, institutions, and cultural markers. Traveling this Southern California highway, I am reminded of where I went to college, where I spent my summers as a child, and where I got my first job. These physical reminders provide a sense of place attachment, continuity, and connectedness that we are rarely aware of but that play a significant role in our psychological development as individuals and in our "place-identity" or "cultural-identity" as members of families or ethnic groups.

But what happens when your places are not marked or, even more to the point, when your personal or cultural history is erased—removed from the urban landscape by physical destruction and omitted from the "sacred" landscapes of history texts? The redevelopment of Paris by Baron George Haussman is still the classic example of the erasure of a working-class and poor people's history in an urban landscape (Harvey 1985). But in the United States, this process has been more subtle; for instance, at a site like Independence National Historical Park in Philadelphia, we have forgotten to record the people who built the buildings (African Americans) or who financed the Revolution (American Jews) or who fed the soldiers (women, mothers, and wives) in our reworking of the national park as a male "white" place. Further, the documentation is missing when one searches for information concerning the histories of "other" people during colonial times.

African Americans in Philadelphia, however, have been fighting to reclaim their history by supporting research, setting up archives, and working to ensure that their history and culturally significant sites are spatially marked and interpreted throughout the city. The African-American community in New York has been successful in contesting the federal government's claims to the African-American Burial Ground, demanding its commemoration and preservation, but it has been less successful in preserving its political heritage, as evidenced by the tearing down of the Audubon Ballroom where Malcolm X was shot. Dolores Hayden (1995) documents how she worked with women of color in downtown Los Angeles to create a monument to a founding black mother's life. Thus, even as histories are erased they are re-searched and rediscovered so that they can be spatially marked in the preserved, conserved, and reconstructed public spaces of the city.

One final way that public space retains meanings is through the ritual use of streets and parks. I have always known that the New Year's Day

Mummers' Parade in Philadelphia was a ritual inversion of Philadelphians' class relations through the aggressive behavior of the crowd and their physical control of the streets. And certainly the Halloween Parade in Greenwich Village, New York, temporarily suspends accepted notions of male and female in an ecstasy of political satire and demonic allegory (Kugelmass 1994). The emerging Labor Day Carnival along Eastern Parkway in Crown Heights, Brooklyn, is another example that highlights how not only social movements such as housing strikes but also temporal, ritual, and culturally defined events can successfully contest a group's position in a city, and at the same time provide many of the spatial markers that give a group a history, spatial rights, and sociospatial representation. These parades are a response to cultural devaluation by the dominant culture and are a contestation of cultural hierarchies and local social controls.

The case of Carnival is particularly telling. This Caribbean-American celebration has become the focal event for a cultural community that is trying to assert its cultural identity and political clout within the tradition of New York City ethnic politics. Begun in the tradition of New York ethnic parades such as the St. Patrick's Day parade, it has become an ornate extravaganza of floats, bands, and costumes, with politicians from around the world as well as from Manhattan participating in this celebration of cultural identity. Recent conflicts between the Crown Heights Caribbean and Lubavitcher communities have added considerable tension to this exuberant cultural and political event that claims the streets of Brooklyn at the same time as the traditional Labor Day parade goes down Fifth Avenue in Manhattan. Carnival is spatially and temporally contesting the white, working-class Labor Day parade as part of the New York Caribbean Americans' struggle for political power and cultural recognition (Kasinitz 1992). Thus, in an ongoing struggle for political rights, cultural devaluation is contested with temporary spatial control of the public spaces of the streets and with rituals of cultural recognition.

So where does this leave us?

This understanding of the political nature and cultural meaning of public spaces leaves us with an obligation to protect, preserve, and fight for them. Vital urban public spaces are at risk and have been vulnerable to the political gaze and pressures of privatization. Equally threatening is the power of computer communication technologies to replace sites of social interaction with Web sites and commercialization.

It has been suggested that public spaces—real, physical places—will be replaced by the "public sphere" of the Worldwide Web. The information highway will provide new ways to connect to others, such that public space will be replaced by "virtual public space," and meaningful conversation and cultural exchange will occur in cyberspace. But in cyberspace we cannot see, hear, touch, and feel each other, much less our environment. The futurist reformulation of social relations in abstract space will increasingly separate human communication and experience from the site of its social production, creating an ever widening gulf between the social spaces where we live and the abstract spaces of technological power and production. Without public space, Castells's most ominous vision of a world where the places of people and the spaces of information flows become completely disconnected could be realized.

Yet we remain embedded in a material world and use it to create meaning and metaphors that transform our lives. Meanings encoded in the landscape are not passive mnemonics that simply add historical contexts for living; rather, they are active translators of everyday practice and human experience. Meaningful public contexts must be conserved for their cultural significance and political importance, and maintained as representational centers of social conflict and cooperation. Through saving public spaces, the image of the placeless, informational city is replaced by an image of active public spaces full of public engagement, intense social interaction, and political struggle for a more tolerant and humane city. Through the making and remaking of public spaces, we retain the spatial and cultural dimensions of democratic political practices.

Recent Costa Rican Presidents
and Their Terms

José Figueres Ferrer	1970–1974
Daniel Oduber Quirós	1974–1978
Rodrigo Carazo Odio	1978–1982
Luis Alberto Monge Alvarez	1982–1986
Oscar Arias Sánchez	1986–1990
Rafael A. Calderón F.	1990–1994
José María Figueres Olsen	1994–1998
Miguel A. Rodríguez Echeverría	1998–2002

BIBLIOGRAPHY

Abu-Lughod, Janet
1994 *From Urban Village to East Village.* Oxford: Blackwell.
Agar, Michael
1986 *Speaking of Ethnography.* Beverly Hills: Sage.
Agnew, John A., John Mercer, and David E. Sopher, eds.
1984 *The City in Cultural Context.* Boston: Unwin.
Agrinier, Pierre
1983 Tenam Rosario: Una posible relocalización del clásico maya terminal desde el Usumacinta. In *Antropología e historia de los Mixe-Zoques y Mayas,* ed. Lorenzo Ochoa and Thomas Lee. Mexico City: Universidad Nacional Autónoma de México.
Alberti, Leon Battista
[1485] 1986 *The Ten Books of Architecture.* New York: Dover Publications.
Alvarado, Pedro de
1969 *An Account of the Conquest of Guatemala in 1524.* New York: The Cortés Society.
Andrews, George F.
1975 *Maya Cities.* Norman: University of Oklahoma Press.
Appadurai, Arjun
1987 Putting hierarchy in its place. In *Rereading Cultural Anthropology,* ed. G. Marcus, 34–45. Durham: Duke University Press.
Archivos, Censo Municipalidad
1993 Municipalidad de San José. Departamento Financiero Sec. Censo. Distrito Catedral 4, Manzana 3, Propiedad 2.
Arciniegas, Germán
1975 *America in Europe: A History of the New World in Reverse.* San Diego: Harcourt Brace Jovanovich.

Arias, Santa
    1993   Empowerment through the writing of history: Bartolomé de Las Casas's
          representation of the Other. In *Early Images of the Americas,* ed. Jerry M.
          Williams and Robert E. Lewis, 163–183. Tucson: University of Arizona.

Arreola, Daniel D.
    1980   Landscapes of nineteenth-century Veracruz. *Landscape* 24: 27–31.
    1982   Nineteenth-century townscapes of Eastern Mexico. *Geographical Review*
          72 (1): 3–19.

Ashmore, Wendy
    1981   *Lowland Maya Settlement Patterns.* Albuquerque: University of New
          Mexico Press.
    1984   Quiriguá archaeology and history revisited. *Journal of Field Archaeology*
          11: 366–386.
    1987a Architectural expression and social complexity in the southeast
          Mesoamerican periphery. Paper presented at the annual meeting of the
          American Anthropological Association, Chicago.
    1987b Cobble crossroads: Gualjaquito architecture and external elite ties. In
          Interaction on the Southeast Mesoamerican Frontier, ed. E. Robinson, 28–
          48. Oxford: BAR International Series 327.
    1989   Construction and cosmology: Politics and ideology in lowland Maya
          settlement patterns. In *Word and Image in Maya Culture,* ed. William F.
          Hanks and Don A. Rice. Salt Lake City: University of Utah Press.
    1991a Of Catherwood and Cauac sky. Paper presented at the annual meeting
          of the Society for American Archaeology, New Orleans.
    1991b Site planning and concepts of directionality among the ancient Maya.
          Latin American Antiquity 2 (3): 199–226.

Aubarbier, Jean-Luc, Michel Binet, and Jean-Pierre Bouchard
    1989   *Les Bastides du Périgord: Domme, Monpazier et les autres.* La Guerche-
          de-Bretagne: Imprimerie Raynard.

Aveni, Anthony, and G. Romano
    1994   Orientation and Etruscan ritual. *Antiquity* 68: 545–563.

Banco Nacional de Costa Rica
    1972   *La Ciudad de San José, 1891–1921.* San José, Costa Rica: Antonio
          Lehmann.

Bateson, Gregory
    1972   *Steps to an Ecology of the Mind.* New York: Ballantine Books.

Becker, Marshall J.
    1982   Ancient Maya houses and their identification. *Revista Española de An-*
          tropología Americana 12: 110–129.

Benevolo, L.
    1969   Las nuevas ciudades fundadas en el siglo XVI in América Latina. *Boletín*
          Centro de Investigaciones Históricas y Estéticas 9: 117–136.

Bigges, Walter
    1588   *Expedito Francisci Draki.* London: N.p.

Booth, John A.
    1998   *Costa Rica: Quest for Democracy.* Boulder: Westview Press.

Borah, Woodrow W.

1972 European cultural influence in the formation of the first plan for urban centers that has lasted to our time. In *Urbanización y proceso social en América,* ed. Richard P. Schaedel et al. Lima, Peru: Instituto de Estudios Peruanos.

1980 Demographic and physical aspects of the transition from the aboriginal to the colonial world. *Comparative Urban Research* 8: 41–70.

Borah, Woodrow W., Jorge E. Hardoy, and Gilbert A. Stelter

1980 *Urbanization in the Americas.* Ottawa: National Museum.

Bourdieu, Pierre

1977 *Outline of a Theory of Practice.* Cambridge: Cambridge University Press.

Boyer, Richard

1980 La ciudad de México en 1628. *Historia Mexicana* 115 (29): 447–471.

Brading, D. A.

1980 The city in Bourbon Spanish America: Elite and masses. *Comparative Urban Research* 8: 71–85.

Braudel, Fernand

1981 *The Structures of Everyday Life: The Limits of the Possible.* Vol. 1 of *Civilization and Capitalism, Fifteenth to Eighteenth Century.* New York: Harper and Row.

Bronner, Fred

1986 Urban society in colonial Spanish America. *Latin American Research Review* 21 (1): 7–72.

Brookes, John

1987 *Gardens of Paradise: History and Design of the Great Islamic Gardens.* London: Weidenfeld and Nicolson.

Burton, William

1993 The publicness of public spaces. Master's thesis, City University of New York.

Calmettes, Claude, Dode Cornu, and Quitterie Calmettes

1986 *Le Bati Ancien en Bastide.* Paris: Electricité de France; Villefranche-de-Rouergue: Centre D'Etude des Bastides.

Calnek, Edward E.

1972 The internal structure of cities in America: Pre-Columbian cities; the case of Tenochtitlan. In *Urbanización y proceso social en América,* ed. Richard P. Schaedel et al., 347–358. Lima, Peru: Instituto de Estudios Peruanos.

1978 The internal structure of cities in America: Pre-Columbian cities; the case of Tenochtitlan. In *Urbanization in the Americas from Its Beginnings to the Present,* ed. Richard P. Schaedel, Jorge E. Hardoy, and Nora S. Kinzer, 315–326. The Hague: Mouton.

Calvo Mora, Joaquín B., comp.

1887 *Apuntamientos geográficos, estadísticos e históricos.* San José, Costa Rica: Imprenta Nacional.

La capital de antaño

1928 *Caja,* November 30, p. 17.

Carr, Stephan, Mark Francis, Leanne Rivlin, and Andrew Stone
1992   *Public Space.* New York: Cambridge University Press.
Carrasco, David
1990a Myth, cosmic terror, and the Templo Mayor. In *The Great Temple of Tenochtitlan,* ed. Johanna Broda, David Carrasco, and Eduardo Matos Moctezuma, 124–162. Berkeley: University of California Press.
1990b *Religions of Mesoamerica: Cosmovision and Ceremonial Centers.* New York: Harper-Collins Publications.
Casey, Edward S.
1996   How to get from space to place in a fairly short stretch of time. In *Senses of Place,* ed. Steve Feld and Keith Basso, 13–52. Santa Fe: School of American Research.
Castells, Manuel
1977   *The Urban Question.* Cambridge: MIT Press.
1983   *The City and the Grassroots.* Berkeley: University of California Press.
1989   *The Informational City.* Oxford: Blackwell.
1996   The net and the self. *Critique of Anthropology* 16: 9–38.
Cervantes de Salazar, Francisco
[1554] 1953   *Life in the Imperial and Loyal City of Mexico in New Spain.* Austin: University of Texas Press.
Chase, Alfonso
1982   Casa del pueblo. In *Obra en marcha: Poesía, 1965–1980,* p. 186. San José: Editorial Costa Rica.
Clark, Mary A.
1997   Transnational alliances and development policy in Latin America: Non-traditional export promotion in Costa Rica. *Latin American Research Review* 32: 71–98.
Clendinnen, Inga
1987   *Ambivalent Conquests: Maya and Spaniard in Yucatan, 1517–1570.* Cambridge: Cambridge University Press.
1991a *Aztecs.* Cambridge: Cambridge University Press.
1991b "Fierce and unnatural cruelty": Cortés and the conquest of Mexico. *Representations* 33: 65–100.
Coggins, Clemency
1980   The shape of time: Some political implications of a four-part figure. *American Antiquity* 45 (4): 727–741.
Columbus, Christopher
1493   *De insulis inventis.* Basle: N.p.
Cortés, Hernán
1524   *Praeclara . . . de nova maris oceani.* Nuremberg: N.p.
[1519–1526] 1971   *Letters from Mexico.* Trans. and ed. Anthony R. Pagden. New York: Grossman Publishers.
1986   *Letters from Mexico.* Trans. Anthony R. Pagden. Intro. by J. H. Elliot. New Haven: Yale University Press.
Cosgrove, D.
1982   The myth and stones of Venice: An historical geography of a symbolic landscape. *Journal of Historical Geography* 8: 145–169.

Coto, Jorge
  1982   Y ahora . . . ¿qué hay bajo la Plaza de la Cultura? *La Nación,* January
     31, pp. 1–4.
Crouch, Dora P., Daniel J. Garr, and Axel I. Mundigo
  1982   *Spanish City Planning in North America.* Cambridge: MIT Press.
Da Matta, Roberto
  1984   Carnival in multiple planes. In *Rite, Drama, Festival, Spectacle,* ed. J.
     MacAloon, 209–240. Philadelphia: Institute for the Study of Human
     Issues.
Davis, Diane E.
  1994   *Urban Leviathan: Mexico City in the Twentieth Century.* Philadelphia:
     Temple University Press.
Davis, Susan G.
  1986   *Parades and Power.* Philadelphia: Temple University Press.
De Certeau, Michel
  1984   *The Practice of Everyday Life.* Berkeley: University of California Press.
De la Torre Villar, Ernesto
  1978   *Guía bibliográfica para la historia y desarrollo de la arquitectura y el
     urbanismo en México.* Mexico City: Coordinación de Humanidades e
     Instituto de Investigaciones Bibliográficas.
Delgado-Gómez, Angel
  1993   The earliest European views of the New World natives. In *Early Images
     of the Americas,* ed. Jerry Williams and Robert E. Lewis, 3–20. Tucson:
     University of Arizona.
Delgado Rojas, Moisés, and Ana Isabel Zúñiga Jara
  1993   *Remodelación y restauración de Parque Central.* San José, Costa Rica:
     Municipalidad de San José.
De Montmollin, Olivier
  1989   *The Archaeology of Political Structure.* Cambridge: Cambridge Univer-
     sity Press.
De Mora, Nini
  1973   *San José: Su desarrollo. Su título de ciudad. Su rango de capital de Costa
     Rica.* San José, Costa Rica: Universidad de Costa Rica.
DePalma, Anthony
  1998   For a famed tortilla, green garnish? *New York Times,* August 25, p. A2.
Díaz del Castillo, Bernal
  1963   *The Conquest of New Spain.* Harmondsworth: Penguin.
Duncan, James S.
  1985   Individual action and political power. In *The Future of Geography and
     Geography in the Future,* ed. R. J. Johnston. London: Methuen.
  1990   *The City as Text: The Politics of Landscape Interpretation in the Kanyan
     Kingdom.* Cambridge: Cambridge University Press.
  1993   Representing power. In *Place/Culture/Representation,* ed. James S.
     Duncan and D. Ley, 232–248. New York and London: Routledge.
Durán Ayanegui, Fernando
  1989   *Mi pequeño bazar.* San José, Costa Rica: Trejos Hermanos Sucs.

Eagleton, Terry
   1986   Marxism and the past. *Salmagundi* 68–69: 271–290.
Edelman, Marc, and Joanne Kenen
   1989   *The Costa Rican Reader.* New York: Grove Weidenfeld.
Elliot, J. H.
   1987   The Spanish conquest. In *Colonial Spanish America,* ed. L. Bethell, 1–58.
          Cambridge: Cambridge University Press.
Escobar, Jesús R.
   1995   The Plaza Mayor of Madrid: Architecture and urbanism for the capital
          of Spain, 1560–1630. *Center* (Washington D.C.: National Gallery of Art)
          15: 63–64.
Fernandez, James
   1992   Architectonic inquiry. *Semiotica* 89: 215–226.
Fernández, León
   1889   *Historia de Costa Rica durante la dominación española (1502–1821).* Vol. 6.
          N.p.
Fernández de Oviedo y Valdés, Gonzalo
   [1535] 1959   *Historia general y natural de las Indias (1535–1547).* Chapel Hill:
          University of North Carolina Press.
Fernández Guardia, Ricardo, ed.
   1985   *Costa Rica en el Siglo XIX.* 5th ed. San José, Costa Rica: Editorial
          Universitaria Centroamérica. Original edition, San José: Editorial
          Lehmann, 1929.
Foster, George M.
   1960   *Culture and Conquest: The American Spanish Heritage.* New York: Viking
          Fund Publications in Anthropology.
Foucault, Michel
   1975   *Discipline and Punish.* New York: Random House.
   1984   Des espaces autres. *Architecture, Mouvement, Continuité* (October): 46–
          49.
Fraser, Valerie
   1990   *The Architecture of Conquest: Building in the Viceroyalty of Peru.* Cam-
          bridge: Cambridge University Press.
Friedman, David
   1988   *Florentine New Towns: Urban Design in the Late Middle Ages.* Cam-
          bridge: MIT Press.
Gade, D.
   1974   The Latin American central plaza as functional space. *Proceedings of the
          Conference of Latin Americanist Geographers* 5: 16–23.
Gage, Thomas
   1655   *A New Survey of the West Indies.* London: E. Cates.
Gasparini, G.
   1978   The colonial city as a center for the spread of architectural and pictorial
          schools. In *Urbanization in the Americas from Its Beginnings to the Pre-
          sent,* ed. Richard P. Schaedel, Jorge E. Hardoy, and Nora S. Kinzer, 269–
          281. The Hague: Mouton.

Geertz, Clifford
  1973   *The Interpretation of Cultures.* New York: Basic Books.
Gibson, Charles
  1964   *The Aztecs under Spanish Rule.* Stanford: Stanford University Press.
Gillespie, Susan
  1989   *The Aztec Kings.* Tucson: University of Arizona Press.
Giroux, Henry A.
  1983   Theories of reproduction and resistance in the new sociology of educa-
          tion: A critical analysis. *Harvard Educational Review* 33: 257–293.
Gonzalez, Nancy S.
  1970   Social functions of the carnival in a Dominican city. *Southwestern Jour-
          nal of Anthropology* 26: 328–342.
González Víquez, Cleto
  1973   San José y sus comienzos. In *Obras históricas,* Vol. 1. San José, Costa
          Rica: Universidad de Costa Rica.
González Zeledón, Manuel
  [1896] 1994   Un día de mercado en la plaza principal. In *Cuentos de Magón,*
          pp. 23–31. San José, Costa Rica: Editorial Costa Rica.
Gossen, Gary
  1996   Maya Zapatistas move to the ancient future. *American Anthropologist* 98:
          528–538.
Gracia Zambrano, Angel J.
  1992   El poblamiento de México en la época del contacto, 1520–1540.
          Mesoamérica 224: 239–296.
Graham, Elizabeth A.
  1991   Archaeological insights into colonial period Maya life at Tipu, Belize. In
          Columbian Consequences, vol. 3, *The Spanish Borderlands in Pan-Ameri-
          can Perspective,* ed. David Hurst Thomas, 319–335. Washington, D.C.:
          Smithsonian Institution Press.
Graham, Elizabeth A., Grant D. Jones, and Robert R. Kautz
  1985   Archaeology and ethnohistory on a Spanish colonial frontier: An in-
          terim report on the Macal-Tipu Project in Western Belize. In *The Low-
          land Maya Postclassic,* ed. A. F. Chase and P. M. Rice, 206–214. Austin:
          University of Texas Press.
Graham, Elizabeth A., David M. Pendergast, and Grant D. Jones
  1989   On the fringes of the conquest: Maya-Spanish contact in colonial
          Belize. *Science* 246: 1254–1259.
Grube, Nikolai, Linda Schele, and Federico Fahsen
  1991   Odds and ends from the inscriptions of Quiriguá. *Mexicón* 13 (6): 106–112.
Grupo de la Agenda Social
  1997   *A la búsqueda del Siglo XXI: Nuevos caminos de desarrollo en Costa Rica.*
          Informe de la Misión Piloto del Programa Reforma Social del Banco
          Interamericano de Desarrollo. San José, Costa Rica: Editorial de la
          Universidad de Costa Rica.
Gudmundson, Lowell
  1996   Costa Rica: New issues and alignments. In *Constructing Democratic*

Governance: Latin America and the Caribbean in the 1990's, ed. J. I. Do-
míguez and A. F. Lowenthal, 78–91. Baltimore: Johns Hopkins Press.

Guillén Martínez, Fernando

1958 *The Tower and the Town Square: An Essay on Interpreting America.*
Madrid: Ediciones Cultura Hispánica.

Gutiérrez, Ramón

1983 *Arquitectura y urbanismo in Iberoamérica.* Madrid: Ediciones Cáedra.

Hall, Carolyn

1985 *Costa Rica: A Geographical Interpretation in Historical Perspective.* Boul-
der: Westview Press.

Hammond, Norman

1982 *Ancient Maya Civilization.* New Brunswick: Rutgers University Press.

Hardie, Graeme

1985 Continuity and change in Tswana's house and settlement form. In *Home
Environment,* ed. Irwin Altman and Carol Werner, 213–236. New York:
Plenum.

Hardoy, Jorge E.

1973 *Pre-Columbian Cities.* New York: Walker and Company.

1978 European urban forms in the fifteenth to seventeenth centuries and
their utilization in Latin America. In *Urbanization in the Americas from
Its Beginnings to the Present,* ed. Richard P. Schae-del, Jorge E. Hardoy,
and Nora S. Kinzer, 215–248. Le Hague: Mouton.

Hardoy, Jorge E., and Ana María Hardoy

1978 The plaza in Latin America: From Teotihuacan to Recife. *Culturas* 5:
59–92.

Harvey, David

1985 *Consciousness and the Urban Experience.* Baltimore: Johns Hopkins University Press.

1990 *The Condition of Postmodernity.* Oxford: Blackwell.

Hayden, Dolores

1995 *The Power of Place.* Cambridge: MIT Press.

Helms, Mary W.

1975 *Middle America: A Culture History of Heartland and Frontiers.* Engle-
wood Cliffs, N.J.: Prentice-Hall.

1988 *Ulysses' Sail.* Princeton: Princeton University Press.

Holston, James

1989 *The Modernist City.* Chicago: University of Chicago Press.

Hulme, Peter

1994 Tales of distinction: European ethnography and the Caribbean. In *Im-
plicit Understandings,* ed. S. B. Schwartz, 157–200. Cambridge: Cambridge University Press.

Hurtado, Gerardo César

1975 *Los parques.* San José, Costa Rica: Editorial Costa Rica.

Hyslop, John

1990 *Inka Settlement Planning.* Austin: University of Texas Press.

Jackson, J. B.

1984 *Discovering the Vernacular Landscape.* New Haven: Yale University Press.

Johnson, Dirk
  1996   Town sired by autos seeks soul downtown. *New York Times,* August 7, p. A8.
Jones, Grant D.
  1989   *Maya Resistance to Spanish Rule: Time and History on a Colonial Frontier.*
    Albuquerque: University of New Mexico Press.
Jones, Grant D., Robert R. Kautz, and Elizabeth A. Graham
  1986   Tipu: A Maya town on the Spanish colonial frontier. *Archaeology* 39: 40–47.
Kasinitz, Philip
  1992   *Caribbean New York.* Ithaca: Cornell University Press.
Keith, Michael, and Steve Pile
  1993   Introduction to Part 2: The place of politics. In *Place and the Politics of Identity,* ed. M. Keith and S. Pile, 22–40. London: Routledge.
King, Anthony D.
  1976   *Colonial Urban Development: Culture, Social Power, and Environment.*
    London: Routledge and Kegan Paul.
  1980   *Buildings and Society.* London: Routledge and Kegan Paul.
Korosec-Serfaty, Perla
  1982   *The Main Square: Functions and Daily Uses of Stortorget in Malmoe.*
    Hassleholm: AM-tryck offset, Nova Series no. 1.
Kubler, George
  1948   *Mexican Architecture in the Sixteenth Century.* New Haven: Yale University Press.
  1978   Open-grid town plans in Europe and America. In *Urbanization in the Americas from Its Beginnings to the Present,* ed. Richard P. Schaedel, Jorge E. Hardoy, and Nora S. Kinzer, 327–342. The Hague: Mouton.
Kugelmass, Jack
  1994   *The Greenwich Village Halloween Parade.* New York: Columbia University Press.
Lang, Jon
  1989   Cultural implications of housing design policy in India. In *Housing, Culture, and Design,* ed. Setha Low and Erve Chambers, 375–392. Philadelphia: University of Pennsylvania Press.
Las Casas, Fray Bartolomé de
  1951   *Historia de las Indias.* 3 vols. Mexico City: Fondo de Cultura Económica.
Lawrence, Denise, and Setha M. Low
  1990   The built environment and spatial form. *Annual Review of Anthropology* 19: 453–505.
Lefebvre, Henri
  1991   *The Production of Space.* Oxford: Basil Blackwell.
Lennard, Suzanne H. Crowhurst, and Henry L. Lennard
  1984   *Public Life in Urban Places.* Southampton: Gondolier Press.
León-Portilla, Miguel
  1992   *The Aztec Image of Self and Society: An Introduction to Nahua Culture.*
    Salt Lake City: University of Utah Press.
Linger, D. T.
  1992   *Dangerous Encounters: Meanings of Violence in a Brazilian City.* Stanford: Stanford University Press.

Lomnitz Adler, Claudio

    1992   *Exits from the Labyrinth.* Berkeley: University of California Press.

López de Cogolludo, Diego

    1688   *Historia de Yucathan Compuesta.* Madrid: Juan García Infanzón.

Loría, Vilma

    1995   San José de noche. In *Relatos de mujeres,* ed. Linda Berrón, 67–69. San José, Costa Rica: Editorial Mujeres.

Lotz, Wolfgang

    1981   *Studies in Italian Renaissance Architecture.* Cambridge: MIT Press.

Loven, Sven

    1935   *Origins of the Tainan Culture, West Indies.* Göteborg: Elanders Bokfryckeri Akfiebolag.

Low, Setha M.

    1985   *Culture, Politics, and Medicine in Costa Rica.* Bedford Hills, New York: Redgrave Publishing Company.

    1992   Symbolic ties that bind. In *Place Attachment,* ed. Irwin Altman and Setha Low, 165–185. New York: Plenum.

    1997a   Urban fear: Building the fortress city. *City and Society,* Annual Review: 53–72.

    1997b   Urban public spaces as representations of culture. *Environment and Behavior* 29 (1): 3–33.

Lungo, Mario

    1997   Costa Rica: Dilemmas of urbanization in the 1990's. In *The Urban Caribbean,* ed. A. Portes, C. Dore-Cabral, and P. Landolt, 57–86. Baltimore: Johns Hopkins Press.

Macleod, Murdo J.

    1973   *Spanish Central America: A Socioeconomic History, 1520–1720.* Berkeley: University of California Press.

Marín, Gloria Violeta

    1991   El parque de antaño. *La Nación,* October 28.

Mark, Mary Ellen

    1997   Disneyland, NYC. *New York Times Magazine,* May 18, p. 56.

Markham, S. D.

    1978   The gridiron town plan and the caste system in colonial Central America. In *Urbanization in the Americas from Its Beginnings to the Present,* ed. Richard P. Schaedel, Jorge E. Hardoy, and Nora S. Kinzer, 471–490. Le Hague: Mouton.

Marshall, Douglas

    1973   *The City in the New World.* University of Michigan: William L.Clements Library.

Matos Moctezuma, Eduardo

    1987   The Templo Mayor of Tenochtitlan: History and interpretation. In *The Great Temple of Tenochtitlan,* ed. Johanna Broda, David Carrasco, and Eduardo Matos Moctezuma, 15–60. Berkeley: University of California Press.

    1990   *The Great Temple.* Mexico City: National Institute of Anthropology and History.

    1992   The Aztec main pyramid: Ritual architecture at Tenochtitlan. In *The*

Ancient Americas: Art from Sacred Landscapes, ed. Richard F. Townsend, 187–196. Munich: Prestel Verlag.

McLennan, Marshall
  1968 The parque-plaza complex in Costa Rica. Department of Geography, Eastern Michigan University. Manuscript.

Merrim, Stephanie
  1993 The counter-discourse of Bartolomé de Las Casas. In *Early Images of the Americas,* ed. Jerry M. Williams and Robert E. Lewis, 149–162. Tucson: University of Arizona Press.

Ministerio de Economía y Hacienda
  1975 Censos de Población de Costa Rica, 1950. San José, Costa Rica: Dirección General de Estadística y Censos.

Ministerio de Economía, Industria y Comercio
  1974 Anuario Estadístico de Costa Rica, 1973. San José, Costa Rica: Dirección General de Estadística y Censos.
  1983 Anuario Estadístico de Costa Rica, 1982. San José, Costa Rica: Dirección General de Estadística y Censos.
  1992 Costa Rica: Cálculo de Población por Provincia, Catón y Distrito. San José, Costa Rica: Dirección General de Estadística y Censos.
  1996 Costa Rica: Cálculo de Población por Provincia, Catón y Distrito. San José, Costa Rica: Dirección General de Estadística y Censos.

Mitchell, Don
  1995 The end of public space: People's Park, definitions of the public, and democracy. *Annals of the Association of American Geographers* 85 (1): 108–133.

Montero Vega, Arturo
  1978 Los parques. In *Poesía Contemporánea de Costa Rica,* ed. Carlos Rafael Duverrán, 197. San José, Costa Rica: Editorial Costa Rica.

Moore, Henrietta
  1986 *Space, Text and Gender: An Anthropological Study of the Marakwet of Kenya.* Cambridge: Cambridge University Press.

Morris, A. E. J.
  1974 *History of Urban Form, Prehistory to the Renaissance.* London: George Godwin, Ltd.

Morse, Richard
  1975 A framework for Latin American urban history. In *Urbanization in La-tin America,* ed. Jorge E. Hardoy, 57–107. Garden City, N.Y.: Anchor Books.
  1980 Introduction. Urban development in Latin America: A special issue. *Comparative Urban Research* 8: 5–13.
  1987 Urban development. In *Colonial Spanish America,* ed. L. Bethell, 165–202. Cambridge: Cambridge University Press.

Morse, Richard, and Jorge E. Hardoy, eds.
  1992 *Rethinking the Latin American City.* Washington, D.C.: Woodrow Wilson and Johns Hopkins University Press.

Motolinía, Toribio de Benavente
  1951 *Motolinía's History of the Indians of New Spain.* Trans. and ed. Francis Borgia Steck. Washington, D.C.: Academy of American Franciscan History.

Mullen, Robert
  1975 *Dominican Architecture in Sixteenth-Century Oaxaca.* Tempe: Arizona
        State University Press.
Mullings, Leith
  1997 *On Our Own Terms: Race, Class, and Gender in the Lives of African
        American Women.* New York: Routledge.
Myers, David J.
  1997 Latin American cities. *Latin American Research Review* 32: 109–123.
Myers, Kathleen
  1993 The representation of New World phenomena: Visual epistemology
        and Gonzalo Fernández de Oviedo's illustrations. In *Early Images of the
        Americas,* ed. Jerry M. Williams and Robert E. Lewis, 183–214. Tucson:
        University of Arizona Press.
Naranjo Coto, Manuel
  1976 *Plaza de la Cultura.* San José, Costa Rica: Banco Central, Litografía
        Trejos.
Oliver-Smith, Anthony
  1986 *The Martyred City: Death and Rebirth in the Andes.* Albuquerque: Uni-
        versity of New Mexico Press.
Palm, Erwin Walter
  1955 *Los monumentos arquitectónicos de la Española,* vol. 1. Ciudad Trujillo:
        Universidad Autónoma de Santo Domingo.
  1968 La ville espagnole au nouveau monde dans la première moitié du XVIe
        siècle. In *La decouverte de l'Amérique,* ed. M. Ballesteros-Garbrois et al.
        10e Stage International d'Etudes Humanistes, Tours 1966. Paris: Librai-
        rie Philosophique J. Vrin.
Parry, J. M., and R. G. Keith
  1984 *New Iberian World,* vol. 3. New York: Hector and Rose.
Parson, Don
  1993 The search for a centre: The recomposition of race, class, and space in
        Los Angeles. *International Journal of Urban and Regional Research* 17:
        232–240.
Patterson, Thomas C.
  1996 Conceptual difference between Mexican and Peruvian archaeology.
        American Anthropologist 98: 499–505.
Peattie, Lisa
  1969 *The View from the Barrio.* Ann Arbor: University of Michigan.
Pendergast, David M.
  1987 Stability through change: Lamanai, Belize, from the ninth to the sev-
        enteenth century. In *Late Lowland Maya Civilization,* ed. Jeremy A.
        Sabloff and E. Wyllys Andrews V, 223–250. Albuquerque: University of
        New Mexico Press.
  1991 The southern Maya lowlands contact experience: The view from
        Lamanai, Belize. In *Columbian Consequences,* vol. 3, *The Spanish Bor-
        derlands in Pan-American Perspective,* ed. David Hurst Thomas, 337–
        353. Washington, D.C.: Smithsonian Institution Press.

1993 Worlds in collusion: The Maya/Spanish encounter in sixteenth- and seventeenth-century Belize. *Proceedings of the British Academy* 81: 105–143.

Pendergast, David M., and Elizabeth Graham
1993 La mezcla de arqueología y etnohistoria: El estudio del período hispánico en los sitios de Tipu y Lamanai, Belice. In *Perspectivas Antropológicas en el Mundo Maya,* ed. María Josefa Iglesias Ponce de León and Frances Ligorred Perramon, 331–353. Madrid: Sociedad Española de Estudios Mayas.

Perin, Constance
1977 *Everything in Its Place.* Princeton: Princeton University Press.
1988 *Belonging in America: Reading between the Lines.* Madison: University of Wisconsin Press.

La pila del Parque Central
1944 *Caja,* January 6, p. 57.

Pile, Steve
1997 Opposition, political identities and spaces of resistance. In *Geographies of Resistance,* ed. S. Pile and M. Keith, 1–31. London: Routledge.

Pred, Alan
1984 Structuration, biography formation, and knowledge. *Environment and Planning D. Society and Space* 2: 251–275.

Quantrill, Malcolm
1987 *The Environmental Memory.* New York: Schocken Books.

Rabasa, José
1993 Writing and evangelization in sixteenth-century Mexico. In *Early Images of the Americas,* ed. Jerry M. Williams and Robert E. Lewis, 65–92. Tucson: University of Arizona Press.

Rabinow, Paul
1982 Ordonnance, discipline, regulation: Some reflections on urbanism. *Humanities in Society* 5: 3–4.
1984 *The Foucault Reader.* New York: Pantheon Books.
1989 *French Modern.* Cambridge: MIT Press.

Rama, Angel
1996 *The Lettered City.* Ed. and trans. John Charles Chasteen. Durham, N.C.: Duke University Press.

Ramírez, Sergio
1973 *Antología del cuento centroamericano.* San José, Costa Rica: Editorial Universitaria Centroamericana.

Rapoport, Amos
1980 Cross-cultural aspects of environmental design. In *Human Behavior and Environment,* vol. 4, ed. I. Altman, Amos Rapoport, and J. F. Wolhwill, 7–46. New York: Plenum.
1982 *The Meaning of the Built Environment.* Beverly Hills: Sage.

Relaciones Geográficas
1890–1900 Relaciones de Yucatán. In *Colección de documentos inéditos relativos al descubrimiento, conquista y organización de las antiguas*

posesiones españolas de Ultramar, 2d series, vols. 11, 13. Madrid: Real Academia de la Historia.

Reps, John W.

1965   *The Making of Urban America.* Princeton: Princeton University Press.

1969   *Town Planning in Frontier America.* Princeton: Princeton University Press.

Revista de Costa Rica en el Siglo XIX

1902   San José, Costa Rica: Tipografía Nacional.

Ricard, Robert

1947   La Plaza Mayor en espagne et en Amérique espagnole. *Annales, Economic-Sociétés-Civilisations* 2 (4): 433–438.

1950   La Plaza Mayor en España y en América. *Estudios Geográficos* 11: 321–327.

Richardson, Miles

1978   La plaza como lugar social: El papel del lugar en el encuentro humano. *Vínculos: Revista de Antropología del Museo Nacional de Costa Rica* 4: 1–20.

1980   Culture and the urban stage: The nexus of setting, behavior, and image in urban places. In *Human Behavior and Environment,* vol. 4, ed. I. Altman, Amos Rapoport, and J. F. Wolhwill, 209–242. New York: Plenum.

1982   Being-in-the-market versus being-in-the-plaza: Material culture and the construction of social reality in Spanish America. *American Ethnologist* 9: 421–436.

Ricoeur, P.

1979   The model of the text. In *Interpretive Social Science,* ed. P. Rabinow and W. Sullivan, 301–340. Berkeley: University of California Press.

Robertson, Douglas L.

1978   A behavioral portrait of the Mexican Plaza Principal. Ph.D. diss., Department of Geography, Syracuse University.

1981   Guadalajara's main square: Some dynamics of change in the Mexican downtown. Paper presented at the annual meeting of the Association of American Geographers, Los Angeles, April.

Rodman, Margaret

1992   Empowering place: Multilocality and multivocality. *American Anthropologist* 94: 640–656.

Rodríguez, Sylvia

1989   Art, tourism, and race relations in Taos: Toward a sociology of the art colony. *Journal of Anthropological Research* 45: 77–99.

1997   The Taos fiesta: Invented tradition and the infrapolitics of symbolic reclamation. *Journal of the Southwest* 39: 33–57.

1998   Fiesta time and plaza space: Resistance and accommodation in a tourist town. *Journal of American Folklore* 111: 39–56.

Rohter, Larry

1996   Costa Rica chafes at new austerity. *New York Times,* September 30, p. A10.

Rouse, Irving

1992   *The Tainos: Rise and Decline of the People Who Greeted Columbus.* New Haven: Yale University Press.

Rutheiser, Charles
    1996 *Imagineering Atlanta: The Politics of Place in the City of Dreams.* New York: Verso.

Samuels, Marwyn, and Carmencita M. Samuels
    1984 Beijing and power of place in modern China. In *The City in Cultural Context,* ed. J. Agnew, J. Mercer, and J. Sopher, 202–227. London: Allen and Unwin.

Sánchez Delgado, Nicolás, and Carlos E. Umaña Ugalde
    1983 San José: Imagen y estructura urbana. *Revista del Colegio Federado de Ingenieros y de Arquitectos de Costa Rica* 78: 20–29.

Sancho, Mario
    [1935] 1984 Recuerdos de Cartago. In *Antología de la literatura costarricense,* ed. Abelardo Bonilla, 516–517. San José: Stvdivm Generale Costarricense, Corporación Costarricense de la Cultura.

Sassen, Saskia
    1991 *The Global City: New York, London, Tokyo.* Princeton: Princeton University Press.

Saville, Marshall H.
    1917 *Narrative of Some Things of New Spain and of the Great City of Temestitan, Mexico, written by the Anonymous Conqueror, a Companion of Hernán Cortés.* New York: The Cortés Society.

Schaedel, Richard P.
    1978 The city and the origin of the state in America. In *Urbanization in the Americas from Its Beginnings to the Present,* ed. Richard P. Schaedel, Jorge E. Hardoy, and Nora S. Kinzer, 31–50. The Hague: Mouton.

Schaedel, Richard P., Jorge E. Hardoy, and Nora S. Kinzer, eds.
    1978 *Urbanization in the Americas from Its Beginnings to the Present.* The Hague: Mouton.

Schell, William J.
    1986 *Medieval Iberian Tradition and the Development of the Mexican Hacienda.* Latin American Series, no. 8. Syracuse, N.Y.: Foreign and Comparative Studies.

Seed, Patricia
    1993 Taking possession and reading texts. In *Early Images of the Americas,* ed. Jerry M. Williams and Robert E. Lewis, 111–148. Tucson: University of Arizona Press.

Shallat, Lezak
    1989 Aid and the secret parallel state. In *The Costa Rican Reader,* ed. M. Edelman and J. Kenen, 221–227. New York: Grove Weidenfeld.

Smith, Michael E.
    1992 Braudel's temporal rhythms and chronology theory in archaeology. In *Archaeology, Annales and Ethnohistory,* ed. A. B. Knapp, 25–36. Cambridge: Cambridge University Press.
    1994 Hernán Cortés on the size of Aztec cities: Comments on Dobyns. *Latin American Population History Bulletin* 25: 25–27.
    1995 The Mesoamerican urban landscape from Teotihuacan to the Aztecs. Paper presented at the Archaeology of Complex Societies conference,

California State University, San Bernardino, October 21.

1996 *The Aztecs.* London: Blackwell.

1997 Aztec city planning. In *Encyclopedia of the History of Science, Technology, and Medicine in Non-Western Cultures,* ed. H. Selin, 200–202. New York: Garland Publishing.

Smith, Neil

1991 New city, new frontier. In *Variations on a Theme Park,* ed. M. Sorkin, 61–93. New York: Verso.

1996 *The New Urban Frontier: Gentrification and the Revanchist City.* New York: Routledge.

Smith, Neil, and Cindi Katz

1993 Grounding metaphor: Towards a spatialized politics. In *Place and the Politics of Identity,* ed. M. Keith and S. Pile, 67–83. London: Routledge.

Solís Zeledón, Rafael

1969 *Delimitación de la región metropolitana de San José.* San José, Costa Rica: Instituto Nacional de Vivienda y Urbanismo.

Sorkin, Michael

1989 *Variations on a Theme Park.* New York: Verso.

Soustelle, Jacques

1961 *The Daily Life of the Aztecs on the Eve of the Spanish Conquest.* London: Weidenfeld and Nicolson.

Spain, Daphne

1992 *Gendered Spaces.* Chapel Hill: University of North Carolina Press.

Stanislawski, Dan

1946 The origin and spread of the grid-pattern town. *Geographical Review* 36: 105–120.

1947 Early Spanish town planning in the New World. *Geographical Review* 37: 94–105.

Stephens, John Lloyd

1949 *Incidents of Travel in Central America, Chiapas and Yucatan.* Vol. 1. New Brunswick: Rutgers University Press.

Stone, Samuel

1974 Aspects of power distribution in Costa Rica. In *Contemporary Cultures and Societies of Latin America,* ed. Dwight Heath, 404–421. New York: Random House.

Todorov, Tzvetan

1984 *The Conquest of America: The Question of the Other.* Trans. Richard Howard. New York: Harper and Row.

Torres Rivas, Edelberto

1993 *History and Society in Central America.* Austin: University of Texas Press.

Toussaint, Manuel, Federico Gómez de Orozco, and Justino Fernández

1938 *Planos de la ciudad de Mexico, Siglos XVI y XVII: Estudio histórico, urbanístico y bibliográfico.* Mexico City: XVI Congreso Internacional de Planificación y de la Habitación.

Townsend, Richard

1992 The renewal of nature at the Temple of Tlaloc. In *The Ancient Americas,* ed. Richard Townsend, 171–186. Munich: Prestel Verlag.

Tozzer, Alfred M.
    1907 *A Comparative Study of the Mayas and the Lacandones.* London: Macmillan Company.

Trullás y Aulet, Ignacio
    1913 *Escenas Josefinas.* San José, Costa Rica: Librería Española.

Turner, Victor
    1967 *The Forest of Symbols.* Ithaca: Cornell University.

Vega Carballo, José Luis
    1981 *San José: Antecedentes coloniales y formación del Estado Nacional.* San José, Costa Rica: Instituto de Investigaciones Sociales.

Villiers-Stuart, C. M.
    1936 *Spanish Gardens.* Batsford: N.p.

Wagner, Henry Raup
    1942 *The Discovery of Yucatán by Francisco Hernández de Córdoba.* Berkeley: The Cortés Society.
    1944 *The Rise of Fernando Cortés.* Los Angeles: The Cortés Society.

Walton, John
    1984 Culture and economy in the shaping of urban life. In *The City in Cultural Context,* ed. J. A. Agnew, J. Mercer, and D. E. Sopher, 76–93. Boston: Allen and Unwin.

Ward-Perkins, J. B.
    1974 *Cities of Ancient Greece and Italy.* New York: George Braziller.

Webb, Michael
    1990 *The City Square: A Historical Evolution.* New York: Whitney Library of Design, Watson-Guptill Publications.

Webster, David
    1997 The study of classic Maya architecture. *Latin American Research Review* 32: 219–232.

Weeks, John M.
    1988 Residential and local group organization in the Maya lowland of southwestern Campeche, Mexico. In *Household and Community in the Mesoamerican Past,* ed. Richard R. Wilk and Wendy Ashmore, 73–96. Albuquerque: University of New Mexico Press.

West, Robert, and John P. Augelli
    1966 *Middle America: Its Land and People.* New Jersey: Prentice-Hall.

Whyte, William H.
    1980 *The Social Life of Small Urban Spaces.* Washington, D.C.: The Conservation Foundation.

Wilk, Richard R., and Wendy Ashmore
    1988 *Household and Community in the Mesoamerican Past.* Albuquerque: University of New Mexico Press.

Williams, Jerry M., and Robert E. Lewis
    1993 *Early Images of the Americas: Transfer and Invention.* Tucson: University of Arizona Press.

Wilson, Chris
    1997 *The Myth of Santa Fe: Creating a Modern Regional Tradition.* Albuquerque: University of New Mexico Press.

Wilson, Samuel M.
  1990   *Hispaniola: Caribbean Chiefdoms in the Age of Columbus.* Tuscaloosa: University of Alabama Press.
World Bank
  1998   *World Bank Atlas.* Washington, D.C.: International Bank for Reconstruction and Development.
Wulff, Vicky Risner, and Setha Low
  1987   Dance/Movement analysis as an anthropological method. Paper presented at the annual meeting of the Society for Applied Anthropology, Oaxaca, Mexico.
Yashar, Deborah J.
  1997   *Demanding Democracy: Reform and Reaction in Costa Rica and Guatemala, 1870s–1950s.* Stanford: Stanford University Press.
Zawiska, L. M.
  1972   Fundación de las ciudades hispano-americanas. *Boletín Centro de Investigaciones Históricas y Estéticas* 13: 88–128.
Zucker, Paul
  1959   *Town and Square.* Cambridge: MIT Press.
Zukin, Sharon
  1991   *Landscapes of Power: From Detroit to Disney World.* Berkeley: University of California Press.
  1995   *The Cultures of Cities.* Cambridge: Blackwell.

INDEX

and spatial boundaries, 159; and tourists, 25; and vendors, 147, 198
Great Temple. *See* Templo Mayor, Tenochtitlan
Grijalva, Juan de, 116
Guatemala, 136
Guevara M., José David, 189
Guillén Martínez, Fernando, 31
Gutiérrez, Ramón, 94

Harvey, David, 36, 49, 128–129
Hayden, Dolores, 36, 245
Hernández de Córdoba, Francisco, 116
Hippodamus, 88
Hispaniola, 96, 97
History: and analysis, 44; of European plazas, 84–100; and first-person narratives, 219, 220; of indigenous plazas, 101–123; and interpretation, 34; and methodology, 38; and photographic documentation, 43; and plazas, 33, 37, 123, 238; and power, 87; and public space, 34, 36, 48, 244–245; of San José, 50, 58–65; and social construction of space, 178; and social production of space, 130; of Spanish American plazas, 51–52; and urban design, 49
Holland, 90, 91
Holston, James, 129
Homelessness, 136–137, 174, 183, 241–242
Hurtado, Gerardo César, 211–215

Iglesia Parroquial, 65
India, 86
Indigenous architecture: and colonial period, 103, 108, 112, 122; and grid-plan plaza-centered form, 106, 120; and Mexico City, 100; and plazas, 83, 101–123; and Spain, 86, 107–109; and Spanish American plazas, 34, 42, 85–86, 100, 104, 107, 119–120, 122, 133, 239; and urban design, 103, 105–109; and urban planning, 85, 86, 114
Indigenous culture, 98, 102–103, 120, 144–145, 195
Instituto Nacional de Vivienda y Urbanismo (INVU), 63
International Council of Monuments and Sites (ICOMOS), 200
International Monetary Fund (IMF), 136, 145
Islam, 86, 92–93, 95, 98
Italian piazzas, 87–89
Izamal, 108, 121

Japan, 86
Jiménez, Bernal, 79
Jiménez, Miguel, 65

Kandy, Sri Lanka, 48
King, Anthony, 36
Korea, 86
Kubler, George, 90, 114, 115

Lamanai, Belize, 108–113, 118–120
Landa, Diego de, 108
Landscape architecture: and crime, 152–153, 198; and cultural meaning, 180; as environmental mnemonic, 239; and Islamic garden, 92–93; and movement maps, 165; and mystification, 181; and Parque Central, 187; and power, 87; and public space, 38, 241; and social relations, xii
Las Casas, Fray Bartolomé de, 96–97
Latin American plazas, 31-33, 35-37, 238. *See also* Spanish American plazas
Laws of the Indies, 85, 89, 92, 95
Lefebvre, Henri, 36, 50, 130, 132–133
Lennard, Henry L., 48
Lennard, Suzanne H. Crowhurst, 48
Lincoln Plaza, New York City, 241
Literature: and Costa Rican plazas, 53; and ethnographies, 207–208; and novels, xi, xiii, 37, 207, 211–218; and Parque Central, 68–77, 134, 207, 211–212; and personal meaning, 49, 238; and plazas, xi, xiii, 33, 207; and poetry, xi, 37, 41, 207; and short stories, xiii, 37, 207
López de Cogolludo, Diego, 117
Loría, Vilma, 81–83, 175
Los Angeles, California, 35, 182, 244, 245
Lungo, Mario, 63

Madrid, Spain, 94
Madriz, Castro, 65
Malcolm X, 245
Market sites, 51, 65, 68–73
Martyr, Peter, 96, 117
Matos Moctezuma, Eduardo, 103
Maximilian (emperor of Mexico), 53
Maya, 101, 107–109, 111–112, 117–119, 133, 185
McLennan, Marshall, 53
Media, 80, 145–146, 148, 181, 185, 186
Memoirs, xi, xiii, 37, 53, 207, 208–210, 238
Mérida, Yucatán, 100, 105, 110, 116–118, *119*, 120, 121
Mexica, 103–104, 106–109, 111–115, 120, 133
Mexico, 36, 51, 52, 53, 89
Mexico City, Mexico: and indigenous architecture, 100; and lateral displacement, 122; map of, *117;* Mérida compared to, 118; new center/old center, 121; and plazas, 32, 53, 105, 115–116; and spatial relationships, 120;